The Complete Idiot's eBusiness

Your eBusiness Do List

When running an eBusiness, it's easy to forget the day-to-day tasks that need to be done to keep your eBusiness on track. Let's face it. You've put a lot of work into building a foundation for your new enterprise. Keeping that foundation solid is an important task in making your eBusiness a success. So, here is a *Do List* of activities that you should do on a daily, weekly, and monthly basis.

Daily To Do

➤ Check your customer service email and respond the same day.

➤ Read new messages in the discussion groups that you participate in and respond to questions and calls for help that match your business offerings.

➤ If you run a bulletin board on your site, respond to all questions from shoppers.

➤ Read and respond to any email discussion lists that you are on.

➤ Check the navigation on your Web storefront for broken links.

➤ If you are using an email auto responder, send a message to it and make sure it's working.

➤ Promote a new product each day from your home page.

Weekly To Do

➤ Check your Web site's position in the search engines.

➤ Review your log files to see which pages are *not* getting hits and make changes accordingly.

➤ Review your advertising placements and see which ones are pulling traffic and which are not.

➤ Update your storefront with new information and products.

➤ Send out your weekly newsletter with product specials.

Monthly To Do

➤ Read your monthly industry and Internet publications.

➤ Create a seasonal promotion for your product or service.

➤ Look for new promotional activities for your Web store.

➤ Create a newsworthy event that can be used in a press release.

➤ Look for new directories and search engines to list your Web store.

ALPHA

PR Do's and Don'ts

Administrating a good publicity campaign takes a lot of work. So mind these Do's and Don'ts of news releases.

- ➤ DO make your press releases short and to the point.
- ➤ DO include all necessary contact information.
- ➤ DO spell-check your release. And do it twice just to make sure!
- ➤ DO keep typefaces large, legible, and readable for both email and faxes.
- ➤ DO write a clear and meaningful subject line. The subject line should reflect the contents of your release.
- ➤ DON'T write unclear press releases. If it doesn't make sense to the reader, it will not be used.
- ➤ DON'T send a release to a publication without knowing the audience or what the publication is all about.
- ➤ DON'T send attached files.
- ➤ DON'T send a word processing document or a zipped file that the contact needs to download, unzip, read into his word processor, determine the compatibility, print, review, and so on.

Top Sites for Posting Your Press Release

PR Web
PR Web offers free posting.

www.prweb.com/submit.htm

PR Newswire
PR Newswire requires an annual fee for posting.

www.prnewswire.com

Business Wire
Business Wire requires an annual fee as well.

www.businesswire.com

URLwire
URLwire will post on demand and charges per posting, but does not have an annual fee.

www.urlwire.com

Internet Wire
Internet Wire will post on demand and charges per posting, but does not have an annual fee.

internetwire.com/release/index.htx

Internet News Bureau
Internet News Bureau charges per posting but does not have an annual fee.

www.newsbureau.com/services

Xpress Press
Xpress Press charges per posting but does not have an annual fee.

www.xpresspress.com

WebPromote
WebPromote charges per posting but does not have an annual fee.

www.webpromote.com/products/prelease.asp

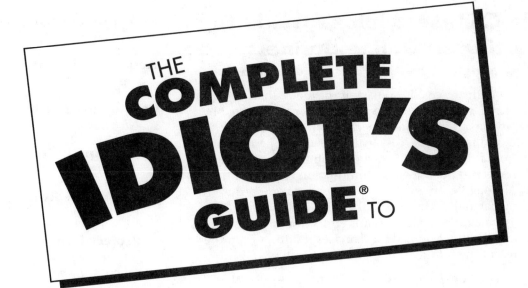

THE COMPLETE IDIOT'S GUIDE® TO

Starting an Online Business

Frank Fiore

ALPHA

A Pearson Education Company

The Complete Idiot's Guide to Starting an Online Business

Copyright © 2000 by Pearson Education, Inc.

International Standard Book Number: 0-7897-2193-7

Library of Congress Catalog Card Number: 99-63885

Printed in the United States of America

First Printing: April 2000

04   03   02   7   6   5   4

Trademarks

Warning and Disclaimer

Associate Publisher
Greg Wiegand

Acquisitions Editor
Angelina Ward

Development Editor
Nicholas J. Goetz

Managing Editor
Thomas F. Hayes

Technical Editor
Bill Bruns

Project Editors
Casey Kenley
Lori A. Lyons

Copy Editor
Sossity Smith

Indexer
Greg Pearson

Proofreader
Kay Hoskin

Illustrator
Judd Winick

Team Coordinator
Sharry Lee Gregory

Interior Designer
Nathan Clement

Cover Designer
Michael Freeland

Copywriter
Eric Borgert

Layout Technician
Steve Geiselman

Contents at a Glance

Contents

About the Author

Frank Fiore has been involved in eCommerce since its inception on the Net. Back in 1982, he was one of the original eCommerce providers for CompuServe where he ran an online service business. He is the author of *Dr. Livingstone's Online Shopping Safari Guidebook*, a direct marketer of products, and an eCommerce consultant for five years. Because of his many years of experience, he knows eCommerce from both sides of the transaction. He's currently the Online Shopping Guide for About.com and an eCommerce columnist for both online and offline publications.

Dedication

This book is dedicated to my mother-in-law and father-in-law, Lois and Alex Peacock, who are happy in the thought that I keep their daughter in the style she's been accustomed to. Lois and Alex—here's how I do it!

Tell Us What You Think!

As the reader of this book, *you* are our most important critic and commentator. We value your opinion and want to know what we're doing right, what we could do better, what areas you'd like to see us publish in, and any other words of wisdom you're willing to pass our way.

I welcome your comments. You can email or write me directly to let me know what you did or didn't like about this book—as well as what we can do to make our books stronger.

Please note that I cannot help you with technical problems related to the topic of this book, and that due to the high volume of mail I receive, I might not be able to reply to every message.

When you write, please be sure to include this book's title and author as well as your name and phone or fax number. I will carefully review your comments and share them with the author and editors who worked on the book.

Email: cigfeedback@pearsoned.com

Mail: Alpha Books
          201 West 103rd Street
          Indianapolis, IN 46290 USA

Foreword

The Electronic Commerce revolution is well and truly under way, and there are undoubtedly fortunes to be made (and lost) on the Internet. It is an exciting time—a time when the old rules of business are being rewritten and a time when a small business can, with a bit of inspiration, hard work, and luck, become spectacularly successful.

It's tempting to rush in and try to grab a piece of the action, only to discover that it just isn't that easy. There are so many options available for setting up a Web store, processing payments, and marketing. How do you pick the best software and services for your business? How do you know you're not being ripped off? What you desperately need is expert guidance at an early stage—a helping hand to point your new business in the right direction and avoid the most obvious pitfalls.

There are many excellent academic studies and technical guides to Electronic Commerce on the market, but up until now there hasn't been a straightforward, streetwise guide for someone who wants to set a up a business on the Net—no book that gives real-world answers to real-world questions. *The Complete Idiot's Guide to Starting an Online Business* fills that gap admirably.

Gordon Whyte

About.com Guide to Electronic Commerce

www.ecommerce.about.com

Introduction

We're living in an historic period of time. A time when anyone with an idea, some guidance, and a lot of hard work can start their own business and share in the fruits of one of the biggest opportunities of the next century—eCommerce.

The Internet—little known to the general public 10 short years ago—has opened the door to virtually anyone wanting to start their own online business. Ten years from now, you and I will be shopping for products and services on the Internet not just through our PCs but through our TVs, telephones, cell phones, PDAs—and yes—even our refrigerators and microwave ovens. We'll be shopping from our homes, our cars, the grocery store, and the mall using hand-held Internet-based personal shopping agents who will know—even anticipate—our shopping needs.

All this and more will open up a vast array of online business opportunities that we can only hint of today—opportunities that *you* can take advantage of to become a cyber-merchant of the twenty-first century.

But what about the Wal-Marts, Macys, and IBMs of the world, you ask? Aren't they going to dominate cyberspace as they dominated "meatspace"? And what about the current crop of eTailers like Amazon, eToys, and CDNow? Would you dare compete with the likes of them?

Well, ponder this. The turn of the next century will look more like the turn of the last. The end of the last century saw the last of the "cottage industries." These home-based businesses went the way of the carrier pigeon as the population marched lock-step into the factories and offices of the Industrial Age. Working for oneself was replaced by working for the firm and individuality was consumed by the faceless corporation.

But the Internet is changing all that and bringing back the "cottage industry."

The Internet levels the playing field and gives any business of any size—home based or not—the image of a larger company that creates the perception in the potential customer that your online business is credible and able to perform. The Internet gives you the power to compete with established brands giving you not only the opportunity of branding your business—but branding *you*!

Sure. It's a long journey from idea to cyber-mogul but as the old sage said, "A journey of a 1,000 miles starts with but a single step."

So, let's shift our eyes away from the future for now and focus on the task at hand—where to begin.

'nuff said. So follow me.

How to Use This Book

The Complete Idiot's Guide to Starting and Online Business begins with an explanation of eCommerce, what to sell, how to sell it, how to plan it, and where to find the money to fund it. Then it gives you the basics of setting up shop on the Web, where to host it, some eCommerce Dos and Don'ts, and how to take orders and ship them. Finally, it covers the essentials of marketing and promoting your new business.

The book is organized in such a way that you can quickly find a topic and get the information you need to set up your own online business.

Part 1, "Staking Your Claim," includes Chapters 1 through 6 and leads you through a process of identifying a need to fill with your new business, exploring the different ways of selling on the Internet, and creating your unique selling position. It also walks you through building a business plan and the ways to fund your new business.

Part 2, "Setting Up Shop," includes Chapters 7 through 11 and shows you how to plan, deign, and set up your online business. It describes eCommerce and Web site essentials and helps you decide whether to build your own or use one of the many store builders available on the Web. It the goes on to explain where and how to host your Web site.

Part 3, "eCommerce Basics," includes Chapters 12 through 14 and covers the basics of eCommerce—the Dos and Don'ts, meeting the customer's expectations, and the importance of informational content and a sense of community on your eCommerce site.

Part 4, "Delivering the Goods," includes Chapters 15 through 17 and explains how to take an order from your site, and how to take credit cards, debit cards, and even personal checks on your Web site. It then describes how to fulfill an order, ship it, and track it. Finally, it covers the essentials of good customer service and how to achieve it.

Part 5, "Promoting Your Online Business," includes Chapters 18 through 23 and shows you how to market and promote your new business through paid advertising, free marketing, give-aways, contests, and promotions. It also gives you the tools on how to market on the Web and the importance of PR and how to use it.

Finally, you'll find a list of valuable eCommerce Internet resources in the Appendix and a Glossary of technical terms so you not only can walk-the-walk of eCommerce but talk-the-talk, too.

Conventions Used in This Book

All through the book, you'll be presented with tips and advice to help you understand the technical language used in the text and to help make your online business more successful.

Important text will be called out with a special typeface. For example if you are instructed to press **Ctrl+C** or select a particular **menu item**, it will appear in **bold**. `Web address` and other `text` that you must type will appear in monospaced type.

In addition you will find special tips and advice in these sidebars:

eTalk

Hey. The Internet is about technology. But that doesn't mean we have to settle for the techno-babble. So look for these sidebars to bring you quickly up to speed on technical terminology.

eTip

Check these out for quick tips and tidbits on how to promote your online business, find much needed resources, and keep your site customer friendly.

eTrend

The Net has a surprising way of quickly making tomorrow today. So, when creating your online business strategy, keep these eCommerce trends in mind.

eWarning

Watch out for these common and not so common eCommerce mistakes. They can quickly stop a customer—and a sale—in its tracks.

Get in the Game

Still here? Hey, time's a-wasting. You're on Internet time now! So turn the page and let's get started!

Part 1
Staking Your Claim

There's gold in them thar cyber-hills, partner—and it's time to stake yer claim!

There's no doubt about it. People are buying online and they could be buying from YOU. If you think your small business idea is too small for eCommerce—think again. There's plenty of room under the eCommerce tent and it's easy to do. So, make that PC of yours double as a cash register and let's get started!

Chapter 1

Putting the "e" in eCommerce

In This Chapter

➤ Discover what eCommerce is and who's doing it

➤ See the opportunity and what it means to you

➤ The numbers tell the tale—find out who's buying online

Just a few short years ago there were no Web sites—now there are more than 100 million of them. According to a survey by NPD Online Research, almost half of all Internet users will have their own personal Web site by the middle of 2000.

And it's not just the number of Web sites that are growing. The population of the Internet is growing, too. According to the U.S. Department of Commerce in 1993, three million people were connected to the Internet. In 1999, 80 million Americans were connected and approximately 200 million people worldwide. Today, thousands of new people are coming online each and every week. Those in business have noticed the numbers and they've seen the handwriting on the wall. Their response? They're opening new Web sites at a furious pace, selling products and services to online consumers.

And so can you.

If you have the right kind of business, the Internet can open up a vast market of customers at a price unheard of even a year or two ago.

What's Happening Here?

eCommerce seems to be everywhere these days. On the radio and TV, in magazines and newspapers—it seems you can't escape the "dot-com" craze. It's everywhere and lots of people are doing it. Your neighbor's kid down the street has dumped his newspaper route and became a cyber-merchant on the Web. Your mother in Florida is cleaning out her garage and her neighbor's by selling the contents on eBay. And your husband is spamming your email list enticing your friends, family, and co-workers to buy his Amway products.

So, what's happening here? And can you still get a piece of the eCommerce pie?

Although at first look, eCommerce (or its more formal name—electronic commerce) seems to be a well-established entity. In reality, eCommerce has been in existence for only a few years. In fact, commerce on the Internet wasn't even allowed until the early 1990s. That's when Vice President Al Gore declared the Internet the Information Superhighway and sought to make the Internet—then a private enclave of the government, researchers, and university professors—open to the general public.

And he did.

eCommerce Is Short for Electronic Commerce

Electronic commerce is quite simply selling online over the Internet. An eCommerce site will display, offer, and sell its product or service electronically through personal computers connected to the Net or through Internet-enabled information devices.

After the doors to the Internet's World Wide Web were flung open to the public, millions flocked to newly formed ISPs, fired up their PCs, and boarded the Information Superhighway. The invention of the Web browser made it easy to surf the Net. Text and images appeared on our monitors enticing us to join in the new global block party. And millions did. And where there's millions of people, there's a potential market; and where there's a potential market business soon follows.

Not too long ago, there was only a scattering of eCommerce sites. A book seller here, a T-shirt seller there—but soon they were sprouting up everywhere on the Web. One of the first online merchants to put eCommerce on the map was Amazon.com. They proved that people would buy books off the Net if you gave them a convenient way to save and to buy. Soon thousands of imitators followed selling everything from flowers, chocolates, and greeting cards to CDs, videos, gifts—even automobiles. Nothing was sacred. Today, you can even buy your funeral arrangements over the Net at WebCaskets.com at www.webcaskets.com.

Now, there's nothing mysterious about eCommerce. If you ever bought an item from a catalog or from an advertisement in a magazine, the purchase process is pretty much the same. The only difference is that instead of purchasing from a person over the telephone or sending a check through the mail, you're conducting the transaction with a mouse through your PC. For the business, the fulfillment process that takes place is no different from taking and fulfilling an order from over the phone.

What puts the "e" in eCommerce is that the transaction is completed electronically and without human intervention. After the order is accepted, the eTailer, or online retailer, fills and ships the order the same way any brick-and-mortar store would. The fact is, a dot-com company faces the same challenges of building a presence, marketing and promoting the business, taking orders, fulfilling and shipping them, and has all the same customer service issues to solve that a no-dot company has.

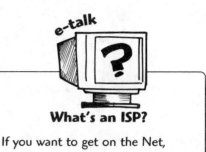

What's an ISP?

If you want to get on the Net, you'll need an ISP. ISP stands for *Internet Service Provider* and provides Internet access to its subscribers. Like a phone company, your ISP connects you to the Internet.

What Is the Big Deal?

What's so special about eCommerce? Why does it offer a unique opportunity to those who go searching for business online?

It's very simple. What eCommerce does is level the playing field.

If you design your business right, the Internet can give your company the image of a large company. Your Web site can make your business look just as large as those that are many times your size. It also can build in a potential customer's mind the perception that your business is as credible as any other that's just a mouse click away.

To "Dot" or Not to "Dot"

The "dot" referred to here is the little dot in .com (www.i-am-in-business-online.com) and identifies a business as an eCommerce company. A no-dot company is a traditional brick-and-mortar business we see in the real world.

Three simple words can make or break your business: It's not location, location, and location as in real estate, but execution, execution, and execution. The dirty little secret of eCommerce is that ideas are easy. It's their execution that determines whether an online business is a success or failure. And in that area—the ability to execute properly—your new business idea has the same chance of succeeding as any other business on the Net—large, medium, or small!

One Man's Testimonial

To see how a one-person operation can flourish, meet entrepreneur Jim Daniels. He started his publishing business with $300. Six months later he was earning enough to quit his day job. Check it out at www.bizweb2000.com/howiquit.htm.

The truth is, the Internet is still an open marketplace for small startups and one-person operations can *and* do build profitable online businesses.

In fact, you don't even need a site to conduct a successful business on the Internet. At person-to-person auction sites like eBay (www.ebay.com), individuals have established their own home-based business buying products and auctioning them off to the highest bidder. Other Net entrepreneurs don't bother to carry inventory at all! Their business model is to set up small content and community sites, join an online merchant's affiliate or associate programs and sell the merchant's merchandise off their site. The merchant takes the order, ships it, and performs all the customer service.

You're probably thinking that heavy hitters with state-of-the-art technology have the eCommerce edge. Or setting up a commerce-ready Web site costs tens of thousands of

eCommerce Success Stories

Do you have to be a well-known merchant to be a success? Not at all! Read how small startups like Just Balls, Flying Noodle, and 1–800 Birthday used the Net to build a successful international business on the Web. Check it out at www.ecommercetimes.com/ success_stories/.

dollars. Well, think again. You can launch a respectable online store for what you spend on video rentals each month. Net companies like Yahoo Store (store.yahoo.com) and iCat (www.icat.com), which we'll discuss in Chapter 9, "Hosting with an ISP," can set up and maintain your online store for as little as $100 a month—and there are some companies that will do it for free!

How Much Is Enough?

You might be wondering if you need to offer shoppers hundreds of products for sale at your online store to be successful. The answer to that question is *no*. Research done by ViaWeb (now Yahoo Store), a host for online merchants, showed that adding more items to an online store doesn't guarantee more sales. Stores that sold less than 10 products had almost as many orders as stores selling 50 products.

Finally, just because the new business model is eCommerce, old business models are not obsolete. Customer service, customer care, a good product or service at a fair price, integrity, and above all proper execution of your business plan are principles that still hold true in business whether it's online or not.

The "Dot-Com" Craze

Recognize these eCommerce companies?

Amazon, CDNow, Cyberian Outpost—they're responsible for what we now call the dot-com craze. When they first hit the Net and opened for business, they were generally ignored by their counterparts in the brick-and-mortar world. The brick-and-mortar crowd saw the Internet as another fad equal to the civilian band radio craze of a couple of decades before. They dismissed it.

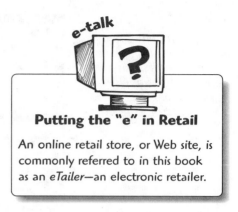

e-talk

Putting the "e" in Retail

An online retail store, or Web site, is commonly referred to in this book as an *eTailer*—an electronic retailer.

That proved to be a mistake. A *big* mistake.

Original no-dot companies like Barnes & Noble, Toys-R-Us, and Compaq were "Amazoned" and soon in a race for their customers who were buying more and more from these electronic upstarts. And if that wasn't bad enough, eTailers like Amazon were flexing their eCommerce muscle and using the inroads made to their online shoppers to sell a wide variety of products competing for the business of even more "no dot" companies (see Figure 1.1).

e-talk

Getting Amazoned

Amazon and its aggressive merchandising first-to-the Net strategy blindsided many no-dot companies who thought that the Net was a fad and not a serious competitor to their real world business. They discovered otherwise. A perfect example is Barnes&Noble which now has to play catch-up to Amazon on the Net.

It seems that if you were a no-dot company you were going no where fast.

Now, dot-com companies are being seen and heard almost everywhere. On TV and the radio, on billboards, in magazines and newspapers. Go to a sports event and right beside the real estate ad on the scoreboard is one for an eCommerce company. And a couple of years ago saw the first "dot com" TV ad on the Super Bowl.

Figure 1.1

Using their ability to reach thousands of potential customers a day, Amazon offers a wide variety of products in many different categories.

Today, there's a frenzied rush to get companies online but success will not necessarily go to the biggest or well known—or even the well funded. Take Toys-R-Us as an example. Being "Amazoned" by eToys, they have yet to create a viable business strategy for selling online. Toys-R-Us is a company with years of experience in its industry, sufficient funds, and good product sources, yet it is unable to create a competitive presence on the Internet.

On the Net, size does *not* matter. You can still build a small- or medium-sized profitable business if you can identify a need, move quickly to meet it, and execute your business plan properly.

The Internet can add tremendous marketing power to a small business. As a dot-com company you can conduct business with both national and international customers with costs far below those of brick-and-mortar stores. Think of it. Because the Internet is global, the cost to reach someone in your local community is the same as it is to contact someone on the other side of the world. Using the technology of the Net, you can take orders and easily and inexpensively build a company's image, provide customer support, make available technical and troubleshooting information, develop prospect lists, and conduct customer surveys with a click of a mouse.

All well and good. But what's the opportunity here?

Just the Stats, Ma'am, Just the Stats

Although eCommerce represents a small part of retail sales today, the potential for eCommerce is immense. Although estimates of retail consumer shopping revenues vary from a low of $4 billion to a high of $36 billion for 1999 alone, Forrester

Research (www.forrester.com) expects U.S. online retail sales to hit $184 billion by 2004. This represents a near astronomical growth from their 1999 estimate of $20.2 billion.

The demographics of the Internet cover the gamut from children, to teenagers, to old and young adults. Ages 18–54 are well represented on the Internet and make up a profitable target market for eTailers on the Net. And who's buying now? Boomers in their peak earning years and seniors with deepening pockets. Close on their heels is Generation X—and the offspring of the Baby Boomers—Generation Y.

MMG eCommerce Clock

Want to know just how many dollars are being spent online—right now? Then check out the real-time eCommerce clock at the Multimedia Marketing Group at www.mmgco.com/clock.html.

Today's eShopper

People who shop online are older than you think. The average age is 43 years old. Online shoppers have a lot of disposable income. The medium annual income is approximately $40,000 a year. But a significant number of people make $100,000 or $200,000 or more a year. People who shop online are much more likely than average to be married and those who shop online are *twice* as likely to be college graduates.

The gender demographics are shifting as well. After the domain of men, more women have come on to the Internet and are making an impact on eCommerce. There are currently 27 million women online in the U.S., according to eMarketer, and they account for 46% of the Internet users in America. And as they continue to grow, NetSmart America predicts they can catch and possibly surpass their male counterparts in the near future.

Internet Economy Indicators

Check out these indicators. They can give you a quick study of the economics driving the Internet. The indicators are derived from analysis of four layers of the Internet Economy: Internet Infrastructure, Internet Applications, Internet Intermediary, and Internet Commerce. Find them at www.internetindicators.com/facts.html.

As far as shopping online, NetSmart found that women account for 75% of major household purchases. NetSmart also found that 53% of women made an online purchase, up from 33% in 1998. Because of their Internet access, 17% of women are doing less catalog shopping and 15% are doing less retail shopping.

Keep Your Eye on the eCommerce Puck

As Wayne Gretzky said: "The real key to success is knowing where the puck is going, not where it is."

To keep track of the eCommerce puck, you need to stay on top of the Internet stats. There are several good sites on the Net that can keep you up to date.

CyberAtlas

www.cyberatlas.com

CyberAtlas can provide you with valuable statistics and Web marketing information, enabling you to understand the online business environment and make more informed business decisions. CyberAtlas gathers online research from the best data resources to provide a complete review of the latest surveys and technologies available.

InternetStats

www.internetstats.com

InternetStats is an excellent source pointing to Web sites having the business and market information, statistics, and trends you need (see Figure 1.2). Although InternetStats doesn't offer numbers directly, it does point you to the proper sites to find the statistic you need. One useful feature is its search engine that you can use to find statistics or market data on a specific industry.

Figure 1.2

InternetStats can point you to a wide variety of statistical sites on the Web. A one-stop-shop for net stats.

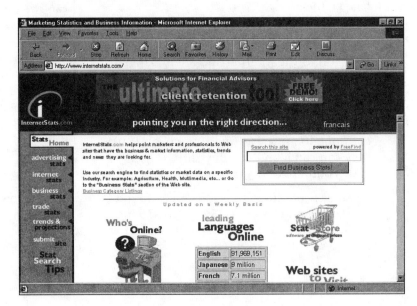

Internet World Statistics Toolbox

✳www.internetworld.com/daily/stats/index.html

Internet World Statistics Toolbox offers a collection of statistics on various Internet and technology related fields such as: eCommerce, Web sites, software, hardware, and who's online.

The Least You Need to Know

➤ The Internet levels the playing field. You can look as big as your largest competitor.

➤ You can still launch a new business online. eCommerce opportunities are growing not decreasing.

➤ As a "dot com" company you can conduct business with both national and international customers.

➤ The cost to reach someone in your local community is the same as it is to reach someone on the other side of the world.

Chapter 2

What's the Big Idea? Identifying a Need

In This Chapter

➤ Learn what types of businesses you can do online

➤ Discover how to choose an idea for your online business

➤ Learn how to identify your customer's specific wants and needs

➤ Determine whether you should sell your own products or those of others

"Find a need and fill it."

That's your first step in starting an online business. The Net can make it easy because it offers you the opportunity to reach and sell to a very targeted market. It's the perfect place for niche marketing.

Here's why.

Let's say you have a product or service that would make someone's life easier—a new way to sew buttons on a garment without a needle and thread. A single product like that could never support a retail storefront. However, on the Net you could reach thousands, even millions of people who could use such a timesaving device.

So, where do you start? With motivation. You need to know what motivates a shopper to buy. Keep in mind that different shoppers are motivated by different things—even at different times. When trying to choose a product or service to sell, keep the following human motivators in mind:

➤ Information

➤ Economic

➤ Entertainment

➤ Social

Niche Marketing

A niche market is one where you meet the needs of a particular consumer audience. For example, selling fitness equipment to health buffs, or hip clothing to teenagers, or foreign films to movie experts.

A great human motivator is the need for information, and that's where the Internet shines. The Internet is like the Library of Congress multiplied millions of times. But it's also a vast information storehouse that is hard to navigate. Provide a ready source of information that meets a shopper's need, and you can turn that shopper into a customer.

A second very strong motivator is economic. It goes without saying that commerce on the Net is a fast growing segment. After all, if you didn't believe that you wouldn't be reading this book! And what motivates a shopper to buy? A quality product, a nice selection, a secure and convenient way to buy—even a great deal! All these and more would entice a shopper to open his wallet and buy from your online store.

Entertainment is another motivator. We all love to be entertained. We'll even pay for it if we feel the value is there. So think about ways of selling entertainment products and services to the online shopper.

Finally, human interaction is a strong motivational force. The opportunity to hobnob with those of similar interests can be turned into a profitable business. Think about community sites that provide live chat or ways for people to meet one another. Fill the need to interact and you can build an effective business on it.

Business Opportunity Scams

If you've been on the Net for any length of time, "they" have pitched you. What I'm talking about are the get-rich-quick schemes that you get via email. These scams masquerading as business opportunities should be avoided like the plague. These are *not* business opportunities! If the business opportunity seems too good to be true—then it is! If you think you've been a victim of a business opportunity scam or just want to learn how to avoid them then go to www.ftc.gov/bizop.

Should I Sell a Product or Service?

That's a good question. Luckily you can easily do either one on the Net. It makes no difference whether you sell a product or a service from your Web site. Both have their advantages and disadvantages.

Selling products online has certain advantages. When selling products, you're not constrained by a limited amount of inventory. When selling products, you can grow your business more quickly because the more products you sell, the more income you make.

The disadvantage of selling products is that they normally require you to stock and ship them. Unless you have a very high profit margin on a product, you have to fulfill a large number of orders to make a reasonable amount of sales.

The advantage of an online services company is that making a profit is quicker and easier because the entire price of the service is paid to you. Also, there is the opportunity to generate repeat business if your clients are pleased with your service. The main disadvantage is there is only so much *time*. We're only human and a person can perform only a certain number of services in a 24-hour period.

Selling services can provide you with immediate revenue but will never give you the biggest bang for your buck in the long run. In short, you can sell only so much of your time, whereas you can sell an unlimited amount of products. The trick is to turn a successful online service into a product. For example, AskMD.com provides electronic health information, an online health opinion—including a second opinion—and sells books, medical products, and supplies (see Figure 2.1). Another example is to have a service that helps people market their online business—like search engine placement—and then sell them a book on how to do it.

Figure 2.1

AskMD is an example of an eCommerce site that has successfully turned an online service into a product.

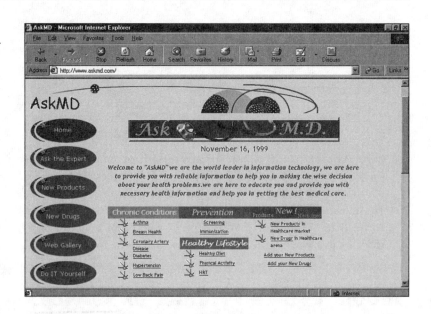

The Main Types of Online Businesses

An online business is not limited to selling just products and services. In fact there are five primary ways of doing business on the Net.

➤ Become an Online Retailer

➤ Become an Online Information Seller

➤ Start an Online Consultation Service

➤ Become an Online Services Seller

➤ Become an Online Subscription Seller

Let's check each one out.

Online Retailers   eTailers, as they are called, are the popular and well known "dot com" companies. They started out selling the basic commodity products—books, videos, and CDs—then branched out to almost every conceivable product that you could buy in the real world. If you become an eTailer, you can sell your own products or market those of another merchant.

Online Information Sellers   Information sellers offer information products for sale. Unlike buying a product, the customer pays for the information and immediately downloads it to his or her computer. A good example of this kind of merchandise is a piece of software. Another is an online newsletter or publication or perhaps a how-to manual that you pay to receive electronically.

Should You Buy an Existing Business?

One online business strategy you might consider is buying an existing eCommerce company. This has several benefits like a current product to sell, a Web site already established, and a customer base to sell to. A good place to start looking for an eCommerce business to buy is at www.bizbuysell.com.

✱**Online <u>Consultation Services</u>**   Consultants are different from Online Information Sellers. They're an online business with a human touch. In this case you might sell advice. Here your customer contacts you directly with a question and you respond personally. This is usually done via email but the business also might offer a live chat room where customers can speak with the consultant or advisor directly.

✱ **<u>Service Sellers</u>**   There are online businesses that just sell services. They perform an actual service on behalf of the customer such as lawyers giving legal advice, CPAs doing taxes, doctors giving medical advice—even Web-site designing and computer programming.

Subscription Sellers   Online businesses that sell subscriptions do just that. A good example of this type of business is the *Wall Street Journal*. Other online businesses might charge membership fees to view the content of their site or participate in one-on-one chat communities.

Should You Sell on Price or Value-Add?

There are two main ways to distinguish your products from your competitors. The first is by price and the second is by adding value. Selling on price is simple—and the least expensive. But you can charge higher prices and still get the sale by adding value to your product offering such as good customer service, guarantees, easy exchange policies, or overnight delivery.

Dr. Maslow I Presume!—Meeting Basic Human Needs

One of the easiest ways to decide on a product to sell is to find a problem then offer a product or service to solve it. The first step is to decide who your target customer is.

Are your customers consumers or other businesses? What are your customers looking for? If your customers are consumers, what are their ages? What are they interested in? What are their needs? If they are businesses, what products and services will help them solve their day-to-day business problems?

Get Product Ideas By Observing Consumer Behavior

Ask yourself these questions. What do people buy and why? What do they want to buy but can't? What do they buy and don't like? What are people buying a lot of? What's trendy and in vogue?

Then you have to decide what to sell them. There are products that sell well online and are easy to fulfill and ship, such as books, software, CDs, housewares, and apparel. Services such as travel packages, information, and professional services work well also. If you're selling products, stick with nonperishable items that are easy to store and ship.

The first step is to analyze your potential customer's needs. The best way to do that is to organize them into the basic human needs. For this, we will need to call on the services of Dr. Abraham Maslow.

Dr. Maslow was a twentieth-century psychologist who spent a lot of time categorizing human needs. If he were alive today and on the Internet, I bet he would have made a pretty effective eTailer. He could easily define a list of human needs and be good at choosing the products to satisfy them.

And so can you.

Meeting Physical Needs

The basic physical human needs are food, shelter, and clothing. If you were going to sell products that solve the problem of finding these physical needs, you would consider these types of products and services.

Physical Needs—Product Ideas

We all need to eat and drink, so selling food products online is a natural. It's something that we all need and is consumable—meaning we can buy the same product over and over. That's good for business. In addition, the food products you sell can be gourmet in nature or ethnic or regional food types that certain customer segments would be want buy.

The need for shelter from the elements is right up there with sustenance. Outdoor products like camping and hunting gear and goods for the patio and garden make very good merchandise to sell on the Net.

Finally, though we might not buy clothing as often as we do food, covering our bodies is a social necessity. Apparel meets both the needs of the fashion conscious and protects us from the elements.

Physical Needs—Service Ideas

Our physical needs can be serviced as well. Many who eat, cook. Providing consumer information on how to cook, what to cook, and where to cook is an information product that makes a very good service to sell online. Perhaps, an "Ask Mr. Chef" site where consumers can ask cooking questions to expert chefs. Here's another idea. We all eat out. Many of us eat out frequently. An online business that lists and categorizes restaurants and their reviews is another service that can be provided online.

As for clothing and shelter, a site could provide the best places to camp in an area or a directory of places to fish and hunt. One might even include the ways to catch, clean, and cook the fish and game that you get. You then have a site that does double duty: where to hunt and fish and how to cook what you catch.

Stumped for Ideas? Try These Techniques

Talk to family and friends. Have a brainstorming session over dinner or drinks. Try and think outside the box. Ask others what they would like to buy and what could be improved. Read the trade magazines and don't just focus on what's happening in your country. Remember, the Net is global and what's a good idea in one country and might not apply to another country.

Meeting Safety Needs

Feeling safe and secure is one of our strongest basic needs. The safety needs of protecting self, family, and home offer an online business the opportunity to sell a variety of merchandise and a nice selection of services to the online consumer. An additional safety concern is our health. Think about these product and services ideas if this is the type of customer that you are targeting.

Safety Needs—Product Ideas

Security products like self-defense items and security devices to use when traveling would make very good products to sell on a Web site. Books and tapes on self-defense are other product ideas. Child safety products like baby seats and identification systems would sell well along with home safes and surveillance equipment.

As for health, diet books, exercise tapes, and health and nutrition products are very big sellers on the Net. First-aid equipment and home medical supplies also are good products to sell as well as products for people with disabilities.

Safety Needs—Service Ideas

Many types of safety services can be delivered online and would make a low-overhead, profitable business. They would include private investigative services, directories of alarm services and their reviews, and emergency alert services for the infirm and elderly.

Another service idea would be to provide nutrition and health information. The Nutrition Guide at About.com is an example of a site that provides a wide variety of information on living a healthy life through nutritious eating (see Figure 2.2).

Figure 2.2

Note the ability to offer products for sale to the visitors that come there for information.

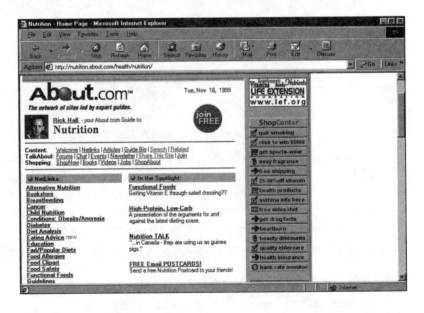

Weight-loss information; nutrition services and guides; and even life, auto, and health insurance can be delivered over the Net.

Belonging Needs

To be loved, to have friends, and to be part of a family fills us with the need to be a part of something greater than ourselves. This need to belong and to express our appreciation for being part of something offers a variety of online business opportunities.

Belonging—Product Ideas

One of the best ways to express our affection for lovers, friends, and family is by giving gifts. Online gift shops are a natural for the Net. When people want to express their affections in a more tangible manner, gifts are one of the best ways to do it. Other products that do just as well are the traditional flowers, cards, and candy. Any of these should be considered as merchandise ideas for your online business.

Belonging—Service Ideas

If you would rather not sell gifts online, then perhaps setting up a gift registry service like the one at www.wishclick.com is the next best thing (see Figure 2.3). This type of service enables visitors to your site to list the actual gifts they want and then inform the potential gift givers. You can then send orders to a gift house that would fulfill and ship them to your customers.

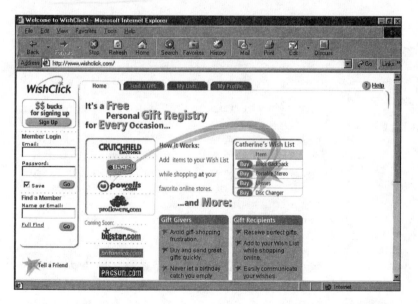

Figure 2.3

Here's a good example of a gift registry service. WishClick matches gift givers to gift recipients.

Another service idea is a genealogy service. Tracing one's roots has become very popular over the last several years—especially with the baby-boom generation. Another popular service that meets the belonging need is an online dating service.

Esteem Needs

We all like to be recognized and feel good about ourselves. Products and services that cater to our esteem needs offer a great opportunity for an online business. How we feel about ourselves and how others perceive us is important to us. Recognition and vanity are strong personal needs that we seek to fulfill.

Esteem Needs—Product Ideas

Beauty and grooming items and other personal care merchandise are the most popular products to sell if your online business is targeting the esteem needs of the consumer. For women, perfume, bath and body lotions, cosmetics, and even fashion products are key items to sell. For men, cologne, razors, and electric shavers would fill the bill.

Next to consider are jewelry items for the ladies—rings, diamonds, bracelets, precious stones—and for men, watches, cufflinks, and rings. Then there are books and videos on personal care, dieting, and products to reverse the aging process.

Can't Think of a Product to Sell? Try This.

You've tried and tried, but still can't come up with a product to sell. Then why not find a merchant who already is selling products—but *not* online—and offer to sell them on the Net. You create the site, the merchant supplies the product, and you both make money.

Esteem Needs—Service Ideas

If meeting the recognition and esteem needs of consumers is your target, then think about these types of services to offer.

Many types of training and educational courses can be offered over the Net, like computer certification classes or real estate courses. You can sell beauty tips to your customers or offer a jewelry appraisal service. Finally, you can offer advice on how to succeed in business or even—after reading this book— offer a course on how to set up your own online business!

Selling Your Creative Work

You don't have to limit yourself to selling other people's products or even services. Consider selling your own creative work.

Ask yourself this. What one thing do you do better than everyone else? Maybe you're a good photographer. Or perhaps, you enjoy writing. Maybe you enjoy working with your hands creating works of art or unique items that can be sold as gifts.

Sit down some evening after work with a pad and pencil or drop by your local coffeehouse and make a list of what you enjoy doing. You might be surprised that what you like to do can be turned into a product or service you can sell online. The key thought here is to do what you enjoy!

Here's a Way to See if Your Idea Is Original

The US Patent and Trademark Office holds the mother of all patent databases. If its been patented; its here. Check out patent descriptions at www.patents.ibm.com.

The Least You Need to Know

➤ The number one rule in starting an online business is "Find a need and fill it."

➤ You only have so much of your time. Selling a service online will give you immediate profitability but you can grow your business more quickly if you sell products—the more you sell, the more income you make.

➤ You must know who your customers are, define their needs, and then fill them.

➤ You don't have to limit yourself to selling other people's products or even services. Consider selling your own creative work.

Chapter 3

WWW—The Wild and Wooly Web

In This Chapter

➤ Find out the different ways you can sell off the Net

➤ Learn what affiliate selling is and what to look out for

➤ Should you sell products without a Web site? Are person-to-person auctions the way to go?

➤ Learn how to use email to sell your product or service

➤ Should you consider setting up shop in an online mall?

You've decided on a need to meet and you've chosen a product or service to meet it. Next task—where to sell it? Luckily the Internet offers you a virtual universe of ways to get your product offer in front of potential customers.

Selling Off the Web—Let Me Count the Ways

It might sound pretty obvious but the first thing to consider when selling your product or service is to find out where your customers congregate. Whether they congregate at your Web site, at auction sites, at classified sites, or at online malls you need to know how to reach them.

When a person wants to set up shop on the Net, the first thing they do is build a Web site. But, there are many alternative ways of selling on the Net that don't require a Web site. You can offer your product or service to potential customers in a number of ways:

➤ Selling from your own Web site with your own product or service.

➤ Selling someone else's product or service from your Web site.

➤ Selling your product at person-to-person auctions.

➤ Selling your product or service through email.

➤ Selling your product or service through online classified ads.

➤ Selling through an online mall.

Any one of these can produce profitable results and help you launch your online business. They each offer their own unique opportunities and challenges.

What's HTML?

Web pages are built using HTML. *HTML* stands for Hypertext Markup Language. The HTML code is a set of commands embedded in a Web page that tells the page what text to display, how it's formatted, and how and where the graphics on a Web page are displayed.

Selling Off a Web Site

Although we will focus on setting up your eCommerce Web site in later chapters, it's good to understand a few of the selling basics connected with selling from a site.

Where you host your Web store and the type of store you need to build depends a lot on what you plan to sell. If you have only a few products to sell, you can list them on a few simple pages with HTML forms to accept orders.

If you have a very large range of products, you will need to build a Web store using a database and an electronic shopping cart.

Another thing to remember is that the more features you add to your store like a database or shopping cart, the more sophisticated the software and hardware you will need. Features like these require a lot of customization and support. Finally, should you consider having your own Web store selling your own products or should you join an affiliate program and sell that merchant's products?

If you don't want the hassle of listing, warehousing, fulfilling, and shipping your own orders, then you should consider Network Selling.

Selling Off a Network

Network selling—or *affiliate programs* as they are called—allow you to sell other merchant's products and services through your site. The advantages: you don't have to source products, warehouse, or ship them. The disadvantages: you only get paid a small commission on each sale.

If Mohammed Won't Come to the Mountain...

Currently, there are over one million Web sites participating in some kind of affiliate program. The products and services sold run the gamut from hard goods such as books, CDs, toys, and movies to credit card applications and marketing programs.

The merchants that offer these programs use them primarily to drive your traffic to their site. They figure if Mohammed—the shopper—won't come to the mountain—the merchant—take the mountain to Mohammed. Web sites in a merchant's affiliate program normally place a merchant's banner on their Web site, hawking a particular product or service.

Keep in mind that you do make a commission if your visitor clicks the banner and buys something from the merchant's site. Chances are though, your visitor will not return to *your* site to buy products in the future after he is aware of the merchant's Web site. So, in a way, you act as a salesman for the merchant and earn a commission when your visitor buys.

The key to making an affiliate program a success for your site is to target your customers. Associate Programs Directory, www.associateprograms.com, lists a wide variety of affiliate programs and also ranks them (see Figure 3.1). If you have a sports site, sell sporting goods or personal electronic equipment—not housewares. If your site caters to women, avoid products that primarily target men.

e-talk

What's an Electronic Shopping Cart?

Just like in a grocery store, you can use an electronic shopping cart at a Web store. By placing items in your electronic shopping cart, you can go from product offer to product offer without having to buy each one separately. When you decide to check out of the Web store, you complete just one order form, pay once, and you're on your way.

e-trend

Catch the Next eCommerce Wave—Syndicated Selling

Syndicated selling or *distributed commerce* is another term for affiliate selling. Forrester Research states that "Syndicated selling will take over...[and] rapidly outpace both Internet shopping malls and destination-only stores." Jupiter Communications reports that affiliate programs account for 11% of the $5.8 billion of consumer transactions online. They project that figure to grow to 24% or $37.5 billion in total sales by 2002.

Then, be sure the products you sell either have a high retail price or that you're paid a high commission on lower-priced products. Remember, you're being paid on commission. Be sure the payment is worth your effort.

Figure 3.1

Check out the Associate Programs Directory's Top 10 affiliate programs.

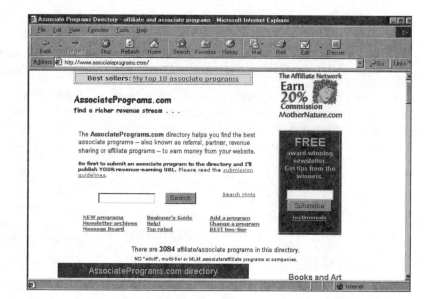

Choosing the right product or service to sell will go a long way in generating a meaningful revenue stream. And don't make the mistake of selecting too many merchant partners. Concentrate on only one—or just a few—programs and then target them to your Web site visitors.

Finally, what kind of help does the merchant offer its affiliates? Most turn mute after the affiliate signs up. But if you're going to sell their product or service, they should offer sales ideas, promotions, and guidance to help you sell their product or service.

A Word of Warning

Affiliate programs are one of the hottest eCommerce plays on the Net. They're easy to join, there are no up front costs, and no costly overhead.

Some programs are either outright scams or structured in such a way that you'll have to sell tens of thousands of dollars of product a month to earn even a meager income. Read the fine print in the Affiliate Agreement that should be posted on a

Get the Real Scoop On Affiliate Programs

Declan Dunn is a well-known affiliate program consultant who understands the pros and cons of affiliate selling. His book *The Complete, Insider's Guide to Associate & Affiliate Programs* is a must read if you're considering joining an affiliate program. Order it at www.linkstosales.com/dunn.html.

merchant's site. See what you are agreeing to do and what the merchant is agreeing to pay you—and when. Some programs are worded in such a way that they will *never* pay you!

Investigate the programs you want to join. Don't pay to join *any* affiliate program and be careful to read the fine print about charging you any fees *after* the sale. Some merchants actually charge back against the commissions you earn and some merchant's will not pay you at all if you don't meet a minimum amount of sales in a period.

Finally, make sure that your sales and commissions are being tracked correctly. Many merchants track their own programs and unless you are completely comfortable with their tracking system, you should consider affiliate programs that use an outside third-party tracking company like BeFree or Linkshare.

Affiliate Tracking Companies—A Good Place to Find Reputable Programs

Third-party affiliate tracking companies like BeFree and Linkshare not only manage and track merchant affiliate programs, but also list reputable ones that do. Check them out at www.befree.com and www.linkshare.com.

Where to Find and Join Affiliate Programs

If you want to go the affiliate selling route, then start with these affiliate program directories. Those listed here are some of the best because they offer advice on choosing a program and—in some cases—even review and rank them.

Your first stop is the Affiliate Times at www.affiliatetimes.com/Info/toprating.htm. The Affiliate Times presents its Affiliate Program Performance Index (APPI) to the top 10 affiliate programs in the APPI index. The index is like a Fortune 500 of Affiliate Programs. The APPI index is calculated by evaluating the top picks of the most respected affiliate program reviewers. It's a good place to start your hunt for affiliate programs.

Get To Know These Gentlemen

There are three affiliate program advisors that you should check out. These three men offer unbiased reviews of many of the most popular affiliate programs on the Net. Check them out. Glenn Sobel's Affiliate Advisor.com at www.AffiliateAdvisor.com, Mark J. Welch's list of Commission-Based Affiliate Programs at www.adbility.com/wpag/bc_main.htm, and Allan Gardyne's AssociatesPrograms.com at www.associateprograms.com.

Then check out the reviewers sites themselves.

- ➤ AssociatePrograms.com at www.associateprograms.com
- ➤ CashPile at www.cashpile.com
- ➤ ClickQuick at www.clickquick.com
- ➤ Revenews at www.revenews.com
- ➤ Clickslink at www.clickslink.com
- ➤ AffiliateGuide at www.affiliateguide.com
- ➤ i-revenue.net at www.i-revenue.net
- ➤ Refer-it at www.referit.com
- ➤ Associate-it at www.associate-it.com
- ➤ 2-Tier at www.2-tier.com
- ➤ Associate Search at associatesearch.com

These sites are your best sources for separating the affiliate wheat from the chaff.

Selling Off Auctions

Selling from your own Web site is not the only way to do business on the Net. Over the last couple of years a whole new way of selling products online has evolved. Its name? Person-to-Person Auctions.

eBay at www.ebay.com pioneered the concept, which was soon followed by a host of imitators including Auction Universe, Amazon, and Yahoo. The advantage of selling off person-to-person auction sites is that there is no need for a Web site. Many home-based businesses have been started and flourish on these auction sites.

One of the reasons the person-to-person auction sites are so successful is the ease of offering your product for bid. At eBay, you simply fill out a form available at their home page, click the **Sell Your Item** icon, and then enter a short, descriptive title of the product and a complete description of the item (see Figure 3.2). Following their instructions, you can even include a picture of your product.

From there, eBay takes over. You set a minimum price that you would sell at—called the minimum bid—and their software automatically assigns a bidding increment. The increments are kept small to encourage more bidding. You can even advertise the existence of your auction to all of eBay.

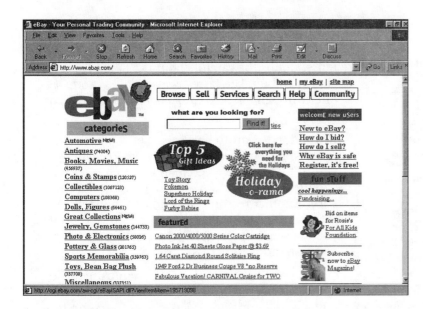

Figure 3.2

The granddaddy of all person-to-person auctions is eBay. You'll find individuals and merchants selling just about any product you can think of—and some you can't.

Other Large Person-to-Person Auction Sites

Besides eBay, there are several other large person-to-person auction sites for you to use to sell your wares.

➤ Yahoo Auctions at `auctions.yahoo.com`— very similar to eBay. List your products with both description and picture.

➤ Auctions.com at `www.auctionuniverse.com`—if you sell antiques, collectibles, and memorabilia, then check out this site.

➤ Excite Auctions at `auctions.excite.com`—similar to eBay and Yahoo Auctions offering you a wide selection of product to sell.

➤ Amazon Auctions at `www.amazon.com`— offers you a wide selection of product to sell.

➤ ZDNet Auctions at `auctions.zdnet.com`—have a technology product to sell like computer desktops, notebooks, and printers? Then sell them here.

What's SPAM?

Spam is unsolicited email. It's the junk mail of the late twentieth century. It clogs email servers around the world and sucks up needed bandwidth on the Net and it's the quickest way to create a bad reputation for you, your company, and your product.

35

What's Opt-In Email?

Opt-in email is the direct opposite of spam. People who opt-in to an email list have said in advance that they are willing to receive unsolicited email from companies on the Net that meet the list criteria. For example, some one who would like to be kept informed of newly released software might opt-in to an email list that announces new software products.

Selling Off Email Lists

Email direct marketing is a hot area for eCommerce. But you must be careful about the email lists you choose to buy. The fastest way to kill a product offer through email is to *spam* your potential customers.

If you don't want to be accused of spamming your recipients, you need to use only *opt-in email lists.* Opt-in lists are targeted email lists that offer you a "politically correct" way to reach your target audience. Another reason to use an opt-in list is your Internet Service Provider or ISP. If your ISP thinks you are sending spam, he will surely cancel your account and your access to the Net.

Opt-in email is more expensive than using unsolicited bulk email but is far more effective and is quickly becoming an effective way to sell on the Internet. The response rate from marketing to the proper opt-in email list can be five to ten times higher than a banner ad.

Here are some rules to keep in mind when selling through email.

➤ **Identify yourself**   Let your prospective customer know who you are right up front. If you've rented an opt-in list, remind them that they opted in. Include a sentence reminding them why they're receiving your email.

➤ **Keep it short—real short—less than one page**   Email is most effective when it's short and simple. After you introduce yourself, give a brief description of your offer. Within the offer, give them a link to click or refer them to the URL of the buying page.

➤ **Provide value for their time**   Make it a compelling or a limited-time offer. Offer something that they couldn't already buy from your site. Perhaps an exclusive offer only made through your email.

➤ **Be ready to apologize**   People's memory can be short and they can forget they opted into the list, or their tastes or needs might have changed. So, if they complain or ask to be removed from your list, respond quickly and politely.

➤ **Make it easy to unsubscribe**   Place your unsubscribe instructions both at the beginning and at the end of your email message. Don't make them call a phone number to unsubscribe. The unsubscribe process should be both fast and simple.

Other Resources Offering Opt-In Email Lists

If you want to email responsibly, then first turn to these sites to purchase targeted opt-in lists.

NetCreations—The first company to collect, categorize, and offer for sale non-spam opt-in email lists is PostmasterDirect (now called NetCreations) at w3.netcreations.com. If you're looking for numbers this is the place. You can choose from more than three million email addresses in 3,000+ categories.

Bulletmail—Bulletmail at www.bulletmail.com gives you a choice of more than 100 targeted, opt-in email lists not available elsewhere. And they target your market by email in a net-appropriate manner. They'll also include an unlimited number of hotlinks in your email to your site offer and even your own email box.

Targ-It—If you want to email using demographic information, then check out Targ-It at www.targ-it.com/. Their lists are all 100% opt-in and have more than 350 lists available for purchase.

Get the Scoop On Email Marketing

Email Marketing News is a monthly email newsletter covering subscription email lists, opt-in, corporate email marketing, advertising in email, email ad techniques, metrics, countering spam, and evolving standards. Check it out at www.emailmarketingnews.com/.

Htmail at www.htmail.com/customer.html gives an interesting twist to their list offer. First they claim that their list will generate as much as a 27% response. Second, they'll guarantee at least a 10% response from your email message or they'll give you your money back.

Finally, The Direct E-Mail List Source at www.copywriter.com/lists/index.htm is a directory of voluntary email marketing lists is a resource for opt-in lists, newsletters, email discussion lists, advertiser-supported email services, and email list brokers where you can advertise without spamming (see Figure 3.3).

Selling Off Classifieds

You've seen the ads, "SWM looking for devout vegetarian into camping, Barry Manilow records, and jell-o wrestling. No freaks."

This is the first type of ad that comes to mind when you say classifieds. But there's another type of classified ad—one that can be used to sell products. The trick is to find the right sites on the Net that cater to businesses and attract customers looking to buy your product or service.

Figure 3.3

The Direct E-mail List Source is a great place to start for both opt-in email lists and ideas for selling your product via email.

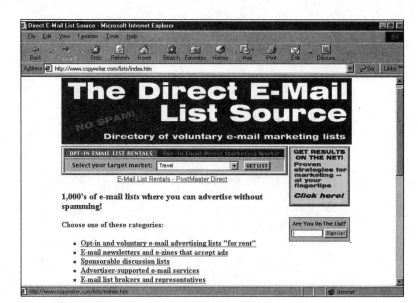

The first stop is a site that is designed specifically for selling products online. It's called Buy & Sell and can be found at www.buysell.com.

One of the most popular classified sites for selling products and services is Yahoo Classifieds at classifieds.yahoo.com. Because of the visitor traffic Yahoo generates to its site, their classified ads are viewed by millions of people each month. But the focus of the ads is usually individuals selling one or two products. Still, you can't ignore the traffic numbers, so it would be worthwhile placing your product for sale there.

The Business Classified Connection, on the other hand, at www.createasite.com/businessclassifiedconnection/classifieds.cgi is focused on business to consumer relationships and offers free business classifieds for marketers, entrepreneurs, and the general business community.

Another classifieds for businesses is i752.com at www.i752.com. They offer a wide variety of items that are essential to today's businesses.

Finally, Promote Plus at promoteplus.hypermart.net/classifieds.html offers a source of low cost advertising through their classified ads. Categories include both business services and products.

Selling Off Online Malls

When eCommerce on the World Wide Web was just starting, online malls were the place to be. They provided a convenient way for shoppers to find a variety of stores in one place. But as stores on the Net developed, the destination sites were the stores themselves and online malls fell from favor.

One of the reasons for this fall from favor was that most of these online malls were nothing more than a directory of stores. The malls didn't add any value to the shopping experience and as the search engines became more mature and efficient, eTailers could be found more easily. The shopping mall that acted as only a directory was not needed any longer.

Some online malls did offer additional value, such as a built-in central purchasing system in the form of a shopping cart. This way you didn't have to pay for shopping-cart software up-front but instead paid for it in higher fees over a period of time. But the main problem was traffic. The malls really didn't advertise and the stores in the malls saw few sales.

Today, online malls are in decline but a new version of them is on the rise.

The major search engines like Yahoo realized a few years back, that they could convert their site visitors into customers. Yahoo was the first to offer an online mall in the form of its Yahoo Store. When you join the Yahoo Store mall as an eTailer, you had the benefit of a major search engine offering its visitors sites to buy the things they were searching for.

Yahoo Store offered the eTailer what the malls didn't—one shopping cart and one interface. Then just last year, Amazon created zShops to compete with Yahoo and upped the ante. Now anyone selling products could open a store on the Net. The result was one return policy, one privacy policy, one shopping cart, one interface, and one customer-support center.

I'll talk more about these do-it-yourself online stores in Chapter 8, "Hosting Your Store for Free." They offer a quick and easy way to get into eCommerce without the large expense.

The Least You Need to Know

➤ Selling from a Web site isn't the only way to do business on the Net. You can use one of several online selling channels available.

➤ You don't have to sell your own products off your Web site. By joining an affiliate program you can sell without the overhead of inventory, fulfillment, shipping, and customer service.

➤ Read the fine print on any Affiliate Program. Make sure you know how, when, and under what conditions you get paid.

➤ Online auctions, email lists, and online classifieds can put you in business immediately.

Chapter 4

Creating a Unique Selling Position

In This Chapter

➤ Learn how to sell on the Net now that the customer is more in control of the transaction

➤ Decide on a pricing model for your business that will attract this new type of buyer

➤ Learn how to differentiate yourself from your competition

Ask a random sample of business owners to tell you what makes them different from their competition and you'd get a blank stare or perhaps a response like "My prices are the lowest." "I guarantee satisfaction." "My products are high quality." "I give great customer service."

Problem is, none of these responses is a *Unique Selling Position* (USP). Many businesses can claim the same things. After you find a need to fill, you must fill it in a unique fashion. A business must know what they offer a customer besides general statements and why they think a shopper should buy from them. That is, what makes them *unique* in the market and in the eyes of a potential customer.

So what is a Unique Selling Position? Let's put it this way. A USP

➤ Gives a your company a unique *advantage* over your competition.

➤ Gives consumers a distinct *reason* to buy from your company.

➤ Portrays in the consumer's mind a compelling *image* of what your business will do for them that others cannot.

Advantage, reason, and image are what your goal should be in creating a Unique Selling Position. Creating a USP is the first thing you need to do before you even consider building your online business. Your USP creates the framework and lays the foundation for your compelling offer. And here's another reason. A good USP also keeps your business pointed in the right direction.

Finally, a good Unique Selling Position helps you deal successfully with the new type of consumer that the Net has created and the different ways of selling that they are demanding.

Commerce Turned on Its Head—The Shopper in Control

A long, long time ago in a Mall far, far away retailers set the price and consumers had little choice but to pay it. Today— because of the Internet—fixed prices are a thing of the past.

In other words, "We're not in Kansas, anymore!"

The pricing of products as we know it has been turned upside down by the Net. The consumer, more and more, is in control of the transaction. Fixed pricing is giving way to all kinds of dynamic pricing schemes ushered in by the technology of the Net. Auctions, reverse auctions, Dutch auctions, comparison shopping, group buying— even bartering—and a host of other buying schemes has put the consumer in control of how much they will pay for an item.

Not that any of this is really new. Auctions, group buying, and bartering have been around in the real world for many years but the Net has made them more efficient. In the real world, it's very difficult for retail stores to change prices after the price tag is applied. But on the Net—prices can be changed in a second.

The technology of the Net offers another advantage to the online consumer—quick and easy comparison shopping. Although most of the Net-based shopping *robots*—or *personal shopping agents* as they are sometimes called—of today are primitive, they are maturing fast. A good example of a comparison-shopping bot is mySimon (see Figure 4.1). They cover the field in the number of merchants and the products shopped. Some day, you and I can simply tell a shopping bot what we want to buy, give it some basic parameters to follow—like size, color, shipping costs, warranties, and return privileges—and it will scamper across the Net searching and negotiating on our behalf for the best deal.

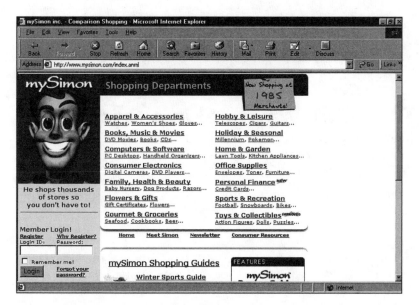

Figure 4.1
*mySimon is a good exam-
ple of a comparison-
shopping bot.*

And what about the consumer? How will their newly won control of pricing impact the design of your new online business? Will they be buying strictly on price alone and will the low price leader win every sale?

Not likely. Consumers buy for different reasons and price is not the only determining factor, although it is an important one. That's why it's important to have a strong Unique Selling Position that explains the *full* selling position of your company. Your full selling position could include one or more of the following:

➤ Pricing policies and discounts

➤ Product selection

➤ Site convenience factors

➤ Customer service and purchase guarantee information

➤ Order security

➤ Shopper communities

➤ Product reviews

➤ Rebates

➤ Personalized services

What's a Bot?

Bot is short for robot. A Shopping bot is a piece of software or service that you can personalize and send onto the Net to search for specific products, services, or information that you request. These intelligent software agents, as they are sometimes called, are becoming more and more popular and will change the face of eCommerce. For a list of shopping bots currently available, check out the BotSpot at www.botspot.com/s-shop.htm.

43

Still, flexible pricing models are going to be very common in the years ahead. When creating your Unique Selling Position it would be wise to understand and incorporate these new models if you want to stay atop the eCommerce wave and not be swamped by it.

There's More Than One Way to Skin a Price Tag

Let's face it. Your online business will succeed or fail based on what you charge a customer. Set prices too high and customers won't buy. Set them too low and you're not profitable. At either extreme you go out of business.

So choosing a pricing model is extremely important.

Fixed Pricing

Fixed pricing has been the norm in U.S. commerce. With fixed pricing, the seller sets the price and the buyer can take it or leave it. But today the fixed pricing model is only one of many on the Net—and one by the way, that doesn't seem to have a very good future.

Tomorrow's pricing models will surpass the fixed-pricing model and include a variety of auction types: online haggling, and aggregate or group buying.

Let's take a look at each one.

Online Haggling

Haggling, though not new in the real world, has come to the Net. This type of pricing model is a one-to-one exchange. You either personally haggle—or negotiate—a price with a seller or you can use an intelligent software agent. You're beginning to see sites use this pricing model because the technology of the Net makes it possible.

eWanted.com at www.ewanted.com and Make Us An Offer at www.makeusanoffer.com (see Figure 4.2) are two examples of haggling services.

Online Auctions

The next flexible selling model is the online auction. As in the real world, online auctions come in three different flavors:

➤ Standard online auctions

➤ Dutch auctions

➤ Reverse auctions

Figure 4.2

At Make Us An Offer, shoppers interact and negotiate with an animated artificial intelligent sales agent over the price of any item.

The *standard online auction* has grown exponentially on the Net over the last few years. It was the first alternative to fixed pricing and the number of sites offering this pricing model has grown steadily. The standard online auction is a seller-dominated market that pits buyers against each other to determine the highest price of an item. The highest bidder gets to buy the item.

A variation of this auction is the *reserve* auction. In this case a minimum price is set for an item and if that price is not reached, the item is withdrawn from sale. A good and venerable example of a standard auction is OnSale at www.onsale.com.

Next is the Dutch auction. Whereas the standard auction sees prices steadily climb, the Dutch auction works backward. Dutch auctions like Klik Klok Productions (www.klik-klok.com) are used when there are many of the same items for sale (see Figure 4.3). In this case many buyers can win a bid and buy as many of the items for sale as they want. The seller who bids the lowest amount for the most items is the winner.

Place an Auction on Your Site

Want to add an auction to your site? Using EasyAuction, you can run an online auction right from your own Web site. And here's the best part, you control the look and feel of your auction and the auction software resides on their server. Check it out at www.EasyAuction.com.

Figure 4.3

At Klik Klok Productions, products in their department store move off the shelves fast. Prices decrease over a period of two minutes.

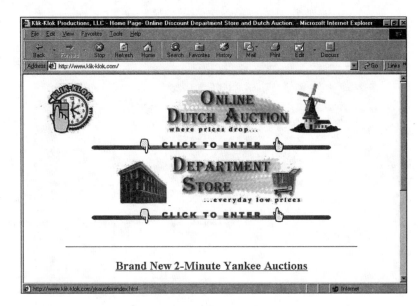

Reverse auctions turn the standard and Dutch auctions on their head. When buyers dominate an auction, the reverse auction is used. In this case buyers name the desired quantity and price of an item or service and sellers bid down to get the sale. Here the seller is competing against other businesses instead of the buyer competing against other buyers. Examples of reverse auctions are Respond.com at www.respond.com and NextTag.com at www.nextag.com.

Group Buying

Demand aggregation, or group buying, is different than the other pricing models. In the other models buyers commit to a price they name and sellers decide whether to accept their offer. In the group-buying model, buyers accept an offer at a maximum price that falls as more buyers decide to buy the product.

It's sort of like an electronic co-op. Buyers band together to negotiate a better price from the seller. Examples of the group-buying model are Accompany at www.accompany.com and Mercata at www.mercata.com.

You should seriously consider these different pricing models when creating your Unique Selling Position.

USP—Your Unique Selling Position

The story goes like this.

FedEx was looking for a Unique Selling Position. They had a new concept of delivering packages overnight and wanted to say that their package delivery service was better than using the services of the buses and airlines. And they needed to say it in one simple phrase.

Up until then if you wanted to ship a small package across the country, you had to ship it on the bus and airlines schedules. It might take up to several days to have your package delivered—and then *you* had to pick it up!

FedEx saw an opportunity here. All they had to do was convince the public that they could deliver their package in a speedier fashion. After much thought, they decided that what differentiated them from their competitors was that they owned their own planes. This meant that customers could ship products on *their* schedule and not the schedule of the airlines and buses.

So what was the USP of FedEx? It was this. "We have our own planes." It didn't fly with the public. They didn't understand it. "So what?" they said. "What does that mean to me?"

So, FedEx went back to the drawing board and came up with this. "When you

Spree.com—A Good Example of Differentiating

Over one million Web sites participate in affiliate programs on Net. So how do you differentiate yourself from those? Spree.com did. Spree.com sells the same products that any other affiliate program does. But they've learned to package the programs in such a way to create a Unique Selling Position. What entices a customer to buy from their Web site? Rebates. Customers who buy get back, as a cash refund, a percentage of the affiliate commission paid to Spree. Check it out at www.spree.com.

absolutely, positively have to have it overnight!" That worked. The pubic responded and rest is commerce history. Consumers didn't care if FedEx had their own planes. They could care less. They didn't care if their packages were delivered by Pony Express. The benefit to the consumer was that their package was delivered overnight right to their door.

There's a lesson here—one that you can use when creating your own Unique Selling Position. Keep in mind WIIFM—What's In It For Me? This is what a customer is looking for when he or she buys. Phrase your USP in those terms and you will go a long way in creating an effective and successful Unique Selling Position.

Another good example is Domino's Pizza. How do you differentiate one pizza service from another? Domino's did by promising to deliver your pizza in "30 minutes or less—or the pizza is free!" One unexpected side effect unfortunately, was that Domino's employees were getting speeding tickets and having car wrecks trying to meet that 30-minute deadline. So be careful how you plan to execute your USP!

Both FedEx and Domino have had a measurable and beneficial USP. They're measurable—"Overnight" and "In 30 Minutes"—and have a unique benefit— "Delivered to Your Door" and "Free If Not Delivered in Time."

Remember that a good USP is specific, measurable, and conveys a customer benefit.

Creating Your USP

So, how do you create a good USP?

Do this. Put this book down, take out a pad and pencil and ask yourself these questions and answer them as *simply* as you can. You're not creating a corporate mission statement here. Keep your responses simple.

➤ Why is my business special?

➤ Why would someone buy from me instead of my competition?

➤ What can my business provide a consumer that no one else can? What's the benefit to the consumer that I can deliver?

Keep your answers specific, measurable, and show a benefit to the buyer. Here's the hard part—answer these questions in just one sentence and make it so anyone can understand it. Test it on your spouse, family, friends, and neighbors and ask them what they think it means.

Before you can build your online business, you must have a clear understanding of what your USP means and how to deliver it through your online business.

Don't Put the eCommerce Cart Before the Horse

Planning your Web site before deciding your Unique Selling Position is bad enough, but even worse is diving into your site design using a lot of pretty graphics and whiz-bang technical tricks. Your job is to sell the customer—not entertain the visitor.

Here are some additional aspects to consider when fleshing out a Unique Selling Position. They're called the four Ps

Pricing   If you're going to compete on price, don't just say you're the lowest—say why. For instance, perhaps you can sell at such a low price because of your ability to source product from the closeout industry, buying products at pennies on the dollar. Play up this uniqueness in your USP.

Positioning   The Marines are looking for just a few good men—not all men, just a few. This is a great positioning statement and makes their business unique and differentiates them among the armed forces. Look for a similar positioning with your business. Perhaps your focus is gender based. Perhaps it's age based. Or perhaps it's interest based like L.L. Bean at www.llbean.com (see Figure 4.4). Sell to a unique segment of the population—not to all of it.

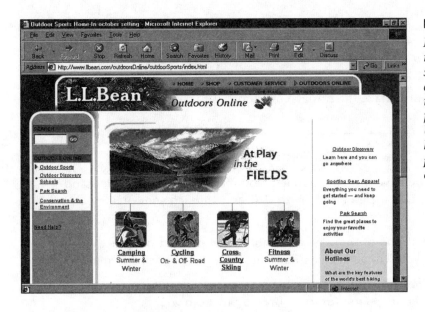

Figure 4.4

L.L. Bean offers a lot of information on outdoor sports and living. Their clothing designers actually test the products in the field. This reinforces their Unique Selling Position by branding them as the place to buy outdoor clothing.

Packaging   Taking a common product that others sell and repackage it in a new way. For instance, take the iMac. It's just a computer, but look at the packaging. Not only did it sell, but it also had a positioning statement with it—get on the Internet in 20 minutes and "Think Different."

Promotion   Finally, look at the promotional possibilities of your product or service. Can you tie your product or service to a season or holiday where you can benefit from the promotional activities and mind set that already exist at that time of year. Or perhaps there are other time-based connections like the birth of a child, birthdays, or anniversaries. The key here is to tie your product or service to activities or life events that are normally promoted by others. You then can identify your USP with those.

Don't Forget the Call to Action!

The hard work you put into a Unique Selling Position is all for naught if you don't have this in your offer: *Ask for the sale!* So many times a business with a great USP and the ability to deliver it forgets to end it with a call to action by asking for the sale.

Above all else remember that your USP is not about you, it's not about your business—it's about your customer. Speak to the needs of the customer—the needs you identified in Chapter 2, "What's the Big Idea? Identifying a Need."

One final thought: Whatever you promise in your Unique Selling Position—be sure you deliver on it. Don't make the mistake of adopting a USP that you can't fulfill.

The Least You Need to Know

➤ Before you can build your online business, you must have a clear understanding of what your USP means and how to deliver it through your online business.

➤ Fixed pricing is just one of the ways to position your product or service on the Net. Design your Unique Selling Position with flexible pricing in mind.

➤ Your Unique Selling Position should give you a unique advantage over your competition, a distinct reason for some one to buy from you.

➤ Unique selection, customer service policies, loyalty programs, rebates, and personalized service can add a unique dimension to your product offerings.

➤ Your Unique Selling Position should be specific, measurable, and convey a distinct customer benefit.

➤ Additional aspects to consider when fleshing out a Unique Selling Position are pricing, positioning, packaging, and promotional attributes.

Chapter 5

The Business Plan—Planning Your Online Business

In This Chapter

➤ Learn what a business plan is and why it's important in creating your online business

➤ Discover where to find sample business plans

➤ Learn the elements of a good business plan

A business doesn't plan to fail—it fails to plan. So if you want your new online business to be a success you'll need to plan for that success. To do that, you'll need a business plan. A business plan acts as a roadmap for your company. It clearly states who you are, what you do, and how you do it.

Besides acting as a plan for the success of your business, there's another reason to write a business plan. If you ever want to raise money from established capital sources like investment banks and venture capitalists, a business plan is essential.

Get a Plan, Man!

If your business plan is, "I plan to be in business," that's not enough. A good business plan helps you focus on your business concept, provide a framework to develop your business idea, serve as a basis for discussion with investors, and gives you a way to measure your business assumptions and performance that can be reviewed over time. It also should give a clear understanding of your business objectives, strategies, and financial viability.

Free Business Plan Template

You can download a free shareware Business Plan Template called Exl-Plan. You can choose from different versions of the software based on the size of your business. Download it at www.planware.org/ exldown.htm.

Every well thought-out business plan has these common elements.

➤ A description of your product or service
➤ An analysis of your competition
➤ A marketing plan
➤ A management plan
➤ A financial plan

A business plan can do something else. Just the process of thinking through all the elements of the plan will help you avoid mistakes and even uncover some hidden opportunities. The process of writing the business plan is just as valuable as the finished product. The very process of planning includes thinking about your business, discussing it with others, researching your market, and analyzing your competition.

Business Plan Tips

Don't kid yourself. Writing a business plan is not easy. It takes a lot of time and hard work. It will take weeks—even months to write a good plan. So here are some general tips that can help you through it.

First, make a list of your new company's strengths, its weaknesses, the market threats and opportunities. Don't write a tome. Keep your plan short and to the point; no more than 20 pages or so. Then nail down your assumptions. Be realistic about your projections and base your assumptions on your market research and analysis.

Free Business Plan Format

You can have a business plan template emailed to you free of charge. The format has been used to successfully raise capital for Capital Connections clients. Ask for it at www.capital-connection.com/ freestuff.html.

Next, make a list of your business risks. Be honest with yourself. Every business has competition. Who are they and how will they impact your business. List other risks like potential changes in your market, personnel challenges, and technology risks. This shows that you've given thought to both the upside and downside of your business.

Don't make statements you can't support. A good business is not built on wishful thinking. Back up your claims with research and analysis. Also, don't use highly technical terms. Keep the wording simple or if you must use technical terms, explain them fully in your plan.

Finally, a business plan is never finished. It's a living document that should be updated frequently as you move through your plan. You'll be surprised how many times you'll modify your activities when new market opportunities present themselves simply because you are in business.

One last thought. Should you hire someone to write your business plan? The answer is "No." Only you have full understanding of your business model. There are many companies that offer business plan writing services and there are a number of software packages on the market that claim to do the same. The truth is, the best they can do is show you a format to follow. You will have to do the research, think through the risks and opportunities, create the marketing hooks, and come up with your financial assumptions— that is, provide the bulk of the material for your plan.

That's all well and good. But what does a business plan look like? Are there sample plans that you could see? The answer to that question is "Yes." In fact, by studying sample business plans you can see how a typical plan is organized and that way you can make sure that your plan covers all the bases.

Test Your Business Plan Skills

Want to experiment on someone else's plan before you write yours? You can. American Express has a business plan exercise that you can use at their Web site. You can test your skills on a fictional business plan and then be rated on how prepared you are to create your own. Check it out at home3. americanexpress.com/ smallbusiness/resources/ starting/biz_plan/try.

Where to Find Sample Business Plans

Before staring on your business plan, it's a good idea to see what a plan actually looks like. Here are two Web sites that provide sample plans for your review. Just remember, these are just samples. They can only give you an idea of how a plan is organized and the type of materials that need to be included. Your business plan will differ dramatically.

Free Newsletter to Improve Your Business Plan

BizPlanIt.Com's free monthly email newsletter provides subscribers with insights and useful business plan advice in every issue. Subscribe at www.bizplanit.com/free/ newsletter1.htm.

First stop is BizPlans.com at www.bplans.com. BizPlans is a very good resource not only for sample business plans but also sample marketing plans. It also provides a Planning Spreadsheet Glossary that explains the details of a business plan spreadsheet. They provide this free service to attract traffic to their site to sell their business plan writing software package. By the way, giving something away to attract traffic to your site is a good thing to keep in mind for your online business.

Now let's discuss the sample plans. First, go to www.bplans.com/sample.htm. On this page you'll see a selection of more than two dozen sample business plans. Select a sample plan to view.

There you'll see the title of the business plan and a brief description of the business (see Figure 5.1). You'll notice that you can either view the plan step-by-step through your browser or download the plan onto your computer for viewing later.

Figure 5.1

Here's an example of a sample business plan from bplans.com, which you can download to your computer for viewing.

Can't decide which sample plan to view? Want to know which plans best match your business concept? Then BizPlans.com offers another useful service called the Plan Wizard at www.bplans.com/planwizard/index.cfm. By answering just a few questions, their Plan Wizard recommends the sample plans on their site that match your business.

If you're looking for real plans—and top-notch ones to boot—then check out the business plan examples at the MootCorp Competition at www.businessplans.org/MootCorp.html (see Figure 5.2). They offer a library of different award-winning business plans. Each was a winner or a finalist in the MootCorp Competition. MBAs from the best business schools in the world were invited to present their business plans to a panel of investors who then chose the best new business ideas.

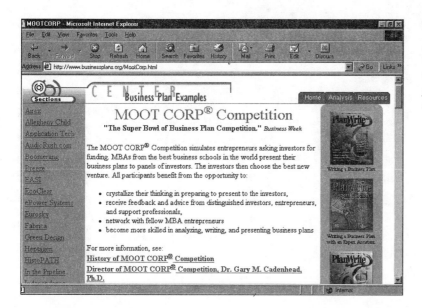

Figure 5.2

At MOOT CORP you can view award-winning business plans by topic—products, services, and Internet services.

Not only do they provide a selection of winning business plans, but they also offer the best example of each specific business plan topic like Best Executive Summary, Best Marketing Plan, Best Operations Plan, and so on.

Now that you have an idea of what a business plan looks like, it's time to write your own.

Great Idea! But Is It a Business?

Coming up with a business idea is relatively easy—it's the execution of it that's hard. A good business plan will go a long way in helping you execute your business idea. So, in this section I'll list the important elements you need to have in your plan, their purpose, and tips to keep in mind when writing each section. Also check out the Center for Business Planning (www.businessplans.org/plan.html) for links to general planning resources on the Net (see Figure 5.3).

e-tip

Create A Quick Mini-Plan

You can write a mini-business plan live on the Web to test your business idea—and it's free. The free process can help you test your business objectives, define its mission, analyze the market, and determine your break-even point. Check it out at www.miniplan.com/index.cfm?affiliate=bplans.

Figure 5.3

This library of resources contains links to sites offering research materials for every possible line of business

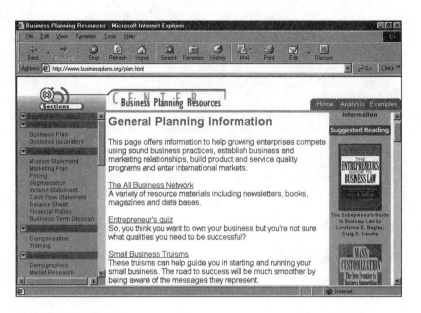

An Online Business Plan Workshop

The Web can teach you how to write an effective business plan. At their site, American Express provides a Small Business Exchange Business Plan Workshop. The workshop actually provides a step-by-step process to create a business plan online. Check it out at `home3.americanexpress.com/smallbusiness/resources/starting/biz_plan/?aexp_nav=sbs_hp_bizplan`.

When you write your business plan, remember to be succinct, to the point, and reader-friendly. Your plan should be no longer than 20 pages—including financials. Make it look professional. Use a word processor, have it bound and have it proofread by someone other than yourself. Nothing looks more unprofessional in a business plan than typos and grammatical errors.

If you're writing your plan for investors, be sure you tell them in your plan how their money will be used and how they'll be rewarded financially for their investment.

Finally, keep in mind that my intent here is not to teach you how to write a detailed business plan. There are many books on the subject that can help you do that. The intent here is to show you the most important elements to include in your business plan.

Get to the Point!—The Executive Summary

Although the executive summary of a business plan comes first, it's the last section that you'll write. To write the summary, you'll be culling information from other sections of your plan.

The executive summary is just that—a quick summary of your business and it's potentially the most important part of your business plan. Keep in mind that if you offer your plan to investors, the Executive Summary is the first and probably the only part of the plan they will read. If it interests them, they'll read further. Others will read it first to get a snapshot of your business and see if your business concept makes sense.

Your Executive Summary should be short—no longer than 2–4 pages and include:

SBA Business Plan Outline

Want a quick outline of a typical business plan? The Small Business Administration (SBA) provides one on their site. Find it at www.sbaonline.sba.gov/starting/businessplan.html.

➤ A brief description of your company and what needs of the customer it will fill.

➤ A description of the product or service you will provide.

➤ What your market is and how you plan to promote and sell your product or service.

➤ A short description of your key management.

➤ The type and amount of investment you will need.

➤ How and when investors will get paid back.

The executive summary is your chance to reach out and grab your readers and get them insanely interested in your business idea. Because this gives the reader the first impression of your business concept, let your friends and family read the summary first. Ask them if it makes sense. You only have a few short pages to pitch your idea so it has to be clearly defined and easily understood.

Avoid these common executive summary mistakes:

➤ **Lacking focus** You have just a few minutes to get your business concept across, and it should be loud and clear in the first few paragraphs of your executive summary. This is where your unique selling position should be displayed. Your USP is brief, to the point, and explains your business quickly and effectively.

➤ **Too wordy** Most times, your executive summary is all that gets read. So, of course, you tend to explain as much as you can about your business opportunity. Don't! Keep each section of the summary as brief as you can. Just touch on the most important points of each part.

➤ **Reads like a preface—not a summary** An executive summary is just that—a summary. It is not an introduction to plan. Look at it as a mini-plan in itself.

➤ **No expression of a unique opportunity**   What's the opportunity? Why should anyone invest in your new business? What will investors receive in return for the risk they are taking? These questions should be answered in the executive summary.

➤ **Fails to generate excitement**   The executive summary is more sizzle than steak. Though it should give the basic details of your business, it should also have a certain amount of hype to it. Remember that you're trying to get people to invest in your idea so make it sound exciting.

Finally, the executive summary is not an introduction, preface, or abstract of your plan—it's your business plan in miniature. So be sure it touches on all the important aspects of your business idea.

Who and What Are You?

An effective business plan includes a clear idea of what your company is and does. You should have decided the type of business entity you are going to be. Is it a corporation, partnership, or sole proprietorship? State in your plan what business you are in. Are you going to be a retailer, distributor, or manufacturer?

You also should include a detailed description of the product or service you will offer. Here's where your unique selling position comes in. Your USP is your identity in the marketplace. It tells you and the reader of your plan in a concise manner who you are and what you do. You also should explain and support why your business idea will work.

The Macintosh evangelist, Guy Kawasaki, once said that the best business to start is one that eases a pain. If you can find a market in pain—and cure it—you'll have a successful business. So, be sure that you clearly state in your plan who's pain you'll be curing—that is, what market problem you are solving—and how you're going to solve it.

Finally, how will customers obtain your product or service? Will they buy it online, over the phone, via fax, through the mail—a combination of all of them? What's your pricing strategy? Will you be the lowest or add value and charge more? And what about your competition? How you differ from them also should be included in your plan. And after your competition learns of your new business, how do you plan to stay ahead of them?

The answers to these questions will help you focus on your business and prepare it for what comes next.

What Is the Market and How Big Is It?

Socrates said, "Know thyself." In business, we say,"Know thy Market."

Your business plan should reflect not only who your customers are, but also the size of the market they inhabit and its trends. From this information you should be able to estimate your sales revenues and company growth over time.

Next, ask yourself where is your market? Is it national, regional, international, or local? You'll need to know the answer to that question when it comes time to create your marketing plan.

When considering a market's size, keep in mind the factors that affect market growth such as social and economic trends, technology innovations, government regulations, and the trends in your particular industry. When selling a product or service online, many if not all of these will affect your online business.

For example, what improvements in Net technology will change the way you offer and deliver your product or service. Is your business positioned to take advantage of the relentless change of the Internet? Within a few short years, consumers will surf the Net with ever increasing speed. Is your business prepared to take advantage of the multimedia possibilities that will be available to the common Net user? What about government regulation? Will sales on the Net be taxed? You should consider how this would affect your online business.

e-tip

Make a List of Your Customer Characteristics

Want to identify the common characteristics of the people that will buy your product or service? You can download a Customer Profile Worksheet at home3. americanexpress.com/ smallbusiness/resources/ starting/biz_plan/market/ toolbox.shtml.

As for sales projections, break them down to best case, worst case, and most likely scenarios. This way you can offer a spectrum of revenue projections.

How Will You Promote Your Product?

Okay. So you know your product, know your customer, and know your market. Now you need to promote your business and market your product or service. To do this, your plan must contain a good marketing plan. A good marketing plan describes your target market (age, gender, geographic location, income bracket, and so on) and specific ways to market, promote, and sell your product or service to that market.

Your marketing plan should include a marketing strategy (how you will find your customers and how you will market to them), an advertising plan and budget (how you will get customers to buy your product and what it will cost to do it), and a public relations plan. *I financial part.*

It also should identify what advertising and promotional vehicles you will use to reach your target market. For instance, what advertising mediums will you use to reach your customer? How often will each be used and what will it cost?

How about Public Relations or PR as it's sometimes called?

Can you attract free PR? How will you do it? What's your PR plan? Will you do it yourself or hire an agency? Every successful PR program has an angle—that is what's press-worthy about your business.

Remember, a strong marketing plan does double duty. It's a roadmap for you and lets a potential investor know that you not only have a good product or service but that you know how to sell it. The business world is littered with failures that had a good product or service and an identifiable market but little or no plan on how to sell into it.

Do You Have the Team to Do It?

It's said that investors invest in people—not ideas. This means that even a good idea has the potential to fail if the right team is not in place to execute it. A good management team can even take a mediocre idea and make it work. Your business plan must demonstrate that you have the right team to execute your plan or if you don't, you have identified the people you need and how to get them.

Tips and Books for Startups

Excellent books and tips for startups from Nolo Press. Be sure to check out their book, *How to Write a Business Plan*. Find them at www.nolopress.com/ChunkSB/ SB.index.html.

Investors are a picky bunch. They want to see a well-rounded team of professionals with experience in every function critical to the business. Duties should be clearly outlined and who on your team is responsible for carrying them out.

Even if you don't plan to raise money with your business plan, you still need to give thought to your management team. Did you cover your bases? Who on your team has responsibility for executing which part of your business plan? Do you have the personnel in place to cover sales, marketing, procurement, accounting, customer service, and fulfillment? If not, who will? Your team should have an array of skills that compliment each other.

Running Through the Numbers

The last element of your plan—and one of the most important—is your financials. This is where your numbers back up what you've been saying with words. The financials will tell the reader when you will turn profitable and how much money you'll need to reach that point.

Your financial plan should show revenue (your sales), expenses, cash flow (how fast you're burning money), your break-even point (when you stop burning money and turn a profit), and, most importantly, the financial assumptions you based your business plan on. It also should include a section on how you plan to use the money you raise from investors. This is called *use of funds*.

Although most financials go out three to five years (and in Internet time that's an eternity), they still are useful to track your assumptions and see how accurate they are after you open for business. As your numbers come in during the first few months to a year, you can review and redo your projections to get a more accurate reading on your first set of assumptions changing them when necessary.

Remember—your business plan is a roadmap, not a destination. It does and will change over time because your business will. You can count on it. After it's done, don't just file it way and forget about it. Update it regularly. Think of it as a process of a constant corporate self-appraisal. Accessing your business goals, strategies, and objectives by updating your business plan on a regular basis will keep your positioning fresh, your competitors at bay, and your business open to new and profitable opportunities.

The Least You Need to Know

➤ A good business plan helps you focus on your business concept and gives you a way to measure your business assumptions and performance that can be reviewed over time.

➤ If you ever want to raise money from established capital sources like investment banks and venture capitalists, a business plan is essential.

➤ Don't make statements you can't support.

➤ A business plan is a living document that should be updated frequently as you move through your plan over time.

Chapter 6

Getting the Dough

In This Chapter

➤ Learn the different ways you can raise the money for your new business

➤ If you're going after venture funding, learn what venture capitalists look for in your business plan

➤ Learn where to look for venture funding

➤ Discover where to post your business plan for investors to see

---

Love might make the world go 'round, but if you're starting a business, it's money that you need. So where do you find it and how do you get it?

First, you have to ask yourself a few important questions. How much do you need? What kind of financing is right for your business? Where will the dough come from? What will you be willing to give up for an investment in your company? All important questions and we will get to them in due time.

So, let's start at the beginning.

Bringing Home the Bacon

Are you ready for money? I know, sounds facetious. Who isn't, right? What I mean is—have you done your homework? Do you know how much money you need—and when? If you took my advice to heart in the last chapter and did a good job on your business plan, your financials will tell you how much you need and when you need it.

A One-Stop Source For Your Startup

Startup.com will handle your company office and operations, enabling you to focus on your core business. They'll supply everything from real estate and space planning to your technology infrastructure to payroll. Find it at www.startups.com.

You spent a lot of time researching your market, now you need to spend time researching your financing options. This is important! You don't want to spend a lot of time chasing financing options that have little or no chance of success. You need to know what financing options are out there and which ones work best for your business.

How Much Do You Need?

The total amount of money you need depends on the size and type of business you have in mind. If it's a service business, your startup and continuing costs will not be as high as with a business that sells products. Selling products is very cost intensive. You might need to warehouse them and ship them. If so, your personnel needs will be high, adding another expense to your business.

The first step in deciding how much you need is to create a budget. You probably do that now with your personal and household bills. The process for a business is the same.

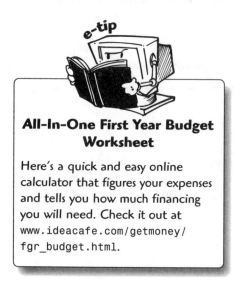

All-In-One First Year Budget Worksheet

Here's a quick and easy online calculator that figures your expenses and tells you how much financing you will need. Check it out at www.ideacafe.com/getmoney/fgr_budget.html.

First figure what cost will be involved. While building your multimillion dollar dream, you still have to feed your family and dog. So calculate how much you need for living expenses. Next, how much do you need just to open the doors of your new business? Will you start the business from home? If not, what are the costs to rent space? Even if you start from home you'll need a separate phone line and answering machine for business. "Daddy can't come to the phone right now" is not the response that a client or customer is looking for when they call.

Finally, you need to know how much your business will need to stay alive until you break even. You're going to burn cash at a certain rate and you'll need to know what that burn rate is.

When doing your budget, be realistic. Underestimate your revenue and overestimate expenses. When budgeting expenses, think of the unexpected: higher than expected phone expenses because of high personnel needs or higher customer service expenses because of more sales. It's these types of expenses that kill a budget quickly.

Also, run several revenue and expense projections. Look at worst case, best case, and several scenarios in between to get a good feel of what your budget should look like. And don't be afraid to test your assumptions with friends, family—and better yet—with professionals. Also, visit Working Solo (www.workingsolo.com) to sign up for their newsletter for tips on growing your business (see Figure 6.1).

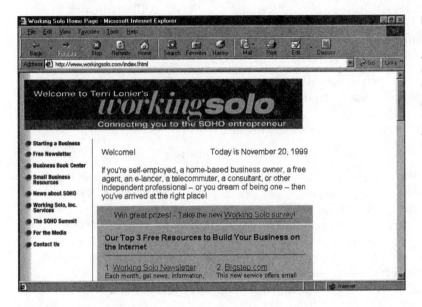

Figure 6.1

Working Solo is a great site for the self-employed or the small business owner. Sign up for their free newsletter for tips, information, and advice for growing your small business.

What Type of Financing Is Right for You?

As they say, one man's meat is another man's poison. So it goes with financing options. Here are some things to consider.

Are you willing to give up a piece of your company for the money you need? How much? And are you willing to give up control? Giving up controlling interest in your company could lead to your removal from management if your investors think you're doing a shoddy job.

If you want to maintain control of your company, you'll either have to give away less for less money, dip into your own pocket, or borrow the cash. If you borrow the money, how much can you afford? You'll have to make payments on any loans. Your budget can tell you what you can afford and how much you can pay back over a time.

Finally, the structure of your company can place restraints on the type of financing available to you. If you decide to be a Sub-Chapter S, Standard C Corporation, or LLC (Limited Liability Corporation) these types of organizations place limits on the number and type of investors you can have.

For example, if you're looking for the big bucks from large investors or venture capitalists, you'll need to have a C Corporation to accept their investment. If you plan on raising a large amount of capital from a group of individuals, a Sub-Chapter S corporation is something to consider.

The main difference between a C and S corporation is who gets the tax write-off for the first few years of losses. In a C corporation, the business gets the write-off. In a Sub-Chapter S, the individuals investing in the corporation get the tax write-off. Usually, when a business starts to turn profitable, the owners elect to change from an S to a C corporation and let the corporation pay the income taxes.

An LLC is a blend of the two. It has all the personal protection of a corporation but also lets the members or investors in the LLC take the tax write-offs personally. But after the business turns profitable and must begin paying income taxes, the LLC might have to incorporate as a C to gain the benefit.

Here's a quick checklist of financing options for your business:

➤ **Angel Investors**   These are individuals who are either entrepreneurs like yourself who have made it or individual wealthy investors looking to help launch new business. The Angel Network (www.angelnetwork.com) is such an example (see Figure 6.2). You could expect investments from $100,000 to $500,000 from an angel investor. The advantage of an angel investor is that they normally take a smaller share of your business than a venture capitalist—and like small investors—stay out of the day-to-day operations of your company. Angel investors understand that what they give you is not a loan but an investment. They don't expect to see the money repaid. That's why they call them angels—the perfect investors!

Figure 6.2

At the Angel Network, you can list your business and funding needs in hopes that Angel Investors will find you and invest in your business.

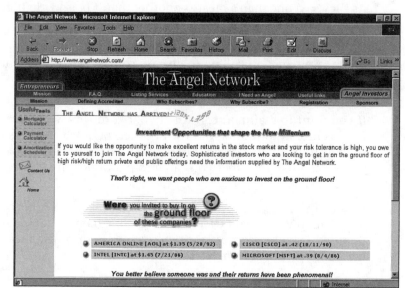

f your balance sheet can support it and you can show
ue stream can meet a repayment schedule, then a
or institution—is an option to consider. To get a loan,
you personally have a good credit history. Being a
no track record, you will almost certainly have to
on the loan. The amount of money raised with this
size of the loan you can qualify for.

ministration (SBA) If you have trouble getting a
guaranteeing your loan or a large portion of it. Being
process is
a lot of
if this is the
you might
cratic red

e-tip

Good Resource for Raising Funds

Garage.com has a very good list of
books about raising funds. Find it at
www.garage.com/resources/
raisingFunds.shtml.

➤ **Private Placement or Seed Capital**
Individuals can be approached asking
them to invest approximately $10,000
to $25,000 apiece to meet the initial
capital requirements of your company.
If your capital needs are small in the
beginning or if you can find a number
of these small investors, this option
might work for you.

➤ **Economic Development Programs**
This is another government-sponsored way to get money. These programs are
found both on the state and federal levels. You can get a free book, *The Small
Business Financial Resource Guide*, that contains a comprehensive list of small
business support programs by writing to the U.S. Chamber of Commerce
Small Business Center at 1615 H St. NW, Washington, DC 20062.

➤ **Customer or Supplier Financing** Here's another money option. Approach
your best customers or even your suppliers. After all, they must like your business concept or they wouldn't be doing business with you. Ask them if they
would like to invest in your business. You might be pleasantly surprised.

➤ **Venture Capital** If you want to sit at the big table and get the big bucks,
then the venture capital route is the way to go. But be warned. It's not easy and
it has its disadvantages. The advantage is you can raise ten, twenty, even a hundred million dollars for your new online enterprise. We'll cover the venture
capitalist option later in this chapter.

Ante Up, Fella!

If after looking at the formal financing options I just described you've decided you're
not ready for them yet, then self-funding is your first step.

Find the Best Rates on Credit Cards

BankRate.com's Bank Rate Monitor lists lots of frequently updated information on which banks and credit card companies are offering the best rates. Check it out at www.bankrate.com/brm/rate/cc_home.asp.

If you don't want to tap into your savings—which you'll need to live on while you develop your business—look to your credit cards. Your credit cards are a ready source of unsecured loans. If you're credit limit is $5,000 to $20,000 or more, you already have at your disposal a pre-approved loan. Another benefit of using your credit card is they free you from having lenders and investors looking over your shoulder all the time.

Okay, so the interest rate is not so great. But if you shop around, you'll find many banks offering short-term introductory interest rates at a fraction of the rates credit cards normally charge. If you have two or three credit cards, they could provide all the capital you need to launch your online business.

And here's another thought. Many credit cards offer rebates or perks of some kind. Find one that offers free air miles for every dollar you spend using their card. Good for ways to pay for all those business trips.

Another way to raise cash is sell what you don't use. In the past, your friendly pawnshop would provide a quick and easy way to unload unwanted items around your house. The pawnshop didn't pay much, but it was a source of ready cash. Today, there are better online options. Simply point your browser at eBay and auction off all that stuff gathering dust in your basement or garage. The money you raise can go towards starting your business.

How Much Do You Love Me? Let Me Count the Money

In many cultures around the world, lending money to family members is an established way of life. But borrowing money from friends and family takes some courage. You're about to take their hard-earned savings and invest it in your online startup with no guarantee of success. Also, unless your uncle is Daddy Warbucks, friends and family are not the sources for large amounts of capital.

If you want to earn the trust of your friends and family, you should be risking most of your needed capital yourself. After all, if *you* don't have confidence in your new business by putting in the maximum you can why should anyone else. The downside to the friends and family option is that family members might show a sudden zealous hands-on interest in your business. When you bring family into your business it becomes by default a family business. If your business does turn into a family affair, then the Family Firm Institute at www.ffi.org is a good resource to check out.

Most importantly, are there any current frictions in your family? Will a business investment by them throw more oil on the fire? You don't want to be the cause—or the recipient—of more family flare-ups. To avoid this, be sure you inform all friends and family of the risks involved in your online business. Better yet, put it all in writing. Make it legal. Have a lawyer draw up a simple promissory note outlining the terms of the loan and how it will be repaid.

Don't Pay to Find Money

Some companies masquerade as venture firms and ask you to pay them money to find investors. Forget it. Real venture firms won't charge you to look at your business plan.

Venture Capitalists

eCommerce is hot and venture capitalists know it. That's why they're pouring hundreds of millions of dollars a year into eCommerce companies. If you're willing to give up part of your company in exchange for the money you need to make your company grow, then venture capitalists—or venture firms—are the way to go.

All venture firms are looking for highly profitable, fast growing, early to mid-stage ventures to invest in. Venture firms raise capital from individual investors looking for 5, 10, even 20 times the return on their investment. Venture firms might invest in nine ventures that fail, but the tenth one will more than make up for the loss of the other nine.

Venture firms also specialize in particular markets and tend to invest in markets they know. Most look for companies that have proven their business concept and need a lot of money to exploit a market and move forward. Fast growth, explosive growth is what they look for. Think of a hockey stick. Venture capitalists want to get in just at that little flat part before the growth soars up the stick. If your company can show meteoric growth in a short amount of time, then you're venture material.

An Entrepreneur's Favorite Letters—I, P, and O

IPO stands for *Initial Public Offering*. In an IPO, shares of your company are sold to the general public in a stock offering. An online entrepreneur makes the big bucks when he or she sells the company—either to some other large firm or to the public in an IPO.

Venture firms look to get their investment out in only a few short years so an IPO is usually their target.

Funding Stages

There are several venture-funding stages to keep in mind when seeking venture capital. Your capital needs dictate the stage of venture funding you look for.

➤ **Early Stage** Early stage funding includes the seed, startup, and first stage. The seed stage represents a small amount of money used to either prove a business concept or product development. Little initial marketing is done at this stage. Startup stage funding goes a little further than seed stage funding. Some marketing has been done, a management team is put in place, and the initial business plan is finalized but products have yet to be sold. First, stage money is used for companies that have launched their business and are selling product.

➤ **Expansion Funding** Expansion stage funding includes second stage, third stage, and bridge funding. After a company is launched and making sales, second stage funding is used to expand the company in size and market share. Although revenue is being generated, it might not be making a profit at this stage. In the third stage of funding, a company has at least broken even and needs funds to achieve profitability. This is the stage in which a business becomes a profitable working enterprise. Funds are used to expand the company farther into its market and build its growing infrastructure. Finally, bridge-funding financing is used to prepare a company for its IPO.

Hunting the Big Game

Finding a venture firm that would be interested in your business concept is not an easy task. Like the old saying goes, "You have to kiss a lot of frogs before you find a prince."

There are several venture-funding directories that you can use to try and narrow your hunt for funds. For example, vFinance.com lists many venture capitalist firms, but one of its best features is the ability to search for firms that invest in specific areas by using their Search by Industry Sector search box (see Figure 6.3).

Corporate Finance network at `www.corpfinet.com/vcapalph.htm` lists many venture capital firms including the type of businesses they invest in, their location, assets under management, and what stage of funding they do. The Web Investor at `www.thewebinvestor.com/online-venture-capital.html` lists a very large selection of venture capital firms with a description of what they invest in and the funding stages they support.

The Next Wave Stocks Web site at `www.nextwavestocks.com/vcindex.html` lists only those firms that specialize in investing in high-tech and Internet companies. Another directory of ventures firms can be found at iEmploy at `www.StartUpUniversity.com/vc/venture_capital_directory.html`. The list includes investment criteria, and full contact information.

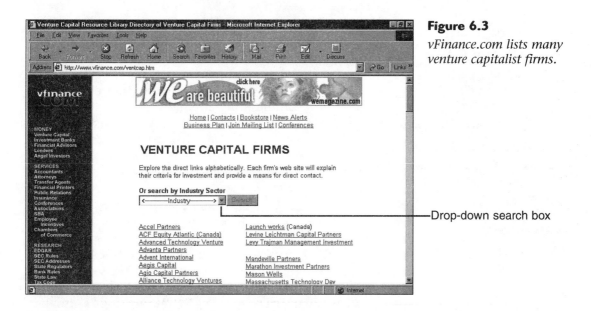

Figure 6.3

vFinance.com lists many venture capitalist firms.

Drop-down search box

Then there's Garage.com at www.garage.com. More than just a directory, Garage.com does seed-level funding for high-tech and Internet startups. For investors, it helps find startup companies that match their investment criteria. For the entrepreneur, it introduces your business to venture firms and—if it likes your business idea—will even help you with your presentation to make it more sellable.

Getting the Venture Capitalist's Attention

After you've chosen a venture capital firm, how do you get their attention? What are the types of things that they look for? How can you improve your odds of being accepted by a Venture firm?

Venture capitalists look at these key things:

➤ **Can they make big bucks?**   If venture firms are going to risk millions of dollars on your business idea, they'll want to know what's the big payoff. They'd rather invest five, ten, twenty million, or more in a 20 billion dollar market than in a 100 million-dollar market. The bigger the market, the bigger the payoff if the business works. To get a venture capitalist's attention right away, show him a big market to exploit.

➤ **Do they invest in your specific market?**   Even if your idea is a good one, if you pitch your idea to a venture firm that doesn't invest in your market you're wasting your time. Venture firms usually specialize in one area. Make sure you're business area coincides with theirs. Also, if you're looking for early stage capital, don't pitch to venture firms that only invest in late stage companies.

Here's Your Resource Library

Venture Capital Resource Library has the links to everything from locating a venture capital firm to details of security law and articles, all related to getting investors. Find it at www.vfinance.com.

➤ **Whose pain are you solving?**   You have to make it very clear not only the market you will serve but also what's the niche you're targeting. If you have a well-defined Unique Selling Position, you'll have a better chance of getting a venture firm's attention. Don't make claims you can't deliver. A venture capitalist will pick up on that real fast. Also, state your weaknesses. This shows the venture capitalist that you have thoroughly thought through your business concept.

➤ **Can you do what you say?**   When you pitch your business idea, be specific on why you can execute it. Remember, ideas are easy—the proper execution of them is the hard part.

Be careful with terminology. Know the semantics of your market like hits, unique visitors, and click throughs. (We'll cover this terminology in Chapter 19, "Speaking the Language of Net Advertising.") Also, be sure you mention your competition—who they are and how you plan to stay ahead of them. Although there are few barriers to competition on the Net, speed and innovation are vital to an online business. Explain how fast you can execute your plan and how you will stay ahead of your competition.

➤ **Do you have the team?**   Venture firms say that they invest in people, not ideas. This tells you that the management team you've assembled or plan to assemble is of vital importance to a venture capitalist. Be specific in presenting their skills. The venture capitalist wants to know that you can deliver on the promise of your business idea.

➤ **Do the numbers make sense?**   Do your homework. Be sure that your assumptions on your market, your expenses, and revenue are airtight—and be ready to defend them. Also, provide clear milestones to measure your success. When will you start to make sales? When will you break even and turn profitable?

Answer these questions to a venture capitalist's satisfaction and you will have their attention.

Use KISS

Don't make the mistake of over complicating your presentation. If it's too complicated to explain, you'll lose a venture capitalist's attention post-haste. Use KISS—Keep It Simple Stupid.

Matchmaker, Matchmaker, Find Me Some Bucks!

Instead of finding investors, have the investors find you. There are several sites on the Net that enable you to meet potential investors such as VentureDirectory.com (www.venturedirectory.com) or even post your business plan and will then match you up with investors looking for new business opportunities (see Figure 6.4). There's a catch, though. Many of them are not free. Prices and/or annual fees range from under a hundred dollars to a few hundred dollars.

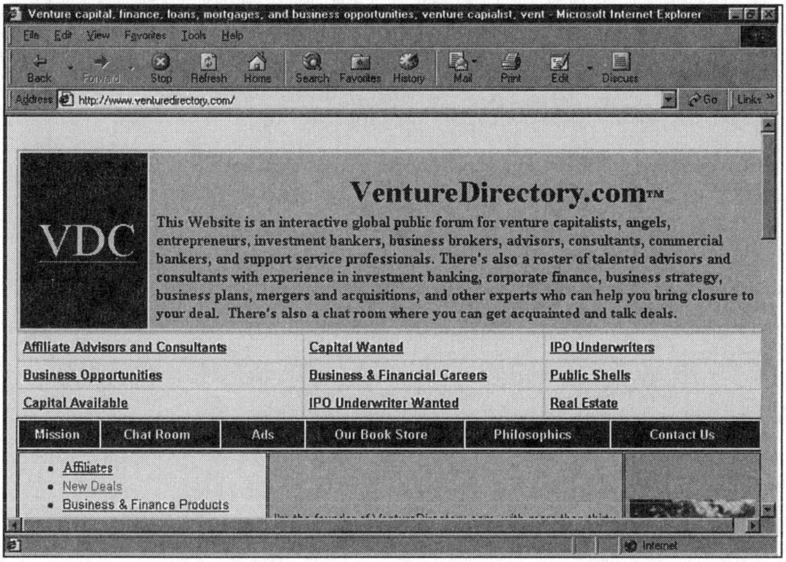

Figure 6.4

VentureDirectory.com is a great place to view and meet investors, angels, and other entrepreneurs. They even have a chat room where you can meet people and make deals.

Here's a list of such sites:

➤ Capital Connection at www.capital-connection.com/entrepreneurapplication.html ($75 one-time fee)

➤ Capital Match at www.capmatch.com ($200 annual fee)

➤ BusinessFinance.com at www.businessfunding.net (Free listing for 30 days)

➤ BizBoard at www.thebizboard.com (One-time $13.95 / 6 months or until funded)

➤ NVST.com at www.nvst.com (Free listing for 90 days then $39.95 a month)

➤ Venture Capital Finance Online at www.vcaonline.com ($30 for one year)

After your business concept is finalized and your business plan finished, don't wait on funding to get started. Whether you need ten million dollars or ten thousand, reach into your pocket and start your business today. You'll find that having an operating business—no matter how nascent—will help you raise money faster than just having a paper plan and an idea.

The Least You Need to Know

➤ Know how much money you need—and when—before you go out looking for funding.

➤ Spend the time researching your financing options and your needs.

➤ If you want a quick and easy loan, use your credit cards to launch your online business rather than approach family members for a loan. You don't want to be the cause, or the recipient, of family flare-ups.

➤ Venture capitalists are looking for highly profitable, fast growing, early to mid-stage ventures to invest in and specialize in specific markets.

➤ There are investor/entrepreneur matching services on the Net, but be aware that they cost money.

➤ Don't wait on funding to get started. You'll find that having an operating business will help you raise money faster than just having a paper plan and an idea.

Part 2
Setting Up Shop

Now that you've hatched that great eBusiness idea, it's time to find a place to roost and establish your own domain—so to speak.

What about costs? No problem. There's a plan out there to fit every eBusiness budget. In some cases, you can even set up shop for free! It all depends on the plan you have for your business, how you want to implement it, and the number and kinds of products or services you want to offer. So come on in and I'll show you how, why, and where to hang your hat!

Getting Started— First Steps

In This Chapter

➤ Learn how to register your domain name

➤ Learn the eCommerce host essentials

➤ See what to shop for when choosing an eCommerce host

Now that you've decided to create on online business, who do you get host it? There are several options—host it yourself, host it at an ISP, or host it at one of the build-it-yourself services on the Web. How do you choose? What do you look for? What are the essentials?

Before you go charging off to create your new online business, there are a number of steps to perform and eCommerce elements to consider. Knowing this information now—upfront—will help you later when considering where to host your site and what services to expect. Finding the right home for your site—one that offers the right eCommerce services—will help you successfully execute your business plan. So, it's important to know what the eCommerce site essentials are when considering a place to roost.

But first things first. Whether you host your site yourself, have it hosted elsewhere, or use one of the build-it-yourself Web-site services, you need to register a domain name.

Registering a Domain Name

If you're serious about doing business on the Net you need to register a domain name. A domain name represents your company and is your URL. For example, Amazon's domain name is www.amazon.com and Wal-Mart's domain name is www.wal-mart.com.

What's a URL?

The URL is the site address that appears in the top window of your browser such as www.yahoo.com. It's the way you find Web sites on the Net. The letters URL stand for *Uniform Resource Locator*.

Just recently, Barnes & Noble acquired a new domain name. It is now known by its long domain name, www.barnesandnoble.com and www.books.com. That, by the way, was some coup. The books.com domain name was the property of another online bookstore. Barnes & Noble wanted it, so they bought the bookstore!

This raises a problem for you. Many of the most popular domain names have been taken. You will probably find that someone has already registered your business name or business type. Creating a unique domain name could be quite a challenge. That is unless you have the deep pockets of a Barnes & Noble to buy an already assigned domain name. The fact is, grabbing a great domain name that reflects your business type or even your business name is getting harder to do.

But what if you want to use a domain name that's already registered? Check out Glenn Sobel's article at www.domainnameadvisor.com/acquisition.htm. He explains the different ways to acquire a domain name owned by another party.

Finally, when choosing a domain name keep it short and memorable. A long domain name with two many letters or with hyphens is hard to remember. Also, make it easy to spell. Lastly, try to choose a name that relates to your core business or business name.

Psst! Wanna Buy a Domain?

Looking for a really good domain name? The one you want is already taken? Then check out the Great Domains Web site. It's a brokerage site that enables you to buy and sell domain names. Another site that buys and sells domain names is 1001 Domains. Find them at www.greatdomains.com and www.1001domains.com.

Where to Start

First, find out whether that nifty domain name you thought up is available. To do that, head over to Network Solutions at www.networksolutions.com (see Figure 7.1). Registering a domain name is not free, and the annual fees you pay depend on how you plan to use it. More on that later.

When you arrive at the Network Solutions site, you'll see at the top of the Web page Register a Web Address with a search box below it. Type the domain name you would like to use to see if it's available. Notice that there's a drop-down box next to the search window. The drop-down box defaults to .com but there are two other choices. One is .org and the other is .net. Because you are setting up a business on the Net, the extension you will use is the .com one. The .org extension is for organizations like the United Way and the .net is for networks on the Internet. When you search, make sure the .com choice is in the drop-down window.

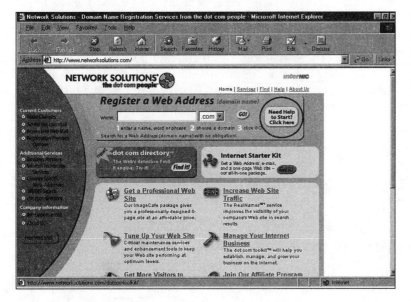

Figure 7.1

The Network Solutions site will walk you through the process of choosing and registering a domain name for your business.

After a quick search, Network Solutions will tell you if that domain name is taken or not. Be prepared to try several variations on your domain name until you find one that has not been registered. You can search as many names as you like—it's free. After you find the domain name you want and it's available, you can proceed to register it at the Network Solutions site.

Here's the Process to Follow

At the Network Solutions home page at www.networksolutions.com, click the **Need Help to Start** box next to the domain name search window.

Get Help Creating a Valid Domain Name

Here's a very useful site to help you choose a domain name. Just enter a few words that represent your domain name and E-gineer's Domainator will create a valid domain name from those words. Try it at www.e-gineer.com/domainator/index.phtml.

You will be brought to a page where you can enter your available domain name to start the registration process. Enter your available domain name and click **Go**.

After your domain name is accepted, you will be told what other Web address for your domain name, if any, is available. These are the .net and .org extensions of your same domain name. Click the **Continue** button to ignore these and continue.

Next, you pay the piper. You have two choices. If you do not have a place to host your site yet, you can reserve your name for when you do. If you've chosen a place to host your Web site, then you need to know your hosting company's *domain name server (DNS)* and *Internet protocol (IP)* information. You will get these from your host provider.

To reserve a domain name for future use, the cost is $119 per address for the first two years. The cost to register a domain name when you have a hosting server is $70 per address for the first two years. You must pay with a credit card to complete your registration at the InterNic site.

Be Sure You Are the Administrative Contact

You will be asked to name both an administrative and technical contact when you apply for a domain name. It is very important that you name yourself, not an employee, as the administrative contact. the administrative contact is the only one who can make changes to your domain registration. Don't be caught having to chase down someone who no longer works for your company to make future changes to your registration.

And that's it. InterNic will send you an email to confirm.

Finally, there are a number of Web sites on the Net that will register your domain for you. They will add their fee on top of the fees that Network Solutions will charge you for registering your domain name. Don't bother. Register your domain name yourself and save the money.

Register Your Misspelled and Alternative Domain Name

Why lose potential customers because they misspelled your URL. Register the obvious misspellings of your domain name and redirect them back to your site. Also register alternative spellings of your name. For example, my company One Minute Shopper.com is registered under oneminuteshopper.com, 1minuteshopper.com, and minuteshopper.com. To further protect yourself, you might consider registering your domain name not only as a .com, but also as a .net or even a .org.

Finding a Home

After you have secured your domain name, it's time to consider finding a home for your new online business. This is called finding a host. A *host* is a computer, or server, on which you place your Web site. The host's server is connected to the Internet, 24 hours a day, 7 days a week. This is how your customers find you and shop at your online store.

Whether you host your pages at free community sites such as AOL, GeoCities, Tripod, or Angelfire, use the do-it-yourself Web-site builder services of Yahoo Store or BigStep. Host at a commercial ISP—or even host your site on your own server—you need to consider some eCommerce site essentials. Later, I'll cover the different types of hosting options in Chapter 8, "Hosting Your Store for Free," Chapter 9, "Hosting with an ISP," and Chapter 10, "Be Your Own Host."

A lot of thought should go into choosing a home for your online business. If your business existed in the real world, you wouldn't set it up in the most expensive part of town and pay exorbitant rent. Nor would you place your store at the end of a pothole-ridden dirt road and expect customers to come to you. You'd also expect the lights to stay on and the police and emergency services to be in the area making it safe for commerce.

So it is with your online business. Your Web site *is* your business and you should expect that wherever you host it, the basic essential services should be available.

eCommerce Host Essentials

Your eCommerce host requirements will vary with the size and type of business that you have. But there are three important criteria that you must address no matter what the size of your online business. They are

➤ Costs

➤ Bandwidth

➤ Tech support

Cost

What you pay is what you get in the eCommerce game and what you get depends on how much control you want over the look and feel of your online store and the services you want to offer the online shopper.

The more elements you want to include in your online business, the higher the cost of creating and maintaining your site—elements such as these:

➤ Product reviews

➤ Special sales sections

➤ Discussion rooms

➤ Live customer service

➤ Personalization

➤ Gift reminder services

➤ Multiple email addresses

➤ Frequent buyer programs

➤ Interactive marketing features

Don't Skimp on Hosting

Go with the best hosting company you can afford—*not* the cheapest. Look for OC3 connections or T3s. Don't use a commercial hosting service that has only T1 connections.

The first question to ask yourself is whether you will buy a server and host your site yourself or outsource it to a hosting service.

Outsourcing

If you're on a budget, you can host an online business for free at community sites like AOL and Tripod, but you'll have little more than a catalog page or two offering a few products that must be purchased through the mail. In addition, because the community sites control the advertising, you'll have no control over the ads placed on your pages. You might well find a competing product advertised on your site.

Another outside hosting option is the all-in-one store such as Yahoo Store. They provide a basic eCommerce site where you can create an online store complete with product pages, shopping cart, and order form. No software is needed, there is very little to learn, and you can do it all through your Web browser. The cost for these types of hosting services ranges from $100 to $500. The downside is that services here are limited. Content and community elements like product news and reviews or chat rooms and discussion boards for customer service—even more than one email address—are normally not available.

⚹*Hosting Yourself*

If you want to create your eCommerce Web site yourself, then you need to look for a commercial ISP who will host your site on his server. CNet at `webhostlist.inter-netlist.com` lists a large number of Web-hosting companies (see Figure 7.2). Costs can range from as little as $30 a month to whatever the market will bear. If you create and maintain your own site, you might be required to do your own programming for a shopping cart, product database, and other essentials for your eCommerce site.

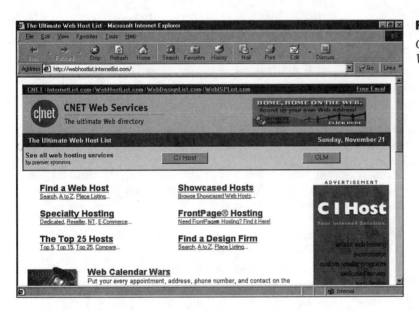

Figure 7.2

CNet has an A-Z list of Web hosting companies.

Finally, even if you host your site on your own server, you need to connect it to the Internet. You can have either a telephone or cable line run to your business and connected to your server, or you can place your server at a hosting service connected to the Net. Costs will vary here depending on how fast your connection is and how close your server is to the backbone of the Net.

This brings up the issue of bandwidth.

How Fast Is Your Connection?

Want to check the page loading time of your Web site? Surf on over to Virtual Stampede and use their Load Time Check service. Find it at www.virtualstampede.com/tools.htm.

Let Your ISP Know Your Marketing Plan

Planning a big marketing push that's going to generate a lot of traffic to your site? Launching a major marketing initiative and not telling your Internet Service Provider could bring your whole site down.

What Is Caching?

Caching is the process of storing Web pages on a server so pages download more quickly.

Bandwidth

For your business to be a success, you want your customers to have a good experience. The customer's experience of your site will either make or break your online business. The first thing a customer experiences is when he or she visits your site is how fast it appears in their browser. A slow loading Web site will probably not be visited again. So a fast download time is essential.

The time it takes to download and view your pages depends on the bandwidth available to your host. The ideal scenario is that your host provider should run his own network rather than buy a network connection from some larger host provider. Your hosting service also should have a good caching system in place and be close to the Internet backbone—the main telephone lines that carry the Internet.

Also, does your host provider have a standard agreement with you to provide additional bandwidth automatically and on demand when unforeseen peaks in traffic hit your site? It's important that it does.

If you're hosting your own site with your own Internet connection, you must have at least a T1 line connected to your server. As your business grows, keep in mind that you'll need more bandwidth requiring larger pipes to handle the traffic coming to your site.

Tech Support

What good is your store if it can't stay open? In the real world, staying open for business requires only some personnel and an unlocked door. On the Internet, however, the reliability of your host server and your Net connection is critical to access to your business.

When shopping for a host, be sure they offer and deliver technical support 24 hours a day, 7 days a week, all year 'round. Can you reach your providers tech support personnel? Does your provider have a tech support telephone number? Can you ask questions via email?

If you're doing self-hosting, you have to ask yourself who will reboot your server at 2 a.m. in the morning when it goes down? Do you have personnel always available to fix any problem that develops?

Protect Your Backups

It is a good idea to back up your Web site each day, but where do you keep the backups? Leaving them on site is just as bad as not backing them up at all. Consider using a remote storage facility company to pick up your backups each day. Check you local yellow pages for companies near you.

And how about a disaster recovery plan? Your entire site can go down due to something as simple as a disk crash or worse—a fire, earthquake, or hurricane. Does your host provider backup your Web site regularly and do they keep the backups off-site? If your site does go down, how long will it take your host provider to get it back up and running again?

If you're self-hosting, do you have the resources set aside to deal with these recovery problems? I guarantee they will happen.

Your Shopping List

Cost, bandwidth, and tech support might be the essential elements to consider when hosting your site, but there are additional items to add to your shopping list when considering a host provider. These are true whether you host through an ISP or self-host your site.

To generate a serious amount of sales at your site, you'll need to accept and process credit card payments. You must have a secure eCommerce server to take orders and process credit cards that encrypts card numbers when sent over the Net. Over the last few years, the media has had a field day telling horror stories about credit cards being stolen while buying over the Net. Truth is, there has never been a documented case of any credit card number being stolen off the Net when using a secure server.

Credit Card Scare Tactics

Simson Garfinkel, author of a book on good privacy encryption software called *PGP : Pretty Good Privacy*, says that sending your credit card over the Internet is no big deal. "By law, if there is no signature, the customer is liable for nothing. If there's a signature, they're liable for $50. The reason the <u>credit-card companies want cryptography is to limit their own liability. It has nothing to do with pro-tecting the consumer.</u>"

But consumer concerns do not fade quickly. So, whether you're hosting through an ISP or hosting yourself, you must have a secure encryption system for credit cards. Shoppers will be looking to see whether your site is secure before they feel comfortable giving you their credit card number. Besides, accepting credit cards at your online store will increase sales dramatically.

While we're discussing security, check to see what kind of security systems your host has in place to prevent break-ins into your server. Ask about their *firewall* protection. A firewall keeps sensitive information on your server out of the reach of hackers and pranksters at best, and credit card thieves at worst.

What's a Firewall?

A Firewall is a security barrier set up between a company's server and the outside world. Firewalls are designed to keep hostile visitors out—a way of protecting the company's internal information.

Your provider should also offer an electronic shopping cart service to your customers. A good shopping cart system gives you control over your products and services *and* makes shopping easy.

Be sure your provider offers an easy, Web-based way to add and subtract items from your product database. A good database not only enables you to manage your merchandise but it also connects to your shopping cart, changing prices and deleting products from inventory as they are sold. The Database also should be able to calculate and add shipping and handling costs to an order and calculate sales taxes that are required by law.

Your hosting service should provide site and traffic analysis reports on a daily basis. These reports are very important and are used to manage your business. They should include at the very least, the number of site visitors, the number and type of pages viewed, where visitors are coming from, how long they stayed on your site, and the URL's that referred them.

How many email address and mailboxes does your hosting service provide? Can they add new email boxes quickly? To run an average size eCommerce site, you need more than webmaster@mysite.com. You should have email addresses for sales, customer service, order status, and general information at the least.

With these items on your shopping list, you're prepared to go out and find a host for your online store.

The Least You Need to Know

➤ Choose then register a domain name at InterNic.

➤ If you don't have a host for your site set up, you can reserve your domain name for use until you've chosen your host provider.

➤ Choose a domain name that's short, memorable, and easy to spell. Choose a name that relates to your core business or business name.

➤ There are three important host essentials: costs, bandwidth, and tech support.

➤ Your hosting shopping list also should include credit card acceptance, shopping cart software, site security, product administration, additional email addresses, and site traffic analysis reports.

Chapter 8

Hosting Your Store for Free

You say you want to sell on the Net but have no programming or technical experience. You want to set up an online store but funds are limited. Or perhaps you have a nice content or community site that attracts a good number of visitors each day and you'd like to turn those visitors into customers.

Well, you're not alone. Thousands of people like you are setting up shop each day on the Net with little or no funds and even less technical know-how. They're using their own personal Web pages or the new free online storefront builders to share in the benefits of the eCommerce revolution. And it's all being done on their own PC through their own Web browser.

No special hardware needed. No software to learn. No technology to buy. Just a few minutes of your time and you can be selling products and services on the Web just like the big boys.

Selling from a Personal Web Page

Soon after the Web became popular, a number of Web-site hosting companies emerged offering free home pages to anyone who would join their community. The price was right—free—and soon hundreds of thousands of cyber-surfers became cyber-squatters. Using the simple tools of the Web-page hosting services like GeoCities, cyber-squatters set up personal home pages by the millions.

At first, they were simple one-page sites for friends and family. But as the personal Web-site hosting companies grew and competition increased, new features and services were offered to those building personal Web pages. In addition, it didn't take long for these people to see that along with offering pictures of their family or acting as a fan site for the Spice Girls or Madonna, you could sell products or offer services over the Web.

It proved to be an inexpensive way to open shop on the Net. Of course, selling from a personal Web site is not the same as having an online store. On the plus side, hosting is free and you can build a Web page quickly using the service's page building tools. On the minus side, there is no shopping cart or a way to take credit card orders. In addition, you can't use a registered personal domain. You must use a cumbersome URL that the Web-page hosting company provides.

For instance, instead of having www.walkingshoes.com, you have to use www.angelfire.com/biz/walkingshoes/index.html—a URL that's long, obscure, and hard to remember. Another trade-off is, whether you like it or not, the company hosting your site for free will place advertising on your site. After all, selling ads on your site is how they make money so you can have a free Web site.

Still, selling from a free personal Web page is a great way to test the eCommerce waters. Whether you have a personal Web page or eCommerce site, you still have the same challenges of drawing traffic to your site and making the sale. On little or no budget and with no out-of-pocket costs, selling from a free Web page could be the best way to test your eCommerce idea.

Free Web-page hosting Sites Review

Looking for a good place to find free Web-page hosting sites? 123 Freepage lists many of the popular free Web page providers. They also review them, listing the advantages of each. Find 123 Freepage at `www.123freepage.com`.

Free Web Page Directory

FreeWebspace.net is the place to find a comprehensive list of free personal Web-page hosting sites. You can even search by the amount of free space each offers. Find FreeWebspace.net at `www.freewebspace.net`.

If you want to set up shop at one of the personal Web-site hosting services then these are the ones to check:

➤ America Online

➤ GeoCities

➤ Angelfire

➤ Tripod

➤ Xoom

America Online

The granddaddy of all personal Web-page hosting services is America Online (AOL). With over 12 million members and growing, many of the AOL members sell products or offer services from their personal Web pages.

AOL calls their Web-page hosting service AOL Hometown (see Figure 8.1). You can find it at `hometown.aol.com/hmtwnpromo/build/index.htm`. As an AOL Hometown resident, you get a free home page, up to 12 megabytes of space, and free special features like a personal chat room.

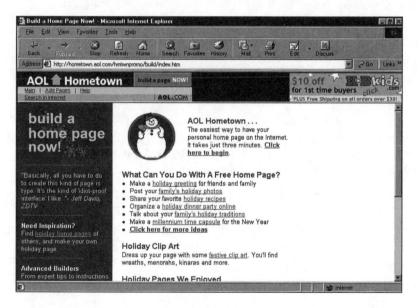

Figure 8.1

Using AOL's Hometown Home Page Builder you can create a personal home page in minutes.

How Much Space Do You Need?

A simple Web site of several pages and a few graphics will fit within 5MB of space. Text takes up very little space, but graphics files are a memory hog. Five megabytes of space should be more than enough if you are selling a product or two, or describing a service. If you plan to have a large number of pictures or graphics on your Web site, then look for hosting services that provide more free space. If not, you might have to pay for the additional space.

Do you need to be a member of AOL to join AOL Hometown? Surprisingly, no. If you use one of AOL's Web-based services like Instant Messenger, Personal Finance Web Center, or My News, you can use the screen name you have to create your AOL Hometown Web page. You can join one of these free services and create a screen name at `publish.hometown.aol.com/_cqr/createsn.adp`.

Unfortunately, many of their other free Web site building services are available only to AOL members.

GeoCities

If AOL is the granddaddy of personal Web pages, GeoCities is close behind. GeoCities was the first such service to hit the Web and quickly grew into the largest personal Web-site hosting service on the Net. GeoCities was so successful that Yahoo! bought it. You can find GeoCities at `geocities.yahoo.com/home/`.

At GeoCities, you can create your home page at one of 40 or more themed communities and have up to 15 megabytes of space to do it. Using the Yahoo! Page Builder, you can build your page in a matter of minutes just by using your browser. You also can add:

➤ Free clip art

➤ News headlines

➤ Stock quotes and charts

➤ Internet search boxes

➤ Interactive features like forms and a guest book

➤ Animation and streaming media

These added features can greatly enhance your eCommerce site by helping to draw visitors who would see your product or service offer. In addition, GeoCities' Pages That Pay Program enable you to easily join a number of affiliate programs from well-known online merchants. Pick the products you want to sell, place the merchant links on your page, and the merchant will process and ship the orders placed by your customers. Pages That Pay lets you check financial reports for all your merchants with one easy-to-use tool (see Figure 8.2). You also get one paycheck for all of them.

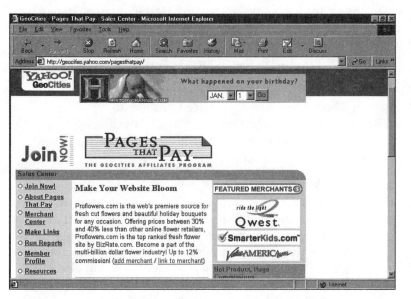

Figure 8.2

Set up business on your GeoCities personal page and earn money without buying or shipping products.

Pages That Pay also helps you promote your online shop quickly and easily. Using the site registration tools you can easily register your site with the popular search engines or send email announcements through your browser.

There might be no such thing as a free lunch, but GeoCities comes close.

Angelfire/Tripod

Angelfire at www.angelfire.lycos.com adds a few whistles and bells to this mix. Like GeoCities, a big portal purchased Angelfire. This time it was Lycos. Besides offering a generous 30 megabytes of space for your Web site, you can also get what the others all lack—a personal URL. Instead of a URL that reads www.angelfire.com/biz/mysitename/index.html you can have a URL that reads www.mysitename.angelfire.com—a much better URL for business.

Like other personal Web page services, you can build a free Web site using Angelfire's online page building tools and free clip art. Or, if you use Microsoft FrontPage or Office 2000 to design your Web pages, you can easily upload them to Angelfire. In addition, you can enhance your Web site with its easy to use Javascripts and polls.

Angelfire's equivalent of GeoCities' Pages that Pay is Commission Central. You can join any number of merchant affiliate programs through Commission Central. You can join as many of them as you want for free with just one form. Like Pages That Pay just pick the products you want to sell, place the merchant links on your page, and the merchant processes and ships the orders placed by your customers.

Angelfire also offers you the opportunity to increase the traffic to your site using its Smart Ads program. Smart Ads is a free banner exchange program. You create the ad banner you'd like and place it on the Web sites of the Smart Ad banner exchange network. In exchange, you place the network's banners on your site. This is a good way to get attention and drive new visitors to your Web site.

Angelfire also has a site traffic program that tells you how many visitors you have and where they're coming from.

Another Lycos-owned personal Web-page hosting service is Tripod at www.tripod.lycos.com. Because the same company owns both Angelfire and Tripod, many of the services offered for personal Web pages are similar.

What's Ftp?

Ftp stands for *File Transfer Protocol.* When you want to send a file—or Web page—from your PC up to a server on the Net, you ftp the file using an ftp program.

Xoom

Xoom, at www.xoom.com, offers everything that Angelfire and Tripod offers—and more. First of all, it offers an easy to use Web-based personal page builder, or you can use the Web pages that you've created and ftp them to its server. Xoom also offers you a way to join merchant affiliate sites to earn money selling product from your site.

What makes Xoom different is this. Xoom offers unlimited space for your Web site so your site can be of any size. It also offers a nice service that can be used for your business called XoomFax that enables you to receive all your faxes at your Xoom email address.

Quick and Easy Online Store Builders

Suppose you've tried selling from a free personal Web page and now want to set up a fully integrated Web storefront. You have little capital in the bank and—even if you had the dough—setting up a secure server and a functional database of products can be technically intimidating. This is a very common situation but easy to overcome.

Beyond the personal Web pages hosting services are the Commercial Service Providers. As eCommerce has heated over the last few years, a host of these Commercial Service Providers have arrived to give you a pure and simple way to open shop on the Net. These Commercial Service Providers can provide you with an integrated browser-based Web storefront, including an online catalog, shopping cart, support for real time credit card payments, advertising, and customer support.

How much do their services cost? Why, they're free!

BigStep, eCongo, and FreeMerchant are three examples of Commercial Service Providers where you can set up and maintain an online store for free. These services give you the opportunity to design and build fully featured, integrated commerce-enabled Web sites, including a host of supporting services.

These free sites offer sophisticated yet easy to use site building through your own browser, and many eBusiness essentials like online catalog with built-in shopping cart, marketing help, credit card clearing, customer communications, comprehensive reports, online customer support, and, of course, site hosting.

BigStep

BigStep at www.bigstep.com offers you six integrated eCommerce functions that help you make your online store a success (see Figure 8.3). And like the personal Web-page hosting services, your URL reads yoursitename.bigstep.com.

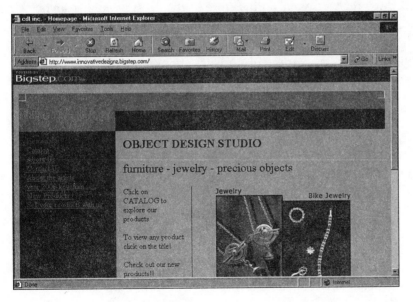

Figure 8.3

Here's an example of a Web store created using BigStep.

BigStep calls these six functions the eCommerce pillars of success—Site building, Catalog Services, Communications, Commerce, Marketing, and Reporting.

Site Building   BigStep says you can build a basic eCommerce site in 10 minutes or less. Their step-by-step process will lead you through building a complete online store that you can finish at your own pace, stopping when you want, and starting again later. You can choose either a basic (the 10 minute path) or advanced path to build your site. You can choose from a selection of professional layouts for setting up most of the pages required on a business site. They even have a logo generator for you to use to create your company logo.

Catalog Services   BigStep enables you to create a catalog to sell products securely and display items efficiently. You can use their catalog services to sell either products or services with multiple pricing structures complete with a secure back-end ordering system. Items in your catalog can be changed as frequently as required.

Commerce   BigStep has made setting up a merchant account to accept credit cards fast, easy, and affordable. Whereas, with most eCommerce services you need to integrate an outside credit card company, Bigstep.com has partnered with Card Services International to provide integrated merchant account services on your site. And there is no set-up fee through Card Services.

Communication   If you want to create an ongoing profitable relationship with your customers, communicating with them is essential. BigStep enables you to collect customer information through an online survey, and the generation of personalized email newsletter.

Marketing   BigStep registers your online store in the most popular search engines and helps you create the keywords that search engines use to categorize Web sites, so customers can better find you.

Reporting   BigStep collects a variety of statistics about your Web site and provides these reports to you covering statistics on your Web site trends and activity like tracking the effectiveness of a targeted newsletter or a search engine submission.

The entire service is free to you. So how does BigStep make money? Will they run ads for other merchants on your site like the personal Web-page hosting services? Nope. BigStep intends to generate revenue from advertisements placed on its own BigStep.com site and through a series of Premium services that will be offered to you to increase your online business.

eCongo

Like BigStep, eCongo at www.econgo.com offers everything you need to set up shop on the Net. And like the personal Web-page hosting services, your URL reads yoursitename.econgo.com.

eCongo offers an easy way to use catalog builder and store administrator. You can have an unlimited number of products for sale complete with descriptions and photos in your catalog. You also can provide contact information and help pages for your shoppers.

eCongo helps you market your Web site. You can build text-based advertisements with their integrated ad builder and each merchant is promoted using streaming text display on a site-by-site basis. You can even trade advertisements with other eCongo merchants through their Merchant Network and eCongo submits your site to popular search engines.

Using eCongo, you can offer your customers multiple payment methods including check, COD, phone ordering, and credit card capture. And like BigStep, eCongo has partnered with Card Services for you to set up a credit card merchant account.

Finally, their free service gives your customers the ability to search your store for products, seven standard customer service email addresses, and a customer service information page. All buyers receive an automated purchase and shipping notification via email after each purchase as well as the ability to check order status 24 hours a day, seven days a week.

Like BigStep, all these services are free to you.

FreeMerchant

FreeMerchant at www.freemerchant.com (see Figure 8.4) offers pretty much the same free eCommerce services that BigStep and eCongo offer, including

➤ Store Hosting

➤ Secure Shopping Cart

➤ Web-Based Store Builder

➤ Unlimited Store Catalog Size

➤ Traffic Logs

➤ eMail Account

➤ Merchant Message Boards

➤ Merchant Banner Xchange

➤ Shipping Calculator

➤ Tax Calculator

➤ Technical Support

But FreeMerchant offers an eCommerce feature that the others do not. Like the other Commercial Service Providers, your URL address is that of FreeMerchant's domain server—yourbusinessname.safeshopper.com. But free hosting for your own domain name is available using their domain name utility. By using this utility program you can make your domain name point to your FreeMerchant site. This is a big plus if you want your business to look even more credible.

One drawback is how FreeMerchant makes its money. They make money by selling and placing banner ads on the bottom of your FreeMerchant site.

Figure 8.4

FreeMerchant lives up to its name—look at all the free services for your free Web store.

eCommerce Enables Your Existing Web Site for Free

Personal Web page hosting services and Commercial Service Providers are a good solution if you don't have an existing site. But what if you do? What if you already have a nice content or community site and want to set it up for eCommerce. Better yet, suppose you want to sell a wide variety of products without the hassle of holding inventory, processing the orders, getting a credit card merchant account, shipping the merchandise, and handling customer service?

The WebPage-O-Matic

Build professional looking Web sites quickly and easily using an awesome free Web-site construction tool called the WebPage-O-Matic. Simply fill out a few fields, click a few buttons, and that's it. WebPage-O-Matic creates, uploads, and even promotes your multi-page Web site for you automatically. Download it at www.AssociatePrograms.com/search/resources.shtml.

You can join one of the hundreds of merchant affiliate programs out there on the Net. Problem is, you have to send your site customers off to the merchant's site and—voilá—they become the merchant's customers not yours. That's the problem with most affiliate programs today.

Affinia—Something Different

Affinia has a different take on building an online store. You do set up your own store but instead of paying you for selling product—they pay you for sending shoppers to their merchants. Whereas the other online store builders pay-per-sale, Affinia uses a pay-per-click model. Find it at www.affinia.com.

But there's hope. A new breed of online merchant has appeared that keeps your traffic—and your customers—on your site when they buy. Their affiliate program treats you like a true partner and not a shill for merchants. These new merchants place a complete store on your site, privately labeled with your company's name. They warehouse the product you sell, process the order, ship it, and handle the customer service. You just sit back and collect the money.

VStore, NexChange, and the One Minute Shopper are examples of this new breed of eCommmerce merchant.

Vstore

With Vstore you can open your own online store in five minutes (see Figure 8.5). Vstore at www.vstore.com can offer your Web site more than one million products to sell, full customer support, order fulfillment, and high-speed hosting and transaction processing. You can choose any number of types of stores to build. A book store, video store, music store, gift store, electronics store, and several others.

Vstore does all the work and takes full responsibility for your customer's purchase. And here's the best part. All products are sold at a discount from list price. And because your store is private labeled with your company name—your customers stay your customers. Vstore does not compete for your sales. You make a commission on each and every sale. Commissions range from 5% to 25% depending upon the product.

Figure 8.5

Open a virtual store on your site with Vstore and you have hundreds of products to sell immediately.

Nexchange

Like Vstore, Nexchange at www.nexchange.com sets up a store on your Web site where you can sell name-brand products from top retailers (see Figures 8.6 and 8.7). You determine what to sell. You can choose from thousands of products in dozens of categories earning 10% to 25% commission on every sale. And because your store is linked to your site, you keep your visitors while they shop and buy.

Figure 8.6

Nexchange can integrate a complete online store into your existing Web site.

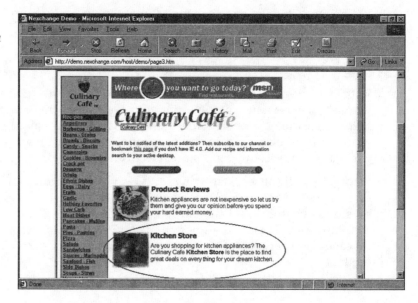

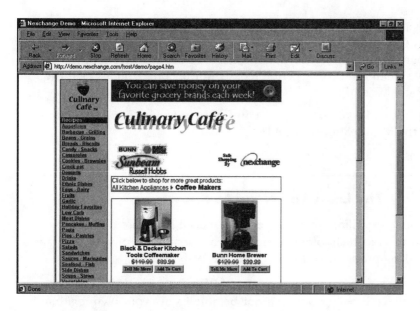

Figure 8.7

A customer can view products for sale on your site and add them to the NexChange shopping cart that is easily integrated into your site.

But unlike Vstore, the look and feel of your store will exactly match the look and feel of your Web site—right down to your site individual navigation links.

One Minute Shopper

One Minute Shopper at www.oneminuteshopper.com goes one step farther. With One Minute Shopper you don't have to create a complete online store like at Vstore or NexChange. You place a small eCommerce application on any page of your site called their MinuteStore. The MinuteStore sells name-brand products at steeply discounted prices and caters to the impulse buyer who visits your Web site.

Not only does your visitor not leave your site—he or she doesn't leave the page they arrived at. Using a series of small pop-up windows, the shopper is lead through a series of product offers, descriptions, and finally an order form when they're ready to buy.

The MinuteStore is a complete eCommerce application that presents limited-time, limited-supply products to your visitors, takes the order, processes it, ships it, and does all the necessary customer service. All you need to do is place a piece of code on your Web page or pages and collect your commission.

Beyond Affiliate Programs

Envision this: A visitor to your site is reading a review of a printer and right next to it is a small icon that says Buy It. And do it without ever leaving your site? They can now. It's called *embedded commerce* and Pop 2 It is doing it. See it at www.pop2it.com.

In addition, there is a prospect-building and customer re-marketing program called the MinuteShoppers Club that is used to promote new products to your customers and prospects in your name. Visitors to your site can join the MinuteShoppers Club and receive exclusive email offers on a periodic basis. If they buy, you also get the commission from the sale.

Commissions range from 15% to 20% on each and every sale whether it's through the MinuteStore or the MinuteShoppers Club.

The Least You Need to Know

➤ You can set up your online store for free. No special hardware needed. No software to learn. No technology to buy. Just a few minutes of your time and you can be selling products and services on the Web.

➤ Keep in mind that if you are using a personal Web-page hosting service or a Commercial Service Provider, you will not be able to use your own registered domain name.

➤ If you don't have a Web site but want full eCommerce capability, use one of the free Commercial Service providers.

➤ If you have an existing Web site and want to eCommerce enable it, use one of the new private labeling store building services.

Chapter 9

Hosting with an ISP

In This Chapter

➤ Set up an online storefront for less than a dollar a day

➤ Learn the difference between Internet Service Providers and eCommerce hosting companies

➤ Learn what eCommerce services to look for in a hosting company

---

Sooner or later (sooner if you have the money in the bank to do so) you'll want to consider running your own eCommerce Web site. The free sites are fine to start with if you have limited funds. But to become a real online business you need more than what the personal Web page providers and Commercial Service Providers can offer.

Let's face it, as a real business you have a number of eCommerce needs that a person with a personal home page does not. And selling other merchants products has its limitations. Free hosting is fine but generally a poor choice if you're going to generate your own transactions and sell your own products on your site. In addition, eBusiness services like customer wish lists, gift certificates, advanced search capabilities, gift reminder services, personal shopping agents, and one-click ordering are not normally available at the free hosting sites.

When you're ready to become a full-fledged eBusiness, you need to ante up and pay the piper.

All-In-One Hosting Services

There are several All-In-One hosting services on the Web to host your online store. An All-In-One hosting service is similar to the free hosting services in that no programming knowledge is required to set up your Web site. You build your store on their server through your browser following a series of quick and easy steps. You don't need to know any HTML or have any prior experience setting up an online storefront—and there is no server to buy.

Multi-Lingual All-In-One Hosting Services

Internet Solutions for Business in England has a multi-lingual Web shop creator called E-Commerce 1. Their shop creator supports more than 500 items for sale in more than 10 native languages. Find it at www.is4b.net/.

Although not free, these services offer low-cost, one-stop solutions for eCommerce. And all claim you can build a store and start taking orders in minutes. Orders are accepted securely and you can retrieve your orders securely whenever you want. All management of your online store is done through your browser and you can add, delete, or change products whenever you please.

Costs vary. Some of these hosting services charge a flat rate based on the number of products you sell whereas others charge for that amount of server space your store takes up. None of the services listed here charge a transaction fee per sale. Steer clear of any service that does.

Here's a list of the largest All-In-One hosting services:

➤ Yahoo! Store
➤ iCat Web Store
➤ eBiz Builder
➤ Shop Builder

You need to decide which plan is best suited for you depending upon the size of your store and the services you would like to provide.

Yahoo! Store

Setting up an online store at Yahoo! Store at store.yahoo.com is quick and easy (see Figure 9.1). You can even test drive your store before you decide to commit to the Yahoo! service. There are no startup costs, no minimum time commitment, and no transaction fees per order. You pay a flat fee per month depending upon the number of products you offer in your store.

➤ A small store (up to 50 items for sale) is $100 a month.
➤ A large store (up to 1,000 items for sale) is $300 a month.
➤ Larger stores cost $300/month for the first 1,000 items, plus $100/month for each additional 1,000 items.

You can either use the Yahoo! Store domain for your online store such as store.yahoo.com/yourstore/ or you can use your own domain name. Yahoo! Store even helps you transfer it to their severs.

An advantage that the other All-In-One hosting services can't offer is the inclusion of your store in the Yahoo! Shopping Search engine. The products in your store are searched and displayed to cyber-shoppers who are looking for the type of products you sell. Ordering through a Yahoo! Store is 100% secure. Credit card orders are encrypted when they're placed online and encrypted when they're sent to you. Yahoo! Store also submits your store to the most popular search engines.

You can retrieve your orders in four ways. View them on the Yahoo! server through your browser, retrieve them as a database file to your computer, have them faxed to you, or if you have your own secure server, have the order posted to it in real time. You can update your store as frequently as you want and you have control over the look and feel of your site to make it unique.

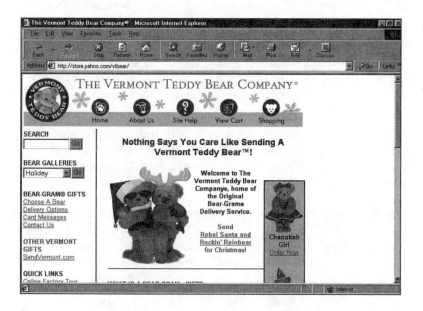

Figure 9.1

Yahoo! Store created a Web store for the Vermont Teddy Bear Company.

Yahoo! Store even supplies you with a set of sophisticated site traffic tracking tools including number of page views, where your visitors came from, what they searched for, and the click paths they used to navigate your site. There's also a Repeat Customer Detector that analyzes each order, which enables you to recognize repeat customers without requiring them to register.

What about the speed of your connection? You should have little worry about bandwidth. Your site downloads fast for your customers because you have the same network connection as Yahoo! itself. After all, your store is residing on their servers.

Credit Card Authorizations

When you take a credit card order and get an authorization, keep in mind that an authorization is just an indication that a card is valid and the customer has enough open credit to charge the sale. It is not a guarantee that you have a valid sale. For example, the card might be stolen.

Finally, Yahoo! Store has a relationship with First Data for credit card processing. If you already have a merchant account you can use their First Data link to process credit cards online. If you don't have a merchant account, you can easily set one up at First Data. Yahoo! Store also supplies you with a set of merchant resources like How to Sell online, site design tips, and a monthly newsletter.

iCat Web Store

Like Yahoo! Store, iCat at www.icat.com offers an easy-to-use Web-based interface to build your online store (see Figure 9.2). There are no setup or transaction fees with iCat. iCat charges by the number of products you offer in your store. Costs range from $9.95 a month for 10 items, all the way up to $249.95 a month for 1,000 items.

One good feature that iCat offers is this: You can build your store and bring it online paying nothing for 30 days. This gives you a chance to see how your eCommerce brainchild does before committing to the iCat service.

iCat offers you the ability to build, manage, and promote your online store using their service. Using their store building wizard, you can have your online store up in no time. And like all the All-In-One hosting services, you can manage your storefront through a Netscape or Internet Explorer Web browser from wherever you are.

Figure 9.2

Here's an example of an iCat store created for Green Thumb Outdoor Wear clothing company.

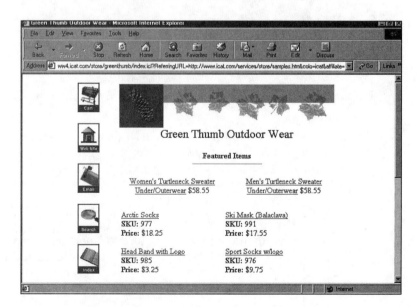

iCat registers you in the top five search engines for free. iCat also directs you to companies on the Web that help you promote your store. Keep in mind that many of these services are not free. If you'd like to use a professional developer to design your Web store or create the graphics for your site, iCat directs you to their Commerce Online Developer Network.

When you build a Web store, your URL is `www.icatmall.com/yourstore/`. But if you have your own domain name, you can use that too. As for orders, iCat alerts you via email when an order is placed at your store. All orders are placed through iCat's secure Web commerce server and you can accept orders via credit cards, checks, or COD.

This Could Be z-Place

Amazon has put a different spin on the All-In-One shop. Although not a real store, you can list your products for sale or for auction at their zShops. You can showcase up to 3,000 listings at a time starting for as little as $10 a month. Find it at `s1.amazon.com/exec/varzea/subscription-signup/`.

If you don't have a merchant account to accept credit cards, iCat helps you establish a merchant account and processes customer credit cards through their Payment Service. When using their Payment Service, all credit card orders are placed in real-time and include fraud protection. iCat's Payment Service carries a one-time setup fee of $300 and a monthly fee of $45.

Finally, a nice feature iCat provides is the listing of your product prices in a number of foreign currencies. This makes it convenient for international shoppers to buy from you.

eBiz Builder

eBiz at `www.e-bizbuilder.com` offers many of the services that Yahoo! Store and iCat provide (see Figure 9.3). They offer four service plans to choose from: eCom Basic, eCom Plus, eCom Gold, and eCom Platinum. Their cost structure is a little different from that of Yahoo! Store and iCat. You don't pay per month for the number of products you offer but the amount of server space your online store uses. There are setup charges for each plan but no transaction fees.

107

Figure 9.3

eBiz Builder was used to create an online flower shop complete with site search functions.

Here are descriptions of the four eBiz Builder service plans:

eCom Basic   This plan gives you 5MB of space and uses eBiz Builder's URL sub-domain name like www.e-bizbuilder.com/yourstorename. The cost for this plan is $12.99 a month with a $35 set up fee.

eCom Plus   Selecting eCom Plus gives you 10 megabytes of space, and uses eBiz Builder's URL sub-domain name. The cost for this plan is $29.99 a month with a $75 set up fee.

eCom Gold   With this plan you receive 20 megabytes of space but you can use your own domain name. The cost for this plan is $59.99 a month with a $150 set up fee.

eCom Platinum   This plan gives you 30 megabytes of space but you can use your own domain name. The cost for this plan is $75.99 a month with a $300 set up fee.

In theory, you could offer an unlimited number of items for sale on eBiz Builder. The only limitation would be the server space that you pay for in your plan and the performance of your site. All the plans except for the eCom Basic plan have these features in common:

➤ Unlimited Inventory
➤ Personal Search Engine
➤ Shopping Cart
➤ Product Sales Receipt

➤ Customer Tracking System

➤ Customer eMail Receipts

➤ Integrated Shipping and Sales Tax System

➤ Credit Card Account Set Up

➤ Accepts Visa and MasterCard

➤ Real-Time Card Processing

➤ Secure Credit Card Transactions

The eCom Basic plan does not offer an email account, total Web site statistics, or Web-based reports. Costs and server space for each plan vary.

eBiz Builder sets you up with a credit card merchant account through QuickCommerce. It's quick, fast, and automatically installed and integrated into your eBiz Builder Web site.

Shop Builder

Like Yahoo! Store, you can test drive an online storefront through Shop Builder. Shop Builder at , offers many of the services of the other three All-In-One Hosting Services (see Figure 9.4). You can build an online store in minutes, take orders securely, make changes to your storefront, track customer sales, and choose from a variety of store layouts. You can even use your own domain name.

Credit card orders are processed in real-time on their secure server, and an email receipt is automatically generated and sent to each customer. You can have your orders faxed to you each day or you can retrieve them from the Web using your browser. You can configure your store to accept orders via phone, mail, or fax by check, credit card, or COD. As for promotion, Shop Builder has an automated system for submitting your store's URL to all the major search engines.

You can use Shop Builder's professionally designed templates to create your store, or you can use HTML to custom-design your store using a Web site design program. Their shopping cart system lets customers see exactly what they've ordered at any time. As for speed, all their stores are connected to the Net via a redundant, fast T1 line.

The cost of their hosting service starts at $20 a month for Starter Store. This allows you to offer up to five items for sale. Their Mini Store gives you up to 20 items for sale for $40 per month, the Small Store up to 100 items for $70 per month, and their Large Store up to 1,000 items for $250 per month. There are no set up or transaction fees and no commitments to continue with their service.

Figure 9.4

Shop Builder supplies a compete set of tools to build, maintain, and manage your online store.

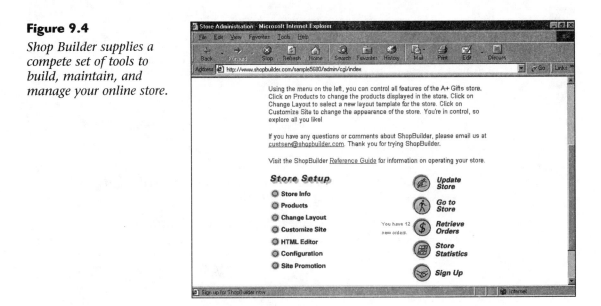

Choosing an ISP Hosting Service

If you have dreams of becoming the next Amazon or CDNow, the All-In-One hosting services will not get you there. You're still constrained by the necessities of these types of hosting services. Sure, you can offer the products you want, take and process a credit card order, have an email account, and use your own domain name. But to be a real eCommerce player you need to take charge of your own destiny and build your own online store.

In addition, if you're planning on raising a large amount of capital from investors or venture capitalists to realize your eCommerce dream, you'll need the flexibility—and credibility—to execute the type of eBusiness that will compete with the large established eCommmerce sites on the Net.

That kind of flexibility and credibility comes only with the control and design of your own site. In Chapter 11, "Building Your Web Store," I cover the essentials of building your own eCommerce Web site. But first you need to learn how to choose the proper Internet Service Provider (ISP) to host your site.

Why host on an independent Internet Service Provider? Why not host your site yourself?

More Is Not Necessarily Better

You don't have to sell hundreds upon hundreds of product to be a successful eTailer. Many eTailers have been successful selling only a dozen or so well defined products to a niche market.

ISPs stand between you and your customer. They are the primary providers and the managers of the servers and other hardware that link the threads of the Web together. Like a fine weaver, they knit together the many diverse pieces of the Internet. If you had to bring all these elements together on your own it would be a costly and—if you're not technically skilled in the ways of the Net—a frustrating experience.

Not any Internet Service Provider will do. If you're in business, you need a dedicated Web hosting company. Dedicated eCommerce hosting companies do one thing and one thing only—they host businesses on the Web. They don't normally offer dial-up accounts to individuals like you and I. This way, your customers won't have to compete for bandwidth to access your online store with online Doom players or people surfing Boyz2Men fan sites. Nothing frustrates a customer more than a slow download time.

Locating your Web site on a qualified ISP's server could take less time than pulling together the necessary services to quickly and safely take sales at your online store. The right ISP can provide your eBusiness with a turn-key eCommerce package that gives you fast credit card processing, end-to-end customer service, a high-speed connection—and gets you up and running in a matter of days.

The Nature of the Beast

Your first task in selecting an appropriate ISP for your online business is to learn about the nature of the beast. You'll find ISPs all over the map—literally. You'll find them in different parts of the country and different in price and service.

At the very bottom of the food chain is the very small ISP. Believe it or not, you can find a person who has set up a server in his basement or spare room that hosts Web sites. Any person can build or buy a Web server, install a T1 line in the back, connect to the Internet, and become an ISP. If you were serious about business, I would leave these people to hosting family and friends' Web pages, multilevel marketing sites, and lawyers' and real estate salesmen's Web sites.

Locating an ISP

To start your hunt for an ISP, check out Yahoo's list of regional ISPs at www.yahoo.com/Business_and _Economy/Companies/Internet _Services/Access_Providers/ National__U_S__/ and the Definitive ISP Buyers Guide at thelist.iworld.com/.

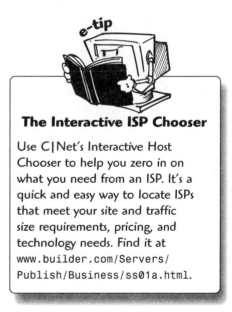

The Interactive ISP Chooser

Use C|Net's Interactive Host Chooser to help you zero in on what you need from an ISP. It's a quick and easy way to locate ISPs that meet your site and traffic size requirements, pricing, and technology needs. Find it at www.builder.com/Servers/ Publish/Business/ss01a.html.

111

They might be cheap in the short run—and they are—but cost you a lot more in time and frustration later on. You're looking for a reliable business partner, not a hobbyist.

You might find that many Web site developers host the sites they design for clients on their own servers. Although these people are more professional and business focused, the downside might be price and a smaller, slower connection to the Internet.

Next up the chain is the dial-up ISP. As I stated before, hosting with a dial-up ISP can have its problems. You need a hosting service that understands business—not Net surfers. If the focus of the ISP is its dial-up customers, the eBusiness services you need might be minimal or even non-existent. Still, there are a few large ISPs that have separate divisions for Web site hosting and dial-up customers and they might be useful if they are nationally based (see Figure 9.5).

Figure 9.5

TopHosts.com offers a directory of hosting solutions for your Web site. Each month they rank the top 25 hosting services.

Following the dial-up ISP is the business Web hosting ISP. These ISPs take eBusiness seriously and focus only on Web business hosting. Prices are competitive, service is good, and technical support for your business is on call when you need it. They also give you dial-up access to your site, usually via ftp to make site changes and additions.

Finally, there's the large business or industrial strength ISP. If your Web site attracts a large amount of traffic, you're going to need one of these ISPs sooner or later. These ISPs offer few bargains, but you can expect to have maximum reliability, 24-hour in-house technical support, mirror sites on both coasts, and a redundant connection to the Internet.

Essential Services

Having to change ISP horses in midstream can be a costly and time-wasting affair. After you're online business is up and running, switching ISPs definitely disrupts your business.

So how can you ensure that you're making the right choice?

First, make a list of the site hosting essentials you'll need for your online store. (We'll get to those in a minute.) Next, try to get referrals from satisfied business people. Referrals are always the safest way to shop for anything.

If you are using a Web site developer to create your Web site, ask for his or her advice. They probably have a few ISPs they would recommend. If not, make a list of ISPs that seem to have eCommerce experience and send them your list of site hosting essentials asking them which ones they can supply. Ask for a written response—and references to Web stores they host—and give them a deadline to do it.

Here are the essential questions to ask an ISP.

Connection Speed

How fast can your customers access your site? Be sure your ISP is using at least T1s or T3s to connect to the Internet. A T1 can carry up to 1.5Mbs (megabits per second), whereas a T3 can carry 45Mbs. Make sure that the ISP is not using a fractional T1 or an ISDN line or buying access from another larger ISP. This affects Web pages' download time.

Another thing that can affect your download speed is the number of clients your ISP has on the server that your site is on. The more Web sites that are on your box, the more hits it gets and the slower your Web pages download. This can happen even if your ISP has a fast connection to the Net. Even if there are just a few Web sites on your server, if one of them is a high-volume site with lots of traffic, it, too, can affect the download speed of your Web pages.

Your hosting contract states how much bandwidth you will be paying for. (How much of a T1 you will be using.) If you exceed that amount of bandwidth at peak times, will they automatically increase it to match the traffic? What will they charge you for the increase? And when it's time to increase your bandwidth, know up front what the incremental costs will be.

e-talk

What's an ISDN?

*ISDN—or Integrated Services Digital Network—*is another way to connect to the Internet. Using an ISDN card and an ISDN connection, your connect speed to the Net is five times faster than a dial-up modem. They require special telephone lines that cost more than normal phone lines.

113

Check Your Page Loading Time

Want to see how fast your connection is by seeing how fast your page loads? Then surf on over to Virtual Stampede and use their Load Time Check program. It's free. Find it at `virtual-stampede.com/tools.htm`.

Finally, ask the ISP about their downtime guarantee—what percentage of the time is their service up and will they guarantee that percentage. A few dollars refunded to you as a downtime penalty cannot make up for lost sales. And while you're at it, ask them about their technical and customer support. Is it 24 hours 7 days a week? It should be.

Space and Site Requirements

An ISP assigns you a certain amount of space on its computer for your Web site. This space allotment usually starts at 5MB and is enough to house the text and graphics of a small to medium eCommerce site. One thing to ask is whether log and mail files are counted in the space allotted to you. If not, you'll need to ask for more.

Next, make sure that the ISP provides a virtual domain or virtual hosting for your online store. This enables you to use the unique domain name you registered with InterNic. Then you can take your domain name off reserved status and locate it on your ISPs server. If you are moving your Web site from one ISP to another, ask if the ISP will move the domain name for you and do all the necessary paperwork for InterNic. This could be quite a hassle if you're new to the mysterious ways of InterNic.

Unlimited Email Addresses and Auto-Responders

Having one personal email address is nice. Having one or two more on Yahoo! or Hot Mail is cool. But neither will do if you're in business. Ask your ISP how many email addresses you are allowed. You need more than one. Your business should have several email aliases for your domain name for different departments of your business.

Be Sure You Have At Least These Email Aliases

You'll need more than one email address for your eCommerce site. Offer at least these email addresses to your site visitors.

➤ info@yourcompany.com—for those requesting general information.

➤ service@yourcompany.com—for customer service requests.

➤ orders@yourcompany.com—for order status questions.

➤ sales@yourcompany.com—for suppliers to contact you.

➤ feedback@yourcompany.com—for general feedback on your site or service.

Make sure that the ISP can provide you with aliases. Also, make sure that each alias can be forwarded to the company email address of the person responsible for that department.

Finally, ask whether the ISP can provide email auto-responders. You can use these auto-responders to automatically reply to certain emails asking for information. For example, when a customer contacts you with a problem, you might create an auto-responder that states you have received their email and their request is being processed. Another type of auto-responder would be an email confirmation of their order and another when their product is shipped.

cgi-bin Access

If you'll be using a shopping cart on your site, generating email messages sent out by Web page forms, or running programs such as polls or surveys, you need access to the ISPs cgi-bin. This is a place on the server that hosts your site where you can run the programs that you have written.

cgi-bin access is critical in supporting a shopping cart application for your online store. Most of these programs are created in the Perl or C++ programming language so you must have access to the ISP's C compiler and Perl interpreter programs. Most ISPs enable ftp access to a cgi-bin directory but not Telnet access. If not, any programming development that you need can be drastically slowed down. Without Telnet access, you won't be able to compile any programs written in C or C++.

You'll have to rely on the ISP to do it. And that can cause a problem. Waiting for your ISP to do your programming can cause considerable delays in executing programs that you need to run your online business. And there's a reason for an ISP's reluctance in granting you access. In some cases, the ISP must give you root access to their server to install and run your program and this can cause a security risk.

Be sure you ask if the ISP enables Telnet access to a cgi-bin directory.

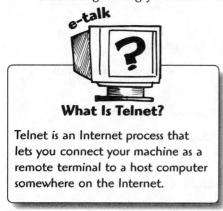

What Is Telnet?

Telnet is an Internet process that lets you connect your machine as a remote terminal to a host computer somewhere on the Internet.

Mailing List Programs

In a short amount of time, you will need a way to contact your customers. You might want to create an email newsletter for them to opt-in to, or email a special offer to a segment of your customer base, or even send an email to all your customers thanking them for their business.

These are all good ways to keep your business in front of your customers and prospects. By communicating periodically with your prospect and customer base, you increase their likelihood of returning to your site to make future sales. If this is your goal—and it should be—then your ISP must provide you with a mailing list program.

One such mailing list program is called Majordomo. At first glance it looks like the name of some Japanese officer but it's really an automated email management program. For example, suppose you want to set up an email discussion group or an email newsletter list. People who visit your Web site can subscribe to your discussion list or email newsletter from a page on your site. Their email address is automatically entered into the Majordomo database and when it's time to send a message, you just compose it and paste it into an email message. Majordomo then sends it to everyone on the email list.

The Majordomo FAQ

Still not clear on Majordomo? Everything you need to know about Majordomo can be found at the Majordomo FAQ. Find it at www.visi.com/~barr/majordomo-faq.html.

In addition, if someone wants to unsubscribe from the list, they can return to your Web site and ask to unsubscribe. Majordomo automatically does it all without any action on your part.

Other Considerations

Most ISPs provide you with unlimited ftp access to your site. You need this to upload your site after it's created and then to make changes when needed. If you're in the software business and want to let customers download demos or if you want to offer some free information for download, you need to have an anonymous ftp capability. This differs from your normal ftp access, which requires a username and password. An anonymous ftp does not. So ask this of any ISP that you are considering.

An ISP also should supply you with a statistical package that can tell you how many people visited your site and from where. (This can tell you which marketing efforts worked and which did not.) The package should tell you the number and types of pages they visited and the path they used to click through your site. (This can help you improve your site navigation.) It should tell you which are your most frequented pages and which are not. (This can help you see which products are popular and which are not.)

Finally, if you're taking credit card orders, be sure the ISP provides a secure commerce server running a *Secure Socket Layer* or *SSL*. This is the standard for credit card security over the Net. And if you plan to use some kind of back-end database for your Web site, be sure that the ISP's operating system is compatible with the system you use to maintain the database.

What Should You Expect to Pay

The price you pay for an eCommerce hosting service varies with services that you need. A typical site with multiple email alias, cgi-bin access, and a T3 connection to the Internet can run anywhere from $20 to $40 a month. If you add SSL security to that you can expect to pay up to $75 a month. If you have a high-volume site, you might be charged additional fees for peak periods of bandwidth.

Remember, ISPs are very competitive. If you like an ISP but its prices are too high, ask if it is possible to match his competitor's price. You never know.

ISP vs Own

The Least You Need to Know

➤ All-In-One hosting services, although not free, offer low-cost, one-stop solutions for eCommerce.

➤ All-In-One hosting service costs vary. Some charge a flat rate based on the number of products you sell whereas others charge for that amount of server space your store takes up.

➤ If you have dreams of becoming the next Amazon or CDNow, the All-In-One hosting services will not get you there. You'll have to build your own site.

➤ If you're in business, you need a dedicated Web hosting company. Dedicated eCommerce hosting companies do one thing and one thing only—they host businesses on the Web.

➤ Having to change ISP horses in midstream can be a costly and time-wasting affair. After your online business is up and running, switching ISPs definitely disrupts your business. So choose well.

➤ Keep in mind the eCommerce site essentials if you want to create a successful eCommerce site.

Chapter 10

Be Your Own Host

> **In This Chapter**
>
> ➤ Discover how to switch ISPs
>
> ➤ Learn what hardware and software you need to build your own Web site server
>
> ➤ Learn whether you should hire a professional to design and build your Web site

Your online business is humming along. Traffic is up, sales are great, and you have Jeff Bezos in your crosshairs. You've gone beyond what an eCommerce ISP or All-In-One hosting service like Yahoo! Store can give you. You're ready to hunt the big game. You're ready to become an Enterprise Site. You're ready to own and maintain your own Web server.

You might be a candidate for an Enterprise Site if:

➤ You're getting tens of thousands of hits a day and your pages are getting slower and slower to download.

➤ Your hits are crashing your ISP's servers.

➤ You need access to sophisticated programs like one-click ordering, advanced product search capabilities, or personal shopping agents that your ISP won't install.

➤ You need to access and update a customized or large database of products and customers—or even direct access to a mainframe computer.

Deciding to go it on your own and owning your own Web server is a serious choice. The costs of building and maintaining an eCommerce Web server are not to be taken lightly. If you do it for ego or the insistence of some computer systems person who wants a new toy, you could greatly damage your successful business.

Are there ways to reduce the risks as you move toward being an Enterprise Site?

Yes, there are. You could co-host your server before you bring it in-house. But first things first. You have to move your site from your current ISP first—and that itself is a challenging task.

Moving Your Web Site

In the realm of eCommerce headaches, moving your Web site to another server ranks right up there with having your site crash. Transferring your Web site to a new server has the potential to disrupt your business, cause you to lose sales—and even customers—if not done correctly.

Here are the problems to prepare for but first a bit of advice. Never assume anything. In moving a site, expect the worst and prepare for it.

First—and most importantly—where are the pages that represent your Web site? Do you have a copy of them on your PC? If you're going to move your site, you must have possession of your Web site pages to transfer them to your new server. If your store is currently running on an All-In-One service like Yahoo! Store, then you have a much larger problem. Because there is no Web site to call your own, you'll need to build one from scratch.

Second, any programs or scripts that you're running on your current ISP need to be moved—or if the ISP provided them for you—replaced or amended to work on your new server. In addition, all the data on customers and products that you have created and stored must be transferred as well. This in itself can be quite an undertaking. Be sure that you maintain a copy of these databases on your computer system.

Third, you have to move your domain name. Sounds simple, right? Not quite. A number of things can go wrong here. First of all, the people at InterNic are nearly impossible to speak to personally. At InterNic you can set up a domain name in a matter of minutes. Making any changes to it can take months!

Here's the problem. InterNic accepts changes to a domain registration from only the Administrative Contact. When you registered your domain name, you were asked to supply an Administrative and Technical Contact. You can see this information at Network Solutions site at www.networksolutions.com/cgi-bin/whois/whois (see Figure 10.1). The Technical Contact is usually someone in technical support where your ISP domain resides.

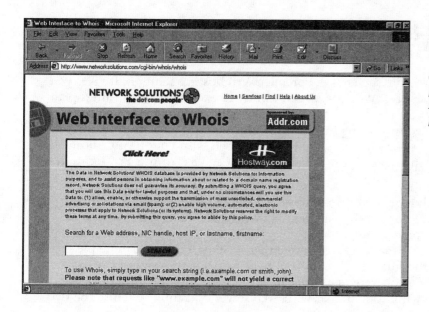

Figure 10.1

Check Network Solution's Whois to view your domain name registration file. Enter your URL and InterNic brings up your file.

Most people make the mistake of having that person be their Administrative Contact as well. If so, you won't be able to make changes to your domain registration—such as moving it to your new server—without the Technical Contact's permission. And only he can do it. Even worse, if the Technical Contact is an employee of the ISP and has left the company, he might be nowhere to be found. So be sure that you are always the Administrative Contact—not one of your employees.

Here's something else to prepare for when you move from an ISP. Service goes from good to poor in a matter of minutes. After the ISP loses you as a customer, he has little motivation in helping you move. After all, you're not his customer anymore, why should he service you. Don't assume your old ISP will cooperate with you—and even if he does—don't assume he'll stick to your timetable.

You might consider withholding any funds due your ISP until the transfer is complete, but I don't recommend it. They could lock you out of access to your site.

To avoid this problem, don't shut down your ISP until your new site is up—and fully functional—on your new server. In fact, run both. When you're confident that your new site is running the way it should, then and only then contact InterNic and point your domain name to the new server. If you're the Administrative Contact on your domain registration, pointing your domain name to the your new server takes only a few days and about a week or so for the Internet to update its records and point your traffic to your new home.

In-House, Co-Located, or Dedicated Host Service?

Having your own Web site server is the premier Web hosting solution. It gives you complete control over your Web site, the flexibility to execute your eBusiness plan, and your site visitors are the only ones using your server. After you've made the decision to use a dedicated server, the first thing you need to do is connect your server to the Internet. You have three choices. Do it you yourself with your own dedicated server and connection in-house, use a dedicated host service, or use a co-location service.

But no matter which type of service you use, you have to decide which software platform you're going to use to run your site. About Guide Gordon Whyte has a Web Store Software Selector at

`ecommerce.about.com/finance/ecommerce/library/blsw.htm` that can help (see Figure 10.2.) Of all the software choices you make for your Web server, the most important will be your software platform—or operating system or OS. Other than DOS, you're probably not too familiar with Web server operating systems. The two most popular are Unix and Windows NT.

Figure 10.2

About Guide Gordon Whyte has created a Web Store Software Selector to help you choose the right eCommerce software system.

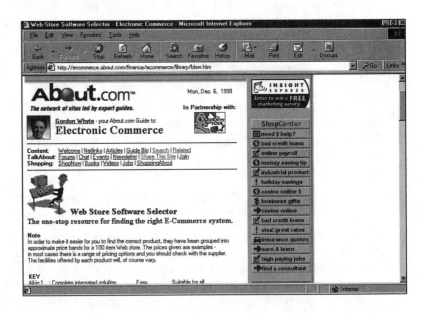

The oldest and most stable of the Web server operating systems is UNIX. UNIX was developed in 1969, and, up until several years ago, was the first choice of server operating systems. Its popularity stems from the fact that it was designed to be a multi-user/multitasking operating system that is perfect for Web servers. But unlike Windows, it is not a graphical OS—it's more like DOS.

Microsoft has been very aggressive in promoting its Windows NT Web server and many businesses have adopted this operation system. There's a problem with Windows NT that you should be aware of. Servers running UNIX have less downtime than those with Windows NT. UNIX servers can normally go months without needing to be rebooted whereas Windows NT servers need to be rebooted much more frequently. And because UNIX is such a popular OS, you should be able to easily find someone who can help you when you have a problem.

UNIX or NT?

Top Host has a very good article that describes the pros and cons of UNIX and NT. Find it at www.tophosts.com/pages/ webhost/ntis.htm.

Hosting your server in-house at your business location is expensive. Not only is there the cost of the Web serving hardware, but also there's the cost of administering the system in-house. This can take a staff of technical people just to keep the server up and running. You need to lease a T1 line, buy routers to connect to the Net, and build firewalls to keep out unwanted guests. Costs for this can start at $20,000 and go up—way up—from there.

Co-Location Host Services

If you don't want to incur the costs of connecting your server to the Internet, you should consider a co-location service provider. This is a good option if you're confident you can maintain a server but don't want the hassle of bringing in an Internet connection in-house. Your server is kept at a high-grade facility that the co-location host provides.

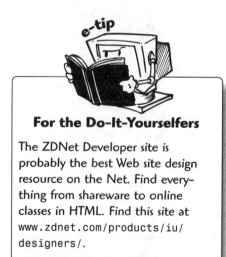

For the Do–It-Yourselfers

The ZDNet Developer site is probably the best Web site design resource on the Net. Find everything from shareware to online classes in HTML. Find this site at www.zdnet.com/products/iu/ designers/.

A definite advantage of this type of service is that their Net connection is usually faster than a simple T1 that you could provide. They will most likely have a T3 line or even a fiber-optics line connected to the Net. It also solves the physical security problem and reduces the chance of the server going down due to power failures.

As for support and service, that's still your responsibility. The co-location host service provider's main job is to connect your server to the Net. When your co-location server goes down, it's up to you to fix it—or pay someone to do it. Are you willing to leave your warm bed at two in the morning to coordinate the repair of your server when it goes down?

Choosing A Web Server

Looking for a good source for help on choosing a Web server? Check out the links at About.com. Find About.com at compnetworking.about.com/ compute/compnetworking/ msubwebserver.htm?terms= choosing+a+server&PM=113_400_T.

As for costs, they're higher than a dedicated hosting service. First you have to buy a server. A low-end server will set you back about $4,000 and a mid-range server about $9,000. Next you need to place your server in rack. A half-rack costs about $500 to $700 a month to rent at the facility. Finally, you have to purchase a router that connects you to the Internet. All total, and assuming you invest in a low-end server, you're initial outlay to get up and running will be about $7,500—not including personnel time for set up and configuration.

Dedicated Host Services

If you still want your own dedicated server but don't want the costs incurred in buying one, setting it up, and connecting it to the Net, then a dedicated host services company is your ticket.

The dedicated host services company supplies your server—fully configured and ready for your site—the rack space, the connection to the Internet, a large bandwidth, back up power, and 24/7 monitoring of your site. One advantage of using a dedicated host service is the speed at which you can add hardware to service unplanned business needs. For example, suppose your site is the subject of a story in *USA Today* or the focus of a TV news story. This news would draw a large number of unexpected visitors to your site.

Check Your Site Performance

Is your Internet provider delivering the speed and service they promised? Then give your Web site a tune up. Use WebSite Garage to measure your site's performance, optimize your graphics, and analyze your site traffic. Check it out at websitegarage.netscape.com/.

If you co-located, you would have to quickly add additional hardware to your site—hardware that was not originally budgeted for. But because the dedicated host company provides all the hardware, upgrading your system to meet the unplanned need would be easy and much less expensive.

In addition, if the traffic subsided, you could simply cancel the use of the new hardware. If you co-located, you would now own an unused piece of hardware. This is very important for an eCommerce site because as the Internet grows, an eBusiness must be prepared to move quickly and add new hardware as the market demands.

Costs for a dedicated hosting service are far less than the co-location option. Because you don't need to buy a server or pay to connect to the Net, your initial costs are very low. You just pay a start up fee of about $900, which includes your server's configuration, and a monthly fee of about $900 a month for the service.

Hosting Requirements

When choosing either a co-location or dedicated hosting service, you should keep a number of requirements in mind.

➤ Are they insured?

➤ Is the physical comsouter environment secure? Are the necessary security precautions in place?

➤ Is the environment kept clean?

➤ Are their technical people knowledgeable? Do they have knowledge of computers and telecommunications? Both are necessary.

➤ What kinds of technical support will they offer? Are they easily reachable? Do they offer the support 24 hours a day 7 days a week? Your online store doesn't close and neither should they.

➤ Can they provide references? What other companies can you talk to that use their facilities? What kind of experience have they had with the service?

➤ Will your site be backed up? How and how often? Do they have a disaster recovery plan in case of a fire or explosion? Do they keep their backups offsite?

➤ What happens if their primary power goes down? Do they have an uninterruptible power supply (UPS)?

Finally, your decision to either go with a co-location or dedicated hosting service—or do it in-house—depends on the monetary and technical resources you have at your disposal.

Free Server Uptime Check

Want to sleep better at night? Here's a free service that checks to see if your server is up and running. It runs a check every 15 minutes and you're emailed if your server goes down. Check it out at uptime.arsdigita.com/uptime/.

Should You Hire a Pro?

Being your own host means that you're serious about building a large business. Designing and building a large eCommerce Web site is no easy task. It's no shame that as a businessperson you might need help with the project.

So, when should you outsource your Web site to a professional?

Check Your Site Performance

Advertising Age's Business Marketing leads you step-by-step through the process of choosing a Web developer. It is quick and easy and directs you to actual developers that meet your needs. Find it at www.businessmarketing.bsource.com/.

➤ When you don't have the technological and design skills in-house.

➤ When you need a professional looking Web site that can compete in looks and credibility with your biggest competitors.

➤ When speed is of the essence—and it always is on the Net—and you want to leverage your limited time and dollars.

It's rare to find a businessperson who also has good technical skills. You not only must know how to write in HTML to create Web pages, but know how to program in Perl, C++, and Java. And then there's graphics for your site—your company logo, navigation elements, and the look and feel of your online store. Creating graphics from scratch requires a good working knowledge of Adobe Illustrator and PhotoShop.

Sure, designing your site yourself saves you money, but if you're going to host it yourself and swim with the big boys, you're going to need professional help. Check out About Guide Jean Kaiser's site at `webdesign.about.com/compute/webdesign/library/designers/bldirectory.htm` (see Figure 10.3). Even if you have a site and are moving it to a new server, you still need help transferring files and reprogramming your site to get it ready for business.

Figure 10.3

If you're looking for a Web designer, About Guide Jean Kaiser has a directory of designers from all over the world.

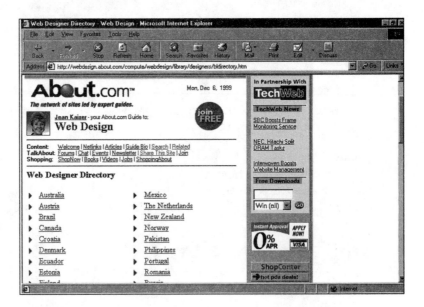

What's It Cost?

So what can you expect to pay? That all depends on what you want in your online store and how big it will be.

If your business is small, expect to pay up to $10,000 or more on setting up an online store. This gets you a pretty good-sized site with a shopping cart. A medium-sized business might spend $10,000 to have its Web site designed. And this doesn't include additional costs for custom graphics and CGI programs such as chat rooms, discussion boards, and polls. These could run thousands of dollars more.

The sky's the limit when designing an eCommerce Web site. Large businesses have been know to spend up to a million dollars or more for all the above—then adding animation, audio, and streaming video to attract shoppers to their site.

Time Is Money

There's another reason for outsourcing to a professional—time.

What Should I Pay?

The Web Price Index Card gives you the average rates for programmers and Web designers to compare against the proposals you receive from Web developers. Find it at netb2b.com/cgi-bin/print_ article.pl/track8/1385.

The Internet moves fast and the Web is littered with companies that did not move fast enough. Speed of execution is critical on the Net. There's a joke that goes, "If you want to pull ahead of your competitor—give him a computer." Don't get bogged down in technology. Go to the people who know. In the real world, time is money. If you're to succeed on the Net, spend money—not time!

The Least You Need to Know

➤ Transferring your Web site to a new server has the potential to disrupt your business, cause you to lose sales—and even customers—if not done correctly.

➤ InterNic accepts changes to a domain registration from only the Administrative Contact, so be sure that you use your name as the Administrative Contact when you register your domain name.

➤ Of all the software choices you make for your Web server, the most important is your software platform—or operating system or OS.

➤ If you want your own dedicated server but don't want the costs incurred in buying one, setting it up, and connecting it to the Net, then a dedicated host services company is your ticket.

➤ Don't get bogged down in technology. Go to the people who know. In the real world, time is money. If you're to succeed on the Net, spend money—not time!

Chapter 11

Building Your Web Store

In This Chapter

➤ Learn the basic essentials of your eCommerce Web site

➤ Discover what software and graphics tools you need to create and maintain an eCommerce Web site

➤ Learn the most important things you need to have on your eCommerce Web site

---

If you've ever built a new house or purchased one, you know that finding a home is just the first step. You still have to furnish it. That goes double for an eCommerce Web site. Whether you've chosen to host your Web store on a free personal Web site service, an ISP, or your own server, you now have the challenge of creating an inviting and useable online store.

So, before you rush out and hastily toss together a catalog of products or services and place them on your server, you have to consider some basic Web site essentials and the tools to provide them if you want your eBusiness to be a success. Knowing these site essentials will prevent you from building into your site fatal errors that are sure to be shopping turnoffs.

These Web site essentials are important if you want to make your customers shopping experience easy, convenient, enjoyable, safe, and reliable. Good eTailer sites make this look effortless, but don't be fooled. A lot of hard work and planning go into creating a successful online store. Just putting up a personal Web page on GeoCities or even using one of the free online store builders such as Yahoo! Store is not enough to make your eCommerce enterprise a success.

Web Site Essentials

Like it or not, your Web site is your "brand." If you can create a positive image—a strong brand—that is memorable, online shoppers will not only be attracted to your site but also return to it over and over.

On the Net, a brand is more than just a graphic design like the Nike swoosh or McDonalds' golden arches. It represents an interactive experience and the online consumer gets this experience through your Web store.

What makes a good online brand? The same thing that makes a good interactive Web site. A good user experience.

Your brand must target a specific audience or market niche. You did that when you created your Unique Selling Position. But just as important, your brand—that is, your Web site—must be useable. A pretty logo is not a brand on the Web. It's the overall user experience your shopper has with your site. This includes the look and feel of the site and its ease of navigation. For some good tips on Web site design, check out About Guide Jean Kaiser's Web site at `webdesign.about.com`. It also includes before, during, and after sales support (see Figure 11.1).

Figure 11.1

Just about everything you need to know about Web design can be found at About Guide Jean Kaiser's Web site.

It's easy to create an adequate eCommerce Web site. What you want to do is create a great online brand that customers will enjoy shopping at and come back to again and again. And to do that you need to keep a set of Web essentials in mind.

Fast Loading Pages

There's an old saying that goes "You can always tell a pioneer by the arrows in his back." Using the latest technology to differentiate yourself from the competition is not the best idea for an online store. In fact, it can be fatal.

If you remember one thing and one thing only in designing your eCommerce Web site, remember the fastest way to drive a customer away from your site is to confront him with a lot of flashy animation, slick Java applets, or require plug-ins to view your site. In other words—stay away from the bleeding edge of Web site design. Even if you include all the proper Web site essentials to your online store, they will be all for naught when your customers are driven away in the first few seconds of their visit.

So, before you move mouse to browser to design your site, keep this in mind. There are millions and millions of potential customers who are still cruising the Web at 28.8Kbps. Design your site with them in mind. All that work you did in finding and choosing a good Web hosting provider with a fast connection to the Web will be irrelevant if you design a technology blotted site that takes the average Web surfer several minutes to download.

Let the other guys stand on the bleeding edge. Forget all the fancy stuff. Forget streaming video, animation, and live audio. Keep your site simple and make it load fast. You only have a few seconds to grab a shopper's attention.

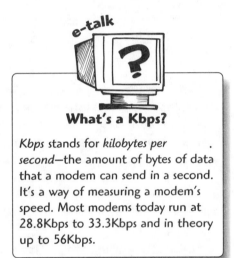

What's a Kbps?

Kbps stands for *kilobytes per second*—the amount of bytes of data that a modem can send in a second. It's a way of measuring a modem's speed. Most modems today run at 28.8Kbps to 33.3Kbps and in theory up to 56Kbps.

Remember to address the technological level of the audience at your Web site. eCommerce will continue to explode over the next 10 years because of the growing number of Internet users. But as the number of new users increases, their level of technological sophistication decreases. Security, good prices, great customer service, easy site navigation, detailed product data, and simple ordering are far more important than cool techno-tricks on your site.

The Right Look and Feel

Your Web site should reflect your Web business. Are you selling products at a steep discount? If so, your site design and look might have more of a warehouse or superstore feel. Or perhaps, you're selling unique or made-to-order creative items. Your site then might have a boutique look and feel to it. If you're running a service business, then a design that displays a professional image would be more appropriate.

The wording you use on your site, the graphic images you choose, the navigational icons you provide—all should reflect the look and feel of your eBusiness. You have only a few moments to get your visitor to look at your site. Your home page—the first page of your Web site—should inform your visitors not only what you sell but also the type of shopping experience they are to expect. Your visitor must be able to quickly determine if you have anything that interests them. Your home page must be designed to entice the shopper inside your online store.

Is Your Web Site Sick?

Does your eCommerce Web site suffer from debilitating diseases such as Clarity Constriction, Image Inflammation, Monitor Myopia, Frames Fixation, Background Blemish, Button Bloat, and Navigation Neuralgia? If so, check out www.wilsonweb.com/articles/7diseases.htm for the cure.

Keep your home page short, fast loading, and to the point. Be brief on you first page. Give the customers enough information to interest them in making a purchase. Then direct them to pages that have more details of your offer.

Finally, try looking at your Web site through the eyes of your customer. Read your Unique Selling Position. Are you targeting the right customer? Does your home page let your customer know exactly what you sell? Does it reflect the other pages on your site? Does it direct the shopper straight to your product offers? Do all your Web pages reinforce the purpose of your site? If the answer is No to any of these, make changes.

Photos and Graphics

Although a picture is worth a thousand words, too many graphics on your site will slow the download of your pages. Make sure you use a graphics person that not only is a good graphic designer but also understands the needs of the Web. He should be skilled in the art of creating good looking but small graphic files for fast downloading.

Image size should be kept small. Nothing is more frustrating to a shopper than to watch the little blue bar at the bottom corner of her screen inch along at a snail's pace. The total amount of graphics on a Web page should not exceed 40K. Try to stick with the basics and use only 256 colors. Use *interlaced* graphic images to keep your visitors' attention while the graphic loads in to their browser.

What's an Interlaced GIF?

Interlaced GIF images help keep your customer's interest as the graphic gradually displays over four passes. Although the download time is the same as noninterlaced GIFS, your customer gets to see it slowly form on the page and might wait instead of clicking off your page.

Keep in mind, that graphics are there to compliment your sales copy—not replace it. They are there to reinforce your sales offer. It's your sales copy that will ultimately sell your product—not the graphic. If you must use a large graphic—such as showing more product detail or a product in use—then place a thumbnail of the picture next to the copy (see Figure 11.2). The page will load quickly and if the customer wants to see a larger image of the product, he can click the thumbnail to expand the image. ValuePrint Pro or Firehand Ember Ultra are two programs that will create thumbnails for you. You can find them at download.com.

There are two types of image formats. One is called the GIF and the other the JPEG. GIF images can be viewed by all Web browsers and work best with graphic images. If you're going to use product photos, then JPEG images are best. They will load much faster than a photo image created as a GIF. Another graphic type to consider is the transparent GIF. These types of images have a transparent background. This is useful if you want the edges of your image to blend into the background color of your page.

Basic Page Elements

Reading off a monitor is tough enough. Don't make it more difficult for your customers by having them scroll through page after page of a product description. Use language that's concise, short, and to-the-point. A Web site is different from a printed catalog page. Don't just dump the product specification sheet on a Web page.

People don't read a Web page—they browse it. Use headlines and subheadlines that describe the product or service concisely. Then follow the headline with supporting copy in more detail. Use short sentences—even bullet points—to make the information easy to read and understand. You're not writing for *Vanity Fair* here. You're trying to make your sales offer as compelling and concise as possible. Use this same formula for other pages on your site, such as Customer Support pages, Company About pages, and so on.

Figure 11.2

This is a good example of the use of thumbnails on a Web page. Click the thumbnail and a large version of the picture appears.

Is there a place for long Web pages? Yes there is. You might want your customer to download technical information on a product for future reference or an instruction sheet that might go with a product that you've created yourself. You could instruct the customer to either wait for the page to load, and then print it, or make it so the customer can download the page as a file to his or her computer. And suppose you need more than one page to describe your product or service offer? Then consider using multiple shorter pages that are linked together.

Each of your Web pages also should have the following elements at the top of the page.

➤ Page title

➤ Page description

➤ Page keywords

The page title resides at the top of your Web page. You can find the title of each Web page in the <TITLE> tag on a page that looks like this:

```
<TITLE>Your Page Title</TITLE>
```

Why is it important to title your pages? Because the top line of your Web page often shows up in search engines such as InfoSeek and AltaVista. By making your title descriptive, people will know right away what's on that page and be more willing to visit your site.

Page Description

The page description normally follows the page title. The page description is what's called a *meta tag* and the code on a Web page would look like this:

```
<META NAME="description"
CONTENT="Your page description
here">
```

Some search engines display the page description tag in their search results. So, a good page description will entice potential customers to view your page and visit your site.

Get the Scoop

Here's your chance to hear what successful professional Web designers have to say about creating a top notch Web site. Check out their interviews at webdesign. miningco.com/msubinterviews.htm.

Page Keywords

Following the title and description tags you'll see the keyword tag that looks like this:

```
<META NAME="keywords" CONTENT="Your keywords'>
```

Page keywords are very important! This is the primary way that most search engines find your Web site. The right choice of key words will make your site rise to the top of a search engine's search results. Because most search engine users only go as far as the first page of search results, its important that your Web site show in the first 10 results or so. We'll talk more on this in Chapter 18, "Marketing Your eBusiness."

Finally, the Web is interactive and your Web site should be too. An essential element of your Web store should be the ability to capture information from your customers. That's how Web page forms are used. Customers or site visitors simply fill out a form on a Web page, press the **submit** button at the end of the form, and the information is immediately emailed to you. Or, if you have access to a programmer, he or she can set up a database that you can access to retrieve the information.

Web page forms can be used in a number of ways. One use is the "Requests for Information." Shoppers can use this form to request further information on your products or service or ask a question about your service guarantee. Customers can use this form to find out about the status of an order or ask to return a product.

Another use for Web page forms is for a Guestbook or Newsletter sign-up. You can ask potential customers to sign your guestbook or subscribe to your email newsletter, and in the process, collect certain information that you could use to market to them later. If you don't have a shopping cart software application on your site, you can use Web page forms to take an order right online. Even if you have a shopping cart program on your site, you could still make this form available to those who want to fill it out and fax their order to you or mail it in with a check.

Now you're ready to build your Web store and to do that you'll need a set of Web site tools.

Web Site Tool Kit

Like any successful builder, the right tools can make the difference between a mediocre outcome and an excellent one. Whether you build your Web store from scratch or maintain it through one of the online store builders, you'll need a specialized set of Web site tools to make it happen. By the way, many of the software programs mentioned here can be downloaded free from download.com (see Figure 11.3).

Figure 11.3

At C/Net's Download.com, you can download many of the programs mentioned either for free or as a trial version.

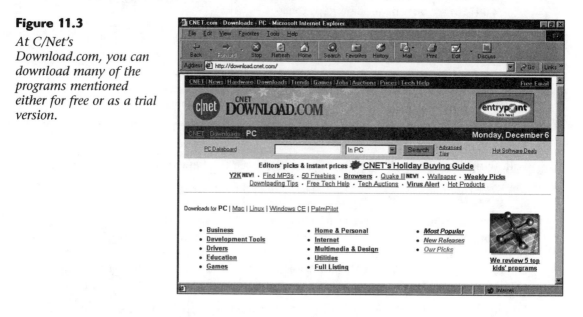

Your Web site toolbox should consist of:

➤ An HTML Editor
➤ Graphic tools
➤ FTP software

An HTML Editor is used to build your Web site from scratch and then edit and maintain your pages after they go live. If you're using an online store builder such as Yahoo! Store, an HTML Editor is not necessary. You create and make changes to your Web store HTML pages right through your browser. And even if you use a Web page builder provided by the personal Web page hosting services such as GeoCities, if you're serious about having a real business online, you would want to create your own Web pages and upload them to the service.

HTML Editors only help you create the actual HTML text pages and Web site structure. You still have to create or find and modify the site graphics you need, such as product images, company logo, and navigational icons. For this, you need a graphics design program.

Finally, after you have your site completed, you need a way to upload your pages to your host server. You need an FTP program to transfer the files on your computer to the server that is hosting your Web store.

So, lets look at the different software packages available to you starting with the HTML Editors.

HTML Editors

There are two ways to create or edit a Web page. The first way is to use an HTML Editor. The second is to use a text pad such as Notepad for the PC. Why use a text pad instead of an HTML Editor?

Text pads, such as Notepad, give you ultimate control over the layout of your Web page. Unlike the HTML Editors, you would code you Web page using raw HTML. That means you must be very familiar with HTML and understand how to use and apply the mark-up language. The HTML Editors, on the other hand, work more like a word processor—some more, others less. In these cases, little to no knowledge of actual HTML is required of you.

Free Site Design Templates

Need help designing your site? Then how about some free site design templates. There are hundreds of these to choose from and many of them are free to download. Find them at toolsforthe.net.

Many developers like to build their pages and Web sites using an HTML Editor for the ease and speed of execution and use a text pad to edit the pages later. That way they are not constrained by the HTML Editor when making upgrades or edits.

The process you use really depends on your knowledge level of HTML and your own personal preferences. For those of us that prefer to use an HTML Editor, here are some of the most popular.

➤ **Macromedia's Dreamweaver** Dreamweaver at www.macromedia.com/software/dreamweaver/. This is a premier WYSIWYG (what-you-see-is-what-you-get) HTML editor. Because is acts like a word processor—that is, WYSIWYG—you would think it would cater to beginners. Unfortunately, it does not. Dreamweaver is designed specifically for the professional Web site developer.

➤ **Homesite** Homesite at www.allaire.com/products/homesite/ is a more user-friendly HTML Editor. It has an easy-to-use interface and also has a WYSIWYG feature that can be turned on or off.

➤ **Adobe Pagemill** As a visual HTML Editor, Pagemill at www.adobe.com/prodindex/pagemill/main.html also has a WYSIWYG interface and includes a simple drag-and-drop interface. Easy to use and full-featured, this is a good choice for beginners. It also integrates with current office and graphics applications, such as Microsoft Word, Corel WordPerfect, Microsoft Excel, Adobe Photoshop, and Adobe Illustrator.

Ask Doctor HTML

Submit your Web page, and Doctor HTML will check it for errors. He'll check spelling, syntax, forms, and table structure—even verify your page links. Find him at www2.imagiware.com/RxHTML/.

➤ **Hotmetal Pro**   Hotmetal at www. hotmetalpro.com/products/ is again for the professional. Its editor offers page creation wizards, and visual and source code editing.

➤ **Microsoft Frontpage**   Microsoft Frontpage at www.microsoft.com/frontpage/ is an HTML Editor designed for nonprogrammers. It's easy to use and integrates fully into the Microsoft Office family of products.

➤ **NetObject's Fusion**   NetObject's Fusion at www.netobjects.com/, a high horsepower WYSIWYG, is a Web site creation and management tool for building small business solutions or your first site.

➤ **Sausage Software's Hot Dog**   Sausage Software at www.sausage.com/ offers a series of editors for both the novice and advanced HTML programmers.

➤ **Arachnophilia**   Arachnophilia at www.arachnoid.com is pretty cool HTML editor for the PC to weave your Web site. And it's free.

Graphics Tools

Let's face it. The Web is a graphical medium. If you want your Web pages to look like more than gray pages of text, you need more than just an HTML Editor. Sooner or later you have to add graphics.

Like with HTML Editors there are two approaches to the problem. First, you download and use the multitude of free clip art that's on the NET, or you can create the graphics yourself. Creating graphics or manipulating photographs takes more skill than writing a Web page. Unlike the HTML Editors, there are no simple graphics design programs. To learn how to create graphics will take quite a learning curve and much of your valuable time.

Unless you plan to use the ready made Web templates available on the Web or the free downloadable clip art, it's best that you find yourself a good graphic designer who knows how to use the following graphic tools.

➤ **Photoshop**   If you're going to have pictures of your product on your Web store, then this is the program to use. Photoshop at www.adobe.com/prodindex /photoshop/main.html gives you the tools to import, crop, retouch, and edit any picture that you would like to use on your site.

➤ **Adobe Illustrator**   Illustrator at www.adobe.com/prodindex/illustra-tor/main.html is the premier graphics design program. Any designer worth his or her salt uses Illustrator to create graphic images from scratch.

Fill Up at the Web Diner

The Web Diner offers tips, tutorials, and Web page templates and a cool set of alphabet icons. All free to download. Find it at www.webdiner.com.

➤ **Paintshop Pro**   Paintshop Pro at www.jasc.com/psp.html has many of the same features as Photoshop but is far less expensive.

➤ **Fireworks**   This is Macromedia's contribution for creating Web graphics. Fireworks' code at www.macromedia.com/software/fireworks/productinfo/ contents.html integrates seamlessly into Dreamweaver and other leading HTML editors.

➤ **CorelDRAW**   Corel at www.corel.com/draw9/index.htm has been around almost as long as Adobe Illustrator and includes a complete suite of graphics tools.

Finding Free Graphics Online

If the thought of learning to use a professional graphics program is too much too bear, then consider using free clip art that's available for use on your Web pages. There are many places on the Net where you can find and download graphics for use on your site. There are hundreds of sites that offer all kinds of images, pictures—even photos—that you can use for free on your site (see Figure 11.4).

The types of free images you can find on the Net are

➤ Animated GIFS

➤ Backgrounds, borders, and textures for your Web pages

➤ Navigational bars, icons, and control pads

➤ Web page templates

➤ Stock photography, royalty free photography, and public domain images

➤ Clip art, icons, and buttons

Figure 11.4

If it's free Web clip art you're looking for, visit Bobbie Peachey's About.com *Web site. You'll find free images from A-Z for your Web site.*

You can find links to many of these sites at two About.com Guide sites. Jean Kaiser, the Web Design Guide, can point you towards dozens of free image sites at webdesign.about.com/compute/webdesign/mlibrary.htm and Bobbie Peachey, the Web Clip Art Guide, at webclipart.about.com lists just about every conceivable resource for finding clip art specifically made for Web sites.

FTP Software

After you have your site designed and edits made on your computer, you have to upload your Web site files to your hosting server. For that, you're going to need an FTP software program. An FTP (File Transfer Protocol) program is quite simple to use. You simply take the complete directory structure of your site that you've created on your personal computer and duplicate it on your hosting server by transferring it over the Net.

Here's an important thing to remember. After you transfer your Web site files to your hosting server, your Web pages go live immediately. So, make sure that you've reviewed, proofread, and tested your pages before you FTP them to your hosting server.

One nice thing about FTP programs is that many of them are *shareware*. This means that you can download and use them for free! Finding them is easy. Just go to C/Net's Download.com, choose **Internet** from the menu page, then **FTP** from the menu page after that. Choose a free FTP program and download it to your computer.

The Six Most Important Things You Need to Have on Your Site

Great creative, catchy copy; good graphics; perfect coding—all these are necessary for a well-designed eCommerce site.

But there are some important fundamentals that must be on your Web store. These fundamentals—let's call them business fundamentals—have little to do with design and technology. These fundamentals are an important element in assuring that your customers quickly know your product offers, have their questions answered, and feel comfortable buying from your site. In other words, it goes back to brand.

Like I mentioned before, your Web site is your brand and your brand is the experience your customer has with your Web store. The quality of the experience an online shopper has with you while visiting your Web store has a lot to do with whether they make a purchase and whether they'll buy from you again. You might get them to enter your store, but potential customers must have sufficient trust to actually buy from you.

If you keep these six important fundamentals in mind, you will go along way toward turning window shoppers into customers.

One: Shop Now!—Start Them Shopping Right Away

If you want the site to sell, (and that's why you're building an eCommerce site, right?) then sell potential customers right on your home page by sending them to your shopping areas from the home page as seen at www.outpost.com (see Figure 11.5). Place your best products in the front of your store—on your home page—and then direct them right to the product page to buy.

Figure 11.5

Outpost.com home page is good example offering impulse buys and holiday specials right on their home page.

Then create opportunities on your home page for impulse buys with a button or icon that says "Buy Now!." That's an important element of sales. Any salesperson worth their salt will tell you to always "Ask for the sale." Also, change your home page frequently. Just as news sites offer fresh content each day, you should offer fresh "content" in the form of "Today's Special" or promote seasonal items on your home page.

At the very least, you should integrate and link to holiday products and timely gift guides from your home page to reflect:

➤ The Christmas holiday season

➤ Winter fun—skiing, skating, and clothing

➤ Mother's Day

➤ Father's Day

➤ Graduation

➤ Summer fun—beach, BBQs, and vacations

➤ Back to school

➤ Halloween

➤ Thanksgiving

➤ Special events—births, birthdays, anniversaries, and weddings

Although your home page should reflect who you are and what you can do for the online shopper, be sure that your home page sells.

Two: About Page—Let Them Know Who You Are

Shoppers would like to know whom they're buying from. So tell them. Have a section linked from your home page to tell them whom they're buying from. Include a history of your business, who's involved, your business philosophy and vision. Here's a chance to tell them your Unique Selling Position and sell the customer on why he or she should buy from you and how you're different from your competition.

Inform the window shopper how you do business, what values you hold, and what's important to the customer. Remember selling on the Net is not about you—it's about the customer. So make sure your About Page reflects this fact. The customer is not interested in you; only what your company will do for him or her.

Finally, you might consider adding a picture of you and your staff and some brief bios on your About Page. Online or off, people still want to do business with other people.

Three: FAQs—The First Place Your Customer Turns To

FAQs, or Frequently Asked Questions, are the first place shoppers will go to if they want quick and easy answers to their questions. A FAQ on your Web store is essential and will save both you and your customers a lot of time (see Figure 11.6).

The object of a FAQ is to list as many questions and answers a shopper might have as possible, such as

➤ Who are you?

➤ Where are you located?

➤ How can I contact you?

➤ What's the cost of shipping?

➤ Do you ship overseas?

➤ What are your return policies?

➤ How do I do a return?

➤ What are your product warrantees?

If you're selling certain categories of products that need a technical explanation, you can include those in your FAQs too.

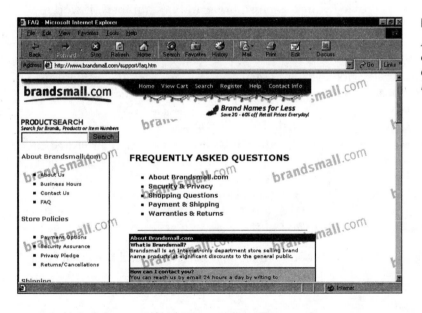

Figure 11.6

BrandsMall has a good example of what an eCommerce FAQ page looks like.

When organizing your FAQ page, list the questions at the top of the page and link them to the answers on the same page. This way, shoppers can read all the questions up front, find what they are looking for, and jump right down the page to the answer with the question included. If you have many questions you might consider breaking the questions up into categories, then creating a menu page of these categories as the main page of the FAQ.

Make sure that you link to your FAQs from your home page. A well-written FAQ will be one of your most popular pages so make it easy to find.

Finally, link your answers to you questions to other pages on your site where appropriate, such as a map to your offices or links to products mentioned in your answers.

Four: Full Contact Information—Address, Phone, Fax, Email

Shoppers want to know that you have a real business. And one of the best ways to show that is to give them a variety of ways to contact you. An email address is not enough. In fact, it could be suspect. Here's the minimum amount of contact information you should have on your contact page:

➤ **Company address**   Display your full company mailing address. If you run your business out of your home, and don't want to use that address, get a private mailbox at one of the commercial pack & ship business, such as Mailboxes Etc (MBE).

➤ **Phone numbers**   Provide your business phone and fax numbers. If working from your home, install a second line or business line. Connect an answering machine to it with a professional sounding message or hire an answering service for after hours or when your line is busy. Also list your fax number on your site.

➤ **Email addresses**   Provide different email addresses for each department or function of your business. At the very least, have a different email address for customer service.

➤ **Toll-free customer service number**   Your credibility as a business increases dramatically when shoppers see that you can be reached through a toll-free customer service number. These are not expensive and are worth the small investment. Publish the toll-free number on your contact page. If you'd rather not staff a customer service phone line, then outsource your 800 number to a service company that will answer your calls on a cost-per-call basis.

A good contact page can help build a level of trust in your business.

FTC Is on the Prowl

The FTC has made it known that if Web sites do not take the initiative in creating good Privacy Policies, it might intervene. If that happens, be prepared to follow government rules and pay the fines when you break them.

Five: Privacy Policy—Get on the Right Side of the FTC

Next to credit card security, privacy issues are second on the list of customer concerns. So, it's becoming vital that eBusinesses post their Privacy Policy on their site. Your customers want to know what you intend to do with the personal information you collect when they place an order on your site.

In a survey of 1,400 Web sites examining the privacy practices of commercial sites on the World Wide Web, the FTC found the vast majority of privacy policies on Web sites to be woefully inadequate.

What does this mean to you?

The FTC will be scrutinizing Web sites to see how they adhere to protecting consumer privacy so it's important that you have a privacy policy on your site. And there's an easy way to do it.

The Direct Marketing Association has a section on their Web site that has an easy-to-use Privacy Policy Page creation form at www.the-dma.org/policy.html (see Figure 11.7). Simply answer the questions and click the **submit** button and the DMA will send you a Privacy Policy Web page to post on your site. The Generate HTML Page button will allow you to see a copy of your statement on the screen as soon as you submit the form.

Figure 11.7

At this Direct Marketing Association's Web page you can create a Privacy Policy page for your Web site.

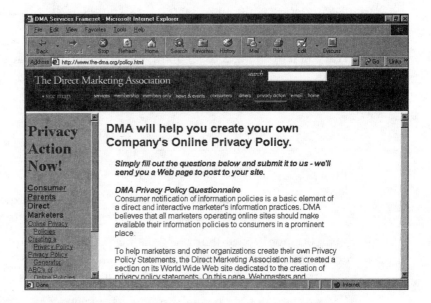

After you get your page, edit the page as needed. You might want to clarify some aspects, add your company name to the title of the page, or make other modifications to make the policy fit in with your site.

That's all there is to it. One last thing: Don't forget to make sure your company abides by your stated policy! The FTC will be checking.

Six: Shipping Policies—Tell Them the Full Cost of Shipping and Handling

Currently, up to 80% of all online shopping carts are abandoned by shoppers before reaching the final check out page. This number is appalling. Picture going to your local grocery store and seeing that 80% of the people filled their shopping carts with food and then left the store leaving them in the aisles! That's what's happening to many online merchants today.

There are a number of reasons for this. Either the customers didn't feel they had enough information about the product to make a buying decision or they still had questions about the credibility of the merchant. But another reason for abandoned online shopping carts is that customers don't like surprises. And one of the worst is being surprised with the true cost of a shipped product at the very end of the transaction.

Your customers need to know before they complete their transaction what the total amount of their order will be including shipping, handling, and applicable taxes. Customers should have the opportunity to see the changes made to the total transaction cost, such as changes to shipping methods and gift-wrapping charges before they check out.

If you want to surprise your customers, surprise them with good offers and great service.

The Least You Need to Know

➤ Your Web site is your brand. It represents an interactive experience and the online consumer gets this experience through your Web store.

➤ Keep your home page short, fast loading, and to the point. Give the customers enough information to interest them in making a purchase. Then direct them to pages that have more details of your offer.

➤ The wording you use on your site, the graphic images you choose, and the navigational icons you provide should reflect the look and feel of your eBusiness.

➤ An essential element of your Web store should be the ability to capture information from your customers.

➤ Great creative, catchy copy, good graphics, perfect coding—all these are necessary for a well-designed eCommerce site.

Part 3

eCommerce Basics

An eBusiness is unlike any kind of business that came before. No matter how sophisticated your offer, your Web store must consider and adhere to some eCommerce basics.

A successful eBusiness today must be more than just a store. Making a sale is more than just posting a picture of a product and a few lines of descriptive text on a Web page. Customers today need information—and lots of it—whether from you or fellow shoppers. They also need a quick and easy way to find what they want on your site and make a purchase. The presentation of your product or service offering and how easy it is to purchase is as important as the offering itself.

So, read on and learn the eCommerce basics that will make your eBusiness a success.

Chapter 12

The 3 Cs of eCommerce

In This Chapter

➤ Learn the successful ingredients of an eCommerce site

➤ Learn how content can help support your online offer

➤ Discover how helping your visitors and customers interact with one another will increase repeat visits to your site

➤ Discover the different types of revenue streams that you can generate from your Web site other than selling a product or service

If you think that a successful Web store is just an electronic catalog—think again. Just slapping together pages and pages of product connected to an online shopping cart might get you sales, but customers don't live on offers alone. Besides the big C of "commerce" there are two other Cs you must consider to make your online store a success.

These are the 3 Cs of eCommerce:

➤ **Content**   Selling your product and service in a context that's relevant to your target audience

➤ **Community**   Creating an online environment in which site visitors and your customers can participate and feel a part of

➤ **Commerce**   The actual offers and revenue generating streams of your Web site

That's the eCommerce site equation—Content builds community, which establishes credibility, which generates sales.

Content—Turn Your Site into a Learning Fountain

Content is King on the Net. People use the Net to learn. That's what drives visitors to a Web site. Content can consist of information and community participation and even your eCommerce offers are considered content. Your site's content—whether it be information, community participation, or a product or service offer—must be interesting enough to make visitors come to your site, stay, and keep them coming back for more.

Encourage Contributions

Offer a way for visitors to submit articles, allowing their experiences to be included on your site or in your newsletter. Not only do you get free help in building your site content but you also gain long-term repeat visits from people whose content is included on your site.

Keep in mind that your content does not have to be closely related to your product, but to your prospective customers' needs and desires. To do this you need to make your Web store not only a place to buy things, but a "Learning Fountain," too. That's what Paul Siegel recommends.

Paul Siegel is an author, an Internet marketing consultant, trainer, and speaker. He is the originator of the Learning Fountain at learningfountain.com (see Figure 12.1). His Learning Fountain is a Web site that influences visitors by helping them learn. He is known for saying "A Learning Fountain is a Web site that attracts prospects—not merely visitors—by helping them learn. While learning, they linger and buy." You should take a leaf out of his book and do the same for your Web store. By the way, his site is a good resource to building your online business.

According to Siegel, The top five popular sites are Learning Fountains. Yahoo! at yahoo.com is a Learning Fountain. The Motley Fool at fool.com and Consumer World at consumerworld.org—even Amazon.com, an eCommerce site—are all Learning Fountains.

Your eCommerce site should be a Leaning Fountain, too. Here's how.

Siegel divides content Learning Fountains into four types: Referrer, Informer, Advisor, and Context Provider.

The Referrer

No one knows the product or service you're selling better than you do. So use this knowledge to help your visitors understand all aspects of the product or service you sell. You might not have all the information they need, but with a little research, you can create a directory of sites on the Net that can provide the information they need and refer them to it.

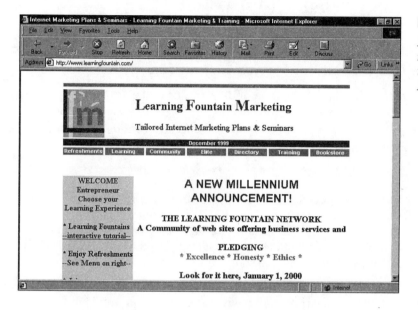

Figure 12.1

Paul Siegel's site is a great resource if you want to turn your site into a Learning Fountain.

For example, suppose you sell computer products. You could provide on your site a long list of product reviews comparing one product you sell to another. That would be a very time-consuming task. So why not refer them to sites that specialize in these reviews, such as SoftGuide at `softguide.com` or ZDNet at `www8.zdnet.com/products/`. Or suppose you sell tools for the do-it-yourself home improvement. You can refer them to ImproveNet at `improvenet.com` where they will direct your customer to design ideas and project estimators.

Another idea is to refer shoppers to places where they can find free stuff, such as at Free Forum Network at `www.freeforum.com` or Free-Stuff.com at `www.Free-Stuff.com`. Shoppers will come to your site just to see your latest links to free stuff on the Net. If you get into the habit of refreshing your links, shoppers will return again and again for fresh referrals.

The Informer

Providing regular updated information on your site that is of practical use to your visitor will bring them to your site and generate repeat visits. Include access to the latest news—even news on your product area—articles, and reminder services.

Add a Calendar Service to Your Site

Sign up for SuperCalendar's affiliate program and offer a calendar to "non-techie" users who have to manage lots of events. In addition to receiving a co-branded calendar, you also have the opportunity to generate revenue when your users sign up for SuperCalendar. Find it at www.SuperCalendar.com.

iSyndicate at iSyndicate.com aggregates free content from over 500 different providers in categories such as Top News and Weather, Sports News, Business and Finance, Entertainment and Lifestyles, Technology, and Health New— even Fun and Games. News providers include CNet, *Rolling Stone* magazine, CBS Market Watch, and *Sporting News*. And most of the content is free to use on your Web site.

A similar site to iSyndicate is Screaming Media at screamingmedia.com (see Figure 12.2). With Screaming Media, you can display news stories based on any keyword that you choose. The story headlines and full stories are integrated into your site pages. A good example of how Screaming Media works can be seen at the eShop Daily at www.mysimon.com/eshop/index.html.

Figure 12.2

ScreamingMedia has a very simple interface and a quick and easy way to add news content to your Web site.

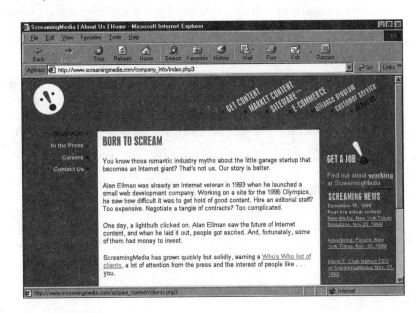

The Advisor

To make a buying decision, many shoppers need advice. By making product advice available to your shoppers, you increase the possibility of making a sale. For advice to work, it must be trusted and credible.

A good example of this kind of advice is at Amazon.com. They pioneered the concept of reader reviews for the books they sell. Anyone who has purchased and read the book being offered for sale can write his or her own review. A peer review looks more objective to a potential customer and increases the possibility of a purchase. Shoppers trust other consumer's opinions more than the advertisers. Amazon.com also sells videos and customers who have bought a video also can review it on Amazon's site.

PriceWonders.com at `www.Pricewonders.com` offers customer reviews of products it sells along with real-time pricing comparison information from online merchants. Although not real peer reviews like Amazon.com, CDNow at `cdnow.com` offers CD reviews from noted music critics and writers. clNet at `www.computers.com` will not only review hardware products, but advise you on the best places to buy them.

Written reviews are great to attract and retain customers and they generate longer visits helping them get more familiar with you and your products. If the thought of page after page of reviews on your site would add too much of an expense, think about using a quick numeric-rating system next to a product—such as one out of five stars. Your shopper can then just pick a rating and that rating could show up next to the product on your catalog page.

Offer a Free Notification Service to Your Site Visitors

People have busy lives and there are lots of things to remember to do. You can offer a free personalized, practical email notification service to your site for visitors to use to keep track of their daily, weekly, monthly, and yearly "things to do." Find it at www.lifeminders.com.

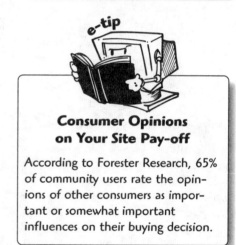

Consumer Opinions on Your Site Pay-off

According to Forester Research, 65% of community users rate the opinions of other consumers as important or somewhat important influences on their buying decision.

The Context Provider

Providing informational tools to shoppers to help them make a buying decision is another important content feature for your Web store. Consider giving the shopper the capability of solving a problem or determining a need in the context of your site using online tools, such as checklists, calculators, evaluators, and simulators.

Let Your Shoppers Find the Exact Time Around the World

If shoppers need to contact a merchant or order by phone he or she should know which time zone they are in. Place a link to World Times on your site and offer this service. Find it at www.hilink.com.au/times/.

Free Currency Converter

A great little service to add to your site is an international currency converter. This way shoppers from anywhere in the world can see what the price of your products is in their currency. Find it at www.xe.net/currency/.

Context-specific information could be either product specific of shopping specific.

First, let's look at the product-specific tools. Suppose you had a mortgage brokerage service on the Web. To help shoppers of your service make a buying decision you might offer them a mortgage calculator on your site. They can calculate their monthly mortgage payment based on the type of mortgage they want, the interest rate, and any other options that would be available with the service. An example of this kind a shopping tool can be found at www.bloomberg.com/cgi-bin/ilpc.cgi.

Investors that visit The League of American Investors at investorsleague.com can run a simulation game that teaches a potential investor how to invest wisely.

Your context-specific information need not be product specific. You could offer several shopping tools at your site that make the shopping experience for consumers more helpful. You could offer some useful general tools at your Web store, such as links to currency exchanges, international holiday listings, and a world time calculator.

One of the best shopping tools that you can provide your customers is a link to a package tracking service. One of the best can be found at the RPS Web site. From their MultiCarrier Trace Page at www.shiprps.com/cgi-win/rmt300ex.exe?func=entry, a customer can track their package after it's been shipped by you by using any shipping company you choose. A great service tool to offer your customers is called LifeMinders at www.lifeminders.com. The LifeMinders program enables Web site visitors to sign up to receive timely, relevant tips and reminders each week about their home and garden, family, auto, entertainment, personal finance, personal events, health, and pets.

Community—Building an Interactive Community

Siegel had one more important Learning Fountain—the Learning Community. People go online not just to be informed but also to interact with other people. Filling this need at your Web store will help you turn shoppers into customers and customers into repeat buyers.

Content can attract shoppers to your site. But to generate a continuous flow of repeat visitors, you need to provide access to an interactive community.

Community is just as important as content when planning an eCommerce site. If done right, community features on your site will increase the number of page-views per visit, giving you opportunities to offer merchandise to your shoppers.

Community features can be used to encourage customers to return to your site. Establishing a Learning Community can help shoppers develop expertise through the interaction with other shoppers who visit your site. Asking questions, discussing problems, raising issues, and the general camaraderie that develops in an interactive community breeds a kind of loyalty that is beneficial to the success of your Web store. And loyalty breeds repeat visits.

Another benefit of an interactive community is that it can add content to you site. Discussion boards and forums, chat rooms, and discussion lists can provide content by their very nature of generating information. You can take a short quote from one of your forums or discussion lists and post it each day on your site as fresh content to generate interest in you product or offer. This type of content can act as a traffic magnet bringing continuous visitors to your site.

Communities can build your business. Think about it. The more times a shopper visits your site the more familiar they are with it. The more familiar they are the more comfortable they might get making a purchase from you instead of some unknown merchant a mouse click away. Look at it this way. Communities are "sticky." Visitors tend to spend longer periods of time at your site than before. The stickier they are the more loyal they get. Loyalty builds trust and trust is the currency of business.

You should include as many interactive community tools as possible on your Web site. The major tools of the interactive community are discussion boards or forums, chat rooms, discussion lists, and newsletters.

Build Your Community with No Programming

"Build Your Own Community" offers software to buy that lets you build guest books, discussion forums, polls, and many more great interactive features including start pages for visitors that direct them right to our site. Find "Build Your Own Community" at www.buildacommunity.com.

Discussion Boards or Forums

Everyone has an opinion and most people want to know that their opinions are taken seriously. Some enjoy helping other people and others have a desire to learn more about a subject, issue, or product. These desires cause people to gravitate to online communities. As word gets out that serious discussions are going on at your Web store and if you can promote those discussions on your site, shoppers will come back on a regular basis to see what's discussed next.

155

Discussion boards and forums—or *message boards* as they are sometimes called—provide a bulletin board of threaded discussions. They start with a series of subjects or questions that readers can post their comments or answers to. Later readers read the posts and add their two cents to the thread of postings—either to the original subject or in response to a reader's posting—until the discussion dies out after available feedback is exhausted.

Visitors to your site are allowed to read any and all posts. But if they want to participate in the discussion, they usually need to register and get a username and password. When they register, this gives you an opportunity to collect some demographic and interest information for marketing uses.

Discussion boards need to be programmed. But if you don't mind using a message board service, you can add a discussion board to your site for free! An example of a free simple discussion board add-on is at Inside the Web at `insidetheweb.com/create.cgi` (see Figure 12.3). Using their Web interface, you can create a customized message board that resides on their server but links to it from your site.

Figure 12.3

Set up a free customized message board on your site with Inside the Web.

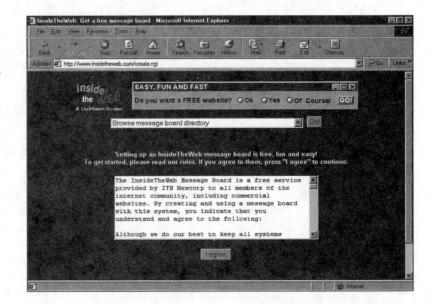

Another free discussion board service and one that offers many options is Delphi Forums at `Delphi.com`. Their administration tools are far more sophisticated than Inside the Web, and they also provide a free live chat room for your site's use.

Chat Rooms

The stickiest interactive community tool of all is the live chat room. Having a live chat room on your Web site can keep visitors on your site for hours at a time. That's a lot of face time for one Web page. During this time, you could place offers on the chat discussion page pitching your products or service. You could even join in the chat about your product or product category identifying yourself as the merchant and offering to answer any questions about your company, its products, and types of products it sells.

There is a downside to chat rooms. Unlike discussion boards where you can read all the messages posted there and remove any that are deemed unfit for your board, chat rooms are open free-for-alls. To supervise them would take a staff of people monitoring them 24 hours a day. To solve this problem, you could open the chat room at certain times of the day when monitoring is available.

Like discussion boards, you don't need to set up a resource demanding chat room on your server or your hosting company's server. There are many free chat services on the Net that you can use by providing a link from your site to the chat services server. As mentioned before, one such service is Delphi at `Delphi.com`. Another free chat service is FreeChat at `www.sonic.net/~nbs/unix/www/freechat/`. You can download the free chat software from their site and install it on your server. After installation, users of your chat room need not download any software. The chat room can be used through their Web browser.

Here's another use for chat. How about real-time customer service? Lands End at `landsend.com` provides live customer service through a chat interface. If you need help with a product, you click the **Live Help** button and it opens a chat window and initiates a chat session with a live customer service representative.

Hello? Is Anybody There?

Nothing kills a chat room tool like people dropping by and asking, "Is anybody there?" and having no response. That is why a chat moderator should always be present when you have your chat room open.

Discussion Lists

Although discussion boards and chat rooms require that shoppers visit your site, there are other ways to build a community with shoppers that do not require a site visit, yet build loyalty and keep your Web store in their mind. One of the best and least expensive ways to build community is through the use of an email discussion list.

A discussion list is a discussion board via email. Subscribers to your discussion list receive emails on a regular basis containing comments that are "echoed" to every other subscriber on the list. Every subscriber on the list receives every post to the list. All posts to the list are done via an email message sent to the list. In a typical discussion list, the listserver software enables a member to send his or her message to the list address, and then broadcasts or echoes that message out to all the list members—all within a few minutes.

A well-executed discussion list can gain wide visibility and a very good reputation for your business and for the products or services you sell. Members of a popular discussion list could number in the thousands and offer a great opportunity to sell your product or service.

Drop Your Programmer—Install Programs Yourself

A multitude of free cgi scripts is readily available on the Web. One such site is Matt's Script archive. He has guest books, counters, discussion boards, and forums—even search engines for your site. Check them out at www.worldwidemart.com/scripts.

And how can you use such a list?

You might use a discussion list as a communications platform for customers who use your manufactured product. If you sell other company's products, you can use the discussion list to inform your subscribers about your product's category. For example, suppose you sell collectible first-edition books. You could form a discussion list for collectors to exchange ideas about collector books. You could participate and answer their questions about first edition books showing off your knowledge of the market and building trust in the eyes of your subscribers for your business.

And where do you get the listserver software to run a list? Do you need to place a program on your site? No. You can use one of several free—there's that great little word again—listserver services on the Net. One is MSN's ListBot at www.listbot.com and another is eGroups at eGroups.com (see Figure 12.4).

There are three types of discussion lists:

➤ Un-moderated discussion lists
➤ Discussion list digests
➤ Moderated discussion lists

An unmoderated discussion list sends all messages received out to all members of the list. If the number of members on the list were small and not very active, then this would not be a problem. But if the list is large and very active, it could generate hundreds of messages a day and swamp the users of the list.

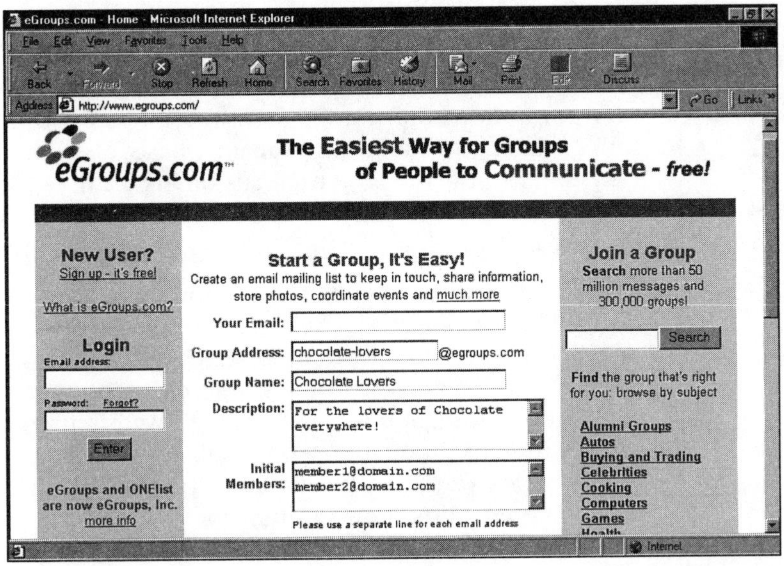

Figure 12.4

With eGroups you can set up your own private discussion list for your shoppers. Your shoppers can send and receive emails, schedule meetings, share files and photos, or have private group chats.

One solution is to create a list digest. The digest collects all the messages sent to the list first, then bundles them, and emails them—in one email—to the list members. The digest can be either daily or weekly.

Another way to cut down on the number of emails to the list is to have a moderated discussion list. You'll find that the free listserver services only provide what's called unmoderated discussion lists. That means that all posts that are sent to the list appear without any review. If you want to control what is said on the list or the number of posts sent to the list, you need to bring the listserver software in-house.

Web Marketing Today (www.wilsonweb.com/reviews/free-lists.htm) has a good review of free mailing list programs. They review eGroups.com, OneList.com, Topica.com, and ListBot.com. The review explains the main features, points out differences and advantages of each.

Newsletters

Unlike discussion boards, chat rooms, and discussion lists, a newsletter is a one-way communication device that does not allow interaction. But it's a very good way to stay in touch with your visitors and keeps your company in the front of their minds. With the typical newsletter, members can subscribe and unsubscribe freely. You need a listserver software such as Majordomo (www.greatcircle.com/majordomo) to manage the list and send out your electronic newsletter.

An electronic newsletter can be used in a number of different ways.

Free Discussion List for Online Marketers

Online Publishers is a moderated discussion list that covers topics of interest for businesses who want to create and improve their email newsletter. Find it at www.ideastation.com/op.html.

How Long Should Your Newsletter Be?

If you have valuable information to say in your newsletter, don't be afraid of your newsletter's length. Give people valuable information on a topic they're passionate about, and they'll read every word.

The most basic use of a newsletter is to keep your subscribers informed as to what's new on your site. You can announce new features, new products, or new promotions that can be used to drive subscribers back to your site on a regular basis. Use your newsletter to nurture potential customers until they're ready to purchase a product from you or sign a contract.

Or you can use your newsletter to send out information that subscribers can use, such as movie, book, or music reviews or upcoming updates to the software they've purchased. You also can enhance your reputation—and get business—through well-written articles in your product or service subject area. You also can archive these information-type newsletters on your site adding more content for shoppers to view when they visit.

There's even a revenue-generating opportunity with electronic newsletters. If your newsletter is unique and offers information or even support that consumers can't get anywhere else, you can solicit paid subscriptions. Or you can ask the manufacturers of your products to sponsor your newsletter, in effect, selling advertising space.

Finally, don't be shy about asking visitors to your site to subscribe. One of the best ways to obtain subscribers is to ask visitors to sign up when they first enter your Web site. Place your subscription offer on your home page and tell them what they'll receive as a subscriber. You also might want to offer an incentive to sign-up, such as a $10 discount coupon or perhaps a free demo of your software.

Commerce—Adding Multiple Revenue Streams

The Net not only evolves quickly but it also quickly evolves those that are on it. Take Yahoo! for example. Only a few short years ago it was a simple search engine. Then it added email, games, investment information, white pages, and other services and became a portal. In its latest incarnation it has added online store hosting and has evolved into an eCommerce site. The other portals, such as Excite, Hotbot, AltaVista, and InfoSeek, are doing the same.

Even eCommerce sites have evolved. Amazon.com sold only books. Now they're selling movies, CDs, electronics, toys, games, and a variety of other products chasing the commerce dream. And what dream are they chasing? It's called *multiple revenue streams*. Multiple revenue streams goes beyond simple product sales. Adding as many of these streams to your site will leverage your site traffic and generate additional income.

Here are some multiple revenue stream possibilities:

➤ **Product or Service Sales Income**   This is the main revenue stream of your Web store. It's what you built your eBusiness around and should be your prime focus. It's the bread and butter of your business and should be your top priority.

➤ **Advertising Income**   After you've built up traffic to your site, you can consider turning some of that traffic into revenue. Advertisers are always looking for ways to get their product or service message out to potential customers. They know that placing ads on Web sites that cater to shoppers that might buy their product is a wise way to spend their advertising dollars. Banner advertising can generate $5 to $75 CPM (cost per thousand per impression). That means you could earn anywhere from .005 cents to .075 cents each time an advertiser's banner-ad is shown to your site visitor. It might not sound like much at first, but if you had thousands and thousands of your site visitors viewing an ad, the dollars add up fast.

➤ **Referral Income**   Another income source is to refer your shoppers to another company's Web site. These are the affiliate programs that we discussed earlier. You might consider referring your shoppers to a non-competitive merchant in exchange for a paid click-through or a percentage of the sale. Income can vary from five cents to $1.00 per click-through or from 5% to 20% of sales.

Develop several of these income streams simultaneously and you can grow your site revenue beyond your product or service offers.

The Least You Need to Know

➤ Just slapping together pages and pages of product connected to an online shopping cart might get you sales, but customers don't live on offers alone. You must offer content, community, and commerce at your Web store.

➤ Remember, the eCommerce site equation—Content builds community, which establishes credibility, which generates sales.

➤ Make your Web site a "Learning Fountain." Become a referrer, informer, and advisor of information.

➤ Building a Learning Community on your site will help you turn shoppers into customers and customers into repeat buyers.

➤ Adding multiple revenue streams to your site will leverage your site traffic and generate additional income.

Chapter 13

Meeting the Customer's Expectations

In This Chapter

➤ Learn what customers expect from a Web store

➤ Learn the Big Five of online shopping and how to apply them to your online store

➤ Discover how to build confidence in your customers so they will buy from your online store

---

To paraphrase President Clinton, "It's the customer, stupid."

Shoppers don't care about your site, your business, or your life. What they care about is themselves. When they come to your site they want to see if there's anything there that interests them. They want to know, "What's in it for them." They come to your Web store with a certain set of expectations. Your job as a Web merchant is to meet those expectations.

And what do they expect?

They expect to find what they came for, a fair price, a good selection of product, great service, and a secure and safe place to shop. In other words, they're looking for the Big Five of online shopping.

The Big Five of Online Shopping

Everything on your site should be about the customer and designed from the customer's point of view. Your customer not only needs a reason to buy, but to buy easily and safely. They want to know right away if their visit to your site is going to save them time and money and if their shopping experience will be a pleasant one. Can they find what they want easily? Can they place an order in a variety of ways? Can they find your customer service pages, shipping and handling fees, and return policies without spending a large amount of time digging through your site looking for them?

These are the customer's expectations and you have to meet them if you want your online business to be a success. If your site is designed with the Big Five of online shopping in mind, you'll provide your customers a pleasant shopping experience and a reason to buy from your online store again.

The Big Five of online shopping are selection, price, service, convenience, and security.

Selection—Do You Have What They Want?

Shoppers come to the Net for the vast selection of product and services that are available at the click of a mouse. Whether shoppers find you through search engines, store directories, or through your own marketing and promotion, after they arrive at your site they want to know you have what they're looking for. Don't build an impression in the shoppers' mind that you sell computer software or have an online bookstore then offer only a small selection of titles.

What's a Search Engine?

Web surfers use search engines—or Web site directories as some of them are called—to find particular Web sites that they're looking for. Yahoo! at yahoo.com, AltaVista at altavista.com, HotBot at hotbot.com, InfoSeek at infoseek.com, and Go at go.com are some of the larger search engines and Web directories.

When building a small to medium-sized business you need to focus your product or service offering. Look at your unique selling position. If done correctly, it tells you the market you're targeting and the unique product or service you're selling. If you've done your homework and created a compelling unique selling position, the shopper will feel that your Web store offers the best selection on the Net.

Offering a good selection to shoppers is not necessarily a numbers game. The quality of your selection is much more important for a small Web business than the quantity. Here are some good examples of small sites that work in large product categories yet deliver a good selection of product offerings for their market.

Music Stores

You don't have to be a CDNow.com or an Amazon.com to be successful selling music CDs on the Web. Acres of Historic Videos & CDs at `stores.yahoo.com/ggroup` (see Figure 13.1) sells hard to find CD sets. Shoppers that come to their Web store will find a good product selection specializing in hard-to-find classic music CD Sets. They organize their offerings into 3-CD sets focusing on subjects like Jazz, Disco, Country, and Pop.

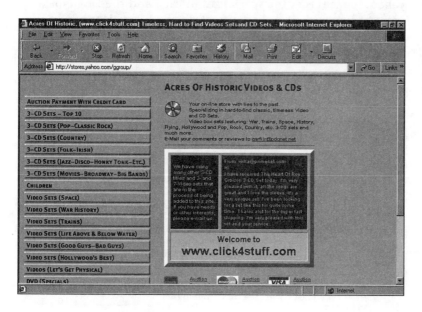

Figure 13.1

Acres of Historic Videos & CDs has carved out a unique niche in the online music sales channel.

Amplified Version at `stores.yahoo.com/amplifiedversion` is a Christian music store and has a good selection of music CDs by Christian artists. Aramusic at `stores.yahoo.com/ara-music` sells Arabic music CDs from Lebanon, Iraq, Syria, and Egypt. And Harmony Marketplace at `stores.yahoo.com/harmonymarketplace` carries the best in barbershop music on CDs.

Software Stores

You don't have to be a NECX (`necxdirect.necx.com`) or CompUSA (`compusa.com`), to competitively sell software on the Net. You can offer a specialized selection of software to shoppers and still give them a good selection in the category you choose.

AccountingShop at `stores.yahoo.com/2020software/` sells only accounting software whereas Bargain Bin Software at `stores.yahoo.com/bargainbins/` sells software starting at $9.95. The Beacon Microcenter Linux Sales Division at `stores.yahoo.com/linuxshop` sells only Linux software.

Pet Stores

The large pet stores on the Net like Petopia (`petopia.com`) and PetsMart (`petsmart.com`) carry a wide variety of pet supplies for all kinds of pets. But a small store like BunnyLuv-Essentials (`stores.yahoo.com/shopbunnyluv`) offers a nice selection of rabbit care supplies, toys, hay, food, and grooming tools. A shopper who comes to their site would be pleased with the selection of product in that subject area.

Cat Faeries at `stores.yahoo.com/catfaeries` specializes in cats, and the Dog-e-bakery at `stores.yahoo.com/dog-e-bakery` offers only gourmet doggie treats. Houndz in the Hood at `stores.yahoo.com/houndzinthehood` (see Figure 13.2) offers only coats for Dachshunds, Mini Poodles, and Italian Greyhounds.

As you can see, you can run with the big dogs of eCommerce if you choose your product or service well and deliver the best selection in that category.

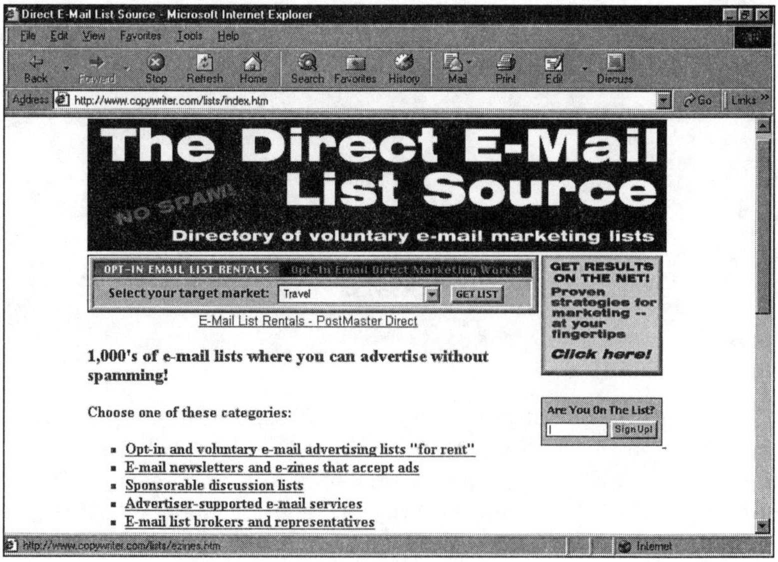

Figure 13.2

The ultimate in niche marketing to a large audience—coats for Dachshunds.

Price—Is Your Price Right?

What kind of price animal is your eBusiness? That's a question you need to answer. And after you answer it, your Web store must demonstrate it.

Do you sell products or services at a discount? Do you want to be a low-cost leader in your market niche? Or are you a value-added reseller? Do you add additional value to products in the form of some kind of service charging a higher price? Do you set the price of the products and services you sell—or does the consumer? What did you decide on as your pricing model back in Chapter 4, "Creating a Unique Selling Position?"

Whatever pricing model you decide, you need to make it very clear to the shoppers that come to your site. Consumers do not like surprises. If you promoted your site as the low-price leader—your prices should show it. If you're a boutique shop and charge better than average prices then show the value you've added to your products or service. Make it very clear what you charge and why and be sure it fits the expectations of your site visitors.

Money Talks—Baloney Walks

If you claim to be the low-price leader, put a shopping bot on your site to prove it. Comparison shopping sites like mySimon at mysimon.com and Bottom Dollar at bottomdollar.com allow you to place their shopping bots on your site for your shopper's use.

Another important thing is not to hide your prices. Nothing annoys a shopper more than going through the process of ordering from you, entering their credit card number, and then being told what the total shipped price is. Be sure that you give your shoppers all the information they need to make a buying decision—upfront—before they buy. A site that does a good job of informing its customers about shipping is DVD Empire at www.dvdempire.com (see Figure 13.3).

Don't draw the customer into the buying process with low prices then surprise them after they place their order with exorbitant shipping and handling charges on the order confirmation page. If you want to see a shopper bolt for the door, this is the way to do it.

Figure 13.3

DVD Empire does a good job of telling the shopper before he orders what their shipping and handling charges will be.

What About International Surcharges?

DHL Airways, the U.S. arm of DHL Worldwide Express will soon let companies go to DHL's Web site and learn what government-imposed charges exist in any country in the world. You can direct consumers to their site to know in advance what the total international surcharges will be. Find it at www.dhl-usa.com/bs.

So how do you inform the shopper of your shipping and handling charges? You can do it in one of two ways.

➤ Provide an easy to find section on your site that lists and easily explains your shipping and handling charges.

➤ Present an order confirmation page to the buyer that lists the price of the product and all applicable shipping and handling charges. Give the buyer the total shipped price before you request their credit card number.

I suggest that you do both. That way the shopper fully understands the total amount of the sale before he or she completes the purchase. And don't forget to include any and all applicable taxes in the total of the sale.

Service—How Do You Measure Up?

You've put a lot of effort into building your Web store. You've created a good selection of product for your market category and priced your product or service to sell. But that's not enough to earn a customer sale. Customers expect to be serviced so customer service is a top priority for your Web site. Because you're not dealing with customers face-to-face, your service policies must instill a sense of trust in your shoppers.

Many current eCommerce companies on the Net today don't understand this simple fact. According to a January 1999 survey by Jupiter Communications at jup.com, only 74% of online shoppers were satisfied with their experience, down 14% from six months prior. Common complaints include slow (or no) responses to customer inquiries. Consumers expect service. Your Web store must deliver it.

Good customer service includes

➤ Email confirmations

➤ Multiple means of contact

➤ Support outside business hours

➤ Guarantees and return policies

Email Confirmations

After a customer clicks the **Place My Order** button, he or she immediately wonders what will become of his or her order. It's only natural that sending an order into the vastness of cyberspace can cause a certain amount of consternation. You can relieve much of your customer's worries—and avoid frustrations—by sending a series of email confirmations that informs the customer of the status of his or her order right through the sales and shipping process.

As soon as the order is placed, an email confirming that the order was received should be sent to the customer. The email message should include a complete record of the transaction, including the following information:

➤ An order number

➤ What was ordered

➤ Who ordered it

➤ Where it will be shipped

➤ Total amount of the sale including all shipping and handling costs

➤ Customer service contact information in case the customer has a question about the order

Don't Include the Customer's Credit Card Number

Remember that when you send any email confirmation to your customer do *not* send his or her credit card number in the email. Email *is not* secure and should never be used to send sensitive information over the Net.

Another email message should be sent confirming that the product ordered is in stock and when it will be shipped. A third email message is sent after the product is actually shipped containing the name and tracking number of the shipping company that was used.

Finally, send an email to your customer after they have received their order asking them for feedback and even offer them a discount on their next purchase if they buy within the next few weeks.

Provide Multiple Means of Contact

Always provide a number of different ways that a customer can contact your customer service department. There are several ways to do this.

List your customer service email address on your Web site and include in it all email correspondence with your customer. In addition, tell people where you are located. Include your company's address, telephone number, and fax number on your Web site. DVD Empire does this very well on their site (see Figure 13.4).

Figure 13.4

DVD Empire lists their complete contact information giving the shopper multiple ways to reach them.

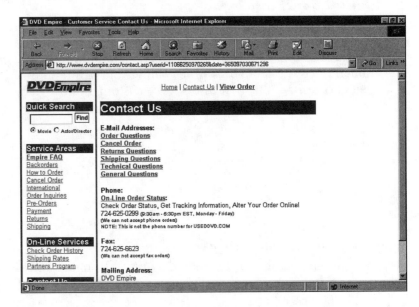

List a telephone number for customer service. Let customers know when a live person will answer the telephone. If you use an answering machine, be sure you leave a message that tells the caller when they can expect their call to be returned.

Invest in a toll-free telephone number and list it on your site. Not only is a toll-free number relatively inexpensive, it goes a long way toward building a level of consumer confidence in your business. If you'd rather not deal with the hassles and expense of staffing a toll-free customer service line, then out-source it. There are many service companies that will do it for you on a fee-per-call basis. Finally, think about offering live chat on your site and use it for customer service.

Provide Support Outside of Business Hours

Although your Web store is available to customers 24 hours a day, 7 days a week, 365 days a year—you are not. So, to support customers outside of normal business hours, be sure your Web store has a FAQ section. Even though a FAQ cannot tell a customer if his product is in stock or when it was shipped, it is useful in providing clear instructions on how to use your product or service and troubleshooting tips in case customers run into trouble after hours.

Remember that it pays to keep all line of communications open with your customers and to provide a quick response to customer emails.

Guarantee the Sale and Provide Clear Return Policies

One of the best ways to gain customer confidence is to offer them a money-back satisfaction guarantee. As an eBusiness, you should offer a money back guarantee with your products and clearly state your guarantee policy on your Web site.

Offer a Satisfaction Guarantee

There's no excuse not to offer your shoppers a 100% satisfaction guarantee. This will build up trust in you and your eBusiness. Some sites like One Minute Shopper.com at oneminuteshopper.com go even further. One Minute Shopper.com offers a 300% Customer Satisfaction Guarantee. 100% satisfaction—send back the product for any reason if not satisfied with a purchase; 100% product warranty—all products will be repaired or replaced if defective; 100% price guarantee—if a shopper finds the price lower on the Net, they get double the difference back in cash.

If you prefer not to offer any kind of money back guarantee, then list your terms of sale and your return policy and procedures on your site. Remember that shoppers don't like surprises. Be sure they understand the terms of their purchase before they push the **Buy Now** button.

Tell the shopper under what conditions he or she can return a product. How many days or weeks do they have to decide to return it? Will they get a refund or a credit? Who pays the shipping back to you? You or them? If the product is defective, who is responsible for replacing it? You or the manufacturer?

Be clear and specific and list all details about your return policy on your Web site.

Convenience—Are You Easy to Do Business With?

When a shopper comes to your Web store, they come to buy. They've got their credit card in hand and they're ready to buy. So, don't let your Web site get in their way.

A Web store with a poorly designed navigation structure will frustrate a shopper. Even though you have a great offer, if the shopper can't easily find it and buy it he'll click off to your competitor and probably will not come back again.

A lot of thought must be given to how a shopper can search for products on your site. If you offer a shopper multiple navigation options it will help them find what they are looking for fast. Have the capability on your site for shoppers to search by:

➤ Product name

➤ Price

➤ Product category

➤ Manufacturer

The more site tools they have to search with the faster they can get to the products they're looking for, and the faster you'll make a sale.

Offer Live Customer Support—Without the Expense

Want to give live customer support on your site to shoppers? Don't want to spend the money for programming? Then use ICQ (www.icq.com/download/), Yahoo Instant Messaging (messenger.yahoo.com), or AOL's Instant Messenger service (www.aol.com/aim/). Shoppers can download the free desktop application and communicate with you real-time if they have a question.

But finding a product to buy is only the beginning. Just as important as price selection and service is convenience. How easy is it to navigate through your site? Getting lost in a site is discouraging and will send the shopper away fast if they can't easily find their way through your Web store. Good site navigation entails telling your visitor where they are, how they got there, how they can get back, and where they can go next.

If your site navigation is done properly, your shoppers should be able to get to where they want to go in just three or four mouse clicks. Be careful when designing the navigation bar on your site. Graphic links to the different sections of your site are nice and give a professional look to you Web store. But also include text links that duplicate your graphic navigation at the bottom of your pages in case your site loads too slowly through a shopper's browser.

Remember, your Web site should be intuitive to navigate. Your site pages should provide a visual map of how to get from one place to another that says, "Here's where I am; this is what I clicked on to get here. If I click on that, I'll go there next."

Security—How Trustworthy Is Your Site?

Good Web sites establish trust. Online shoppers can be a very skeptical bunch. They've been trained by the media to expect all kinds of online scams that are waiting to pick their pockets. If up to now you've given them a reason to buy from you, now they have to trust you enough to plunk down their money.

Build Trust in Your Site with Shoppers

Shoppers are looking for proof that your site is trustworthy to deal with. A good way to do this is join *eTrust* or the *Better Business Bureau (BBB)*. eTrust certifies that the personal information you give a site is protected and the BBB shows that you abide by the BBB way of doing business. You can join these organizations online at etrust.com and bbbonline.org/businesses/privacy/index.html.

You build trust on your Web site in two ways:

➤ The customer knows his credit card number is secure when placing an order on your site.

➤ The customer knows that the private personal information he or she gives you is kept personal and private.

Make Shoppers Comfortable Using Their Credit Card on Your Site

Credit card companies state that you are responsible for the first $50 of fraudulent charges if your card is stolen. Offer to cover the $50 credit card company charge if the shopper is a victim of credit card fraud while shopping at your store.

Credit Card Ordering

Shoppers are very concerned about using their credit cards to make purchases online. So there are two things you can do to help your customers feel secure enough to place an order on your Web site.

First, be sure that your Web store is running on an SSL secure server. Check with your ISP or Web hosting service and be sure your store is either running on an SSL secure server or that they can make it available to you. If your transactions are not being placed through an SSL secure server, then find an ISP or hosting service that will provide it.

Shoppers can see right away if your server is secure by looking in the bottom left corner of their browsers. If they see a broken key or an unlocked lock, they know that their order will not be placed securely.

Second, after an order is taken at the secure server, many times the order information must be emailed to you for processing. If so, be sure that the email method is using some kind of encryption key. You can avoid all this if your SSL secure server sends the information encrypted to your credit card company for process and charges the customer's credit card.

Some shoppers just will not place an order online with their credit card no matter how secure it is. For these types of customers, provide a toll-free telephone number for them to use and call in their order to you. Also provide an order form on your site that they can print, fill out, and fax to you.

Privacy Policies

After credit card security, privacy issues come next on a shopper's list of concerns. As I said before, this is an area that the FTC is very interested in and is watching closely. So be sure that your Privacy Policy clearly states the following:

Have Shoppers Rate Your Site

BizRate (`bizrate.com`) has exclusive real-time access to more than 60% of all customers making online retail transactions. To participate, you simply allow BizRate to solicit feedback from all your customers who make a purchase at your site. BizRate solicits feedback twice, once at the point-of-sale, and again after the expected date of fulfillment. Feedback covers 10 service attributes, from ease of ordering to product shipping and handling.

➤ What information is collected when shoppers buy from you

➤ How you use this information

➤ What do you intend to do with it

Finally, make your Privacy Policy accessible right from your home page.

The Least You Need to Know

➤ Everything on your site should be about the customer and designed from the customer's point of view.

➤ Offering a good selection to shoppers is not necessarily a numbers game. The quality of your selection is much more important for a small Web business than the quantity.

➤ Don't draw the customer into the buying process with low prices then surprise them after they place their order with exorbitant shipping and handling charges on the order confirmation page.

➤ Customers expect to be serviced so customer service is a top priority for your Web site. Because you're not dealing with customers face-to-face, your service policies must instill a sense of trust in your shoppers.

➤ Good Web sites establish trust. Establish trust through secure online ordering and a clear Privacy Policy.

Chapter 14

The Seven Cardinal Sins of eCommerce

In This Chapter

➤ Learn the seven cardinal sins of eCommerce and how to avoid them

➤ Discover examples of good and bad Web site designs.

I was raised in the Roman Catholic tradition. I have fond memories of the Catholic grammar school I attended while I was a kid. And on these occasions I recall Sister Mary Theresa. I remember her clearly for her quick wit in class and hard ruler across the knuckles. She also taught me one of my first religion classes that all good Catholic children were required to take.

And like all good Catholic children we were taught to avoid the seven cardinal sins of Vanity, Greed, Lust, Envy, Gluttony, Wrath, and Sloth.

Now that I'm an Internet professional, I can see a strong resemblance of the seven cardinal sins taught to me as a child to the seven cardinal sins of eCommerce.

So, here they are and some ways to avoid them.

Vanity—Going It Alone

There's a saying that goes "You can do anything on the Internet—but you can't do it alone." In the world of eCommerce outsourcing is not an evil word. Many new Web stores fail to succeed due to a lack of professional design and programming know-how. The biggest challenge to a new eBusiness is not so much the technical aspects—although they are important—but how best to execute your business plan.

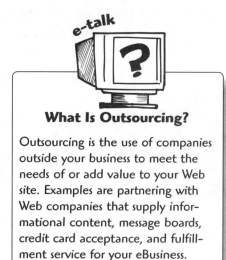

What Is Outsourcing?

Outsourcing is the use of companies outside your business to meet the needs of or add value to your Web site. Examples are partnering with Web companies that supply informational content, message boards, credit card acceptance, and fulfillment service for your eBusiness.

Too few businesses on the Net use the resources available to them for order taking, credit card clearing, site hosting, store building, and so on. You can spend valuable time and resources building a site, hiring professionals to do the necessary programming, buying software and hardware, and paying advertising agencies. Instead, partner with companies on the Net that supply free or nearly free resources to set up and run your business.

Sure, having a store on Yahoo! or selling other merchant's products through an affiliate program is not as glamorous as having your own custom online business. But if you're just starting out in the world of eCommerce or have limited funds, partnering with other sites on the Web is a smart thing to do.

Even if you have the wherewithal to build a custom one-of-a-kind Web store, you can still partner with other sites to save your time and money. In Chapter 11, "Building Your Web Store,"you saw how you can set up a Web store for free. In Chapter 12, "The 3 Cs of eCommerce," you found ways to include information content and community elements on your site by partnering with content and community providers that syndicate their programs to sites free of charge.

In the chapters to follow, you will see where on the Net you can accept credit cards without the hassle of setting up a credit card merchant account by partnering with Web companies like iBill (`ibill.com`) and ccBill (`ccbill.com`) (see Figure 14.1). You will also see you dozens of ways you can promote your site free.

Figure 14.1

At ccBill you can accept credit cards on your site without going through the expense and time of getting a merchant account.

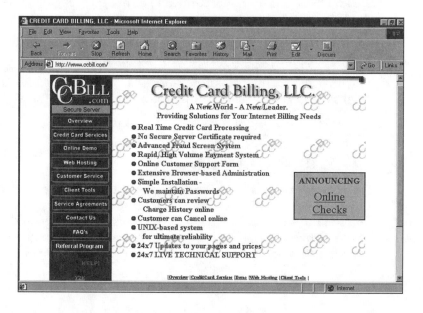

But you can't do it alone. There is a lot of help out there in cyberspace. Learn to use it by partnering with other Web companies.

Greed—Forcing a Square Peg into a Round Hole

Your product sells well in the real world. Why shouldn't they sell just as well online? Right? Wrong! Just because a particular product sells well in retail stores, it's easy to think that it will, by necessity, sell well online. Take a hard look at what you're trying to sell.

Look at the product—even the service—you are going to sell over the Net and ask yourself these questions.

➤ Can my product or service be pictured and clearly understood through electronic means only? Until *virtual reality* becomes a reality, viewing a product through cyberspace will never replace the hands-on experience of the real world. Yes, there are attempts at adding 3D to an eCommerce site such as Boo.com (boo.com). But such a site is programming intensive and visitors need to have a fast connection to view the product offerings properly. So, pick a product to sell that does not require the shopper to physically handle before he or she can purchase it. If your product or service requires a personal sales touch, you might have problems selling it online.

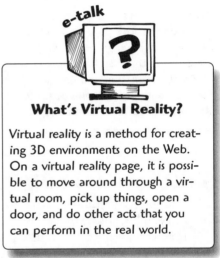

What's Virtual Reality?

Virtual reality is a method for creating 3D environments on the Web. On a virtual reality page, it is possible to move around through a virtual room, pick up things, open a door, and do other acts that you can perform in the real world.

➤ Is your product heavy or bulky? Will it cost an exorbitant amount to ship the product to a customer? Selling refrigerators, washing machines, and wide-screen TVs might be a good idea but think of the shipping costs to the customer and actually handling these items in your warehouse.

➤ Do your products carry a high product liability? Some products if not handled properly can cause physical harm or property damage. Be sure that the products you sell and even the service you offer are covered by liability insurance. Find out who's responsible if someone is injured using your product or if your service does not deliver as promised.

Be sure you have all these questions answered before you set out to sell your product or service on the Net. Before you offer your product or service to the public, evaluate its suitability for online sales.

Envy—Keeping Up with the Nerds

When a potential customer hits your site, is the first thing they see a straight offer to buy, or a song and dance routine of Java applets, animated icons, or other special effects that wastes the time—and delays the sale—of your visitor?

What's a Splash Page?

A splash page is a first or front page of a Web site. This page usually contains a clickable logo or message, announcing that you have arrived. The real information and navigation for the site lies behind this page on the home page or welcome page.

People don't care to be entertained with the equivalent of elevator music when they're looking to take action. Who cares if your competitor's Web site won "Cool Site of the Day." What counts in business is making sales. Don't force customers to sit through a flashy, long *splash page* before getting to the site's home page. Don't make potential customers wait for a variety of images to appear, move around, and disappear from the screen before the home page appears. You can be sure that they'll be gone before your flashy animations are through.

Finally, be sensitive to customers with older systems. If your site has a lot of flashy graphics, offer a text-only option for viewing your site.

Gluttony—Is It Bigger than 60K?

That pretty graphic on your home page that takes several minutes to load? Get rid of it. People want simplicity over cool graphics. Faster loading is better than eye candy. If your total page size is more than 60K, put it on a diet. GMBuy at www.gmbuypower.com (see Figure 14.2). In fact, most designers agree that a page should not be more that 48K and that includes graphics.

Figure 14.2

GMBuyPower has a bloated front page that takes a long time to download on a 28.8 modem.

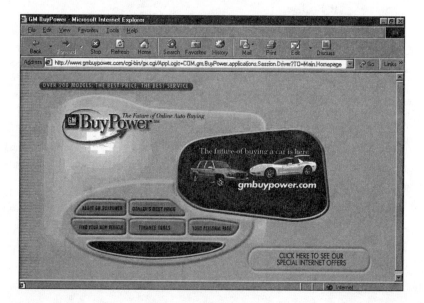

If you're selling products on your Web site, there's no getting around the need for product shots. If you need to place a lot of product shots on a page, use thumbnails—smaller sized pictures—instead. If the shopper wants to see a larger version of the product, they can click it and be sent to a Web page that contains only that product along with a detailed description and buy button.

To create a good customer experience, use graphics only when they serve the customer's goals.

Sloth—Neglecting Security and Customer Convenience

You want to make visitors comfortable while they are shopping on your site. You do that buy making your site easy to do business with and offering a safe and secure way for shoppers to buy with their credit cards at your site.

People are concerned about sending their credit card numbers over the Net. Sure. People are getting more comfortable with the idea, but that doesn't mean you should sit there like a bump on a log and not soothe the fears of your visitors by telling them—and I mean tell them—that your site is secure and they can safely send their card number to you over the Net.

Tell them upfront—on your home page—that their credit card purchases are secure like OfficeMax does, www.officemax.com (see Figure 14.3). Direct them to a page on your site that explains how the customer's credit card number is protected when they use it on your site. To make them feel more secure, promise to pay the $50 liability charge that the shopper would incur from their bank if their card number were stolen when used on your site.

Figure 14.3

OfficeMax tells the shopper right up front on their home page that the shoppers' credit card purchases are secure. Then OfficeMax links the shoppers to a page detailing their security precautions.

Keep a Running Total

Keep a view of what's in a customer's shopping cart on every page of your site. It could be a simple text box that says, "You have 3 items in your shopping cart—total amount $26.95." This is a useful service to provide for your shoppers.

Make it easy for your customers to shop around your store by adding an online shopping cart. Think about this. You just bought a product at your neighborhood store. To buy another one, you need to pay for it, leave the store, and enter it again. Sounds silly right? Well, without a shopping cart on your site, that's exactly what you're asking your customers to do.

If you really want to drive customers away from your site, make it hard to navigate (see Figure 14.4). According to a recent research paper by Creative Good, Inc., "Thirty-nine percent of test shoppers failed in their buying attempts because sites were too difficult to navigate." Make your site navigation simple—not cute. Use labels such as Contact Us, About Us, Our Catalog, Services We Offer, or Shop Now. Forget naming sections Joy Ride, Buzz the Bean, or Cool Stuff.

Figure 14.4

Visiting the SAAB USA Web site brings this to mind, "Where am I and where do I go from here?" This site is a good example of poor navigation.

Don't be lazy with security and convenience. Place your Web store on a secure server and provide an easy-to-use shopping cart and site navigation system for your customers.

Lust—You Gotta Love Those Plug-Ins

Get this. You walk into your favorite retailer and at the door you're stopped and told to go down the block and get a special pass before you can enter the store. You comply, right? In your dreams! Or, how about this? You're at the checkout counter ready to pay but you're told to go across the street and buy a special wallet to complete the purchase.

Well, that's what you ask a visitor to your site to do when you tell them that they need a plug-in to view your site or a special *eWallet* to make a purchase. People don't want to have to download anything to view your site or buy from you. Don't lust after some cool way to display the goods and content of your site or offer a convenience that's inconvenient to get.

Help Your Shoppers Fill Out Order Forms

No one likes to fill out order forms every time he goes to a new site to buy. That's why eWallets are the latest shopping trend to hit the Web. Consumers fill in all their purchasing information once and then when they go to a Web store the eWallet fills in the order form for them. There is a problem with most eWallets, though. Consumers have to download them onto their computers. But using a service like Microsoft Passport, the consumer enters their purchasing information onto Passport's secure Web site. No downloads are necessary. When they buy at a Web store that accepts the Passport eWallet, shoppers can enter their information easily into the order form. Consider making your Web store Passport enabled. Find it at passport.com.

But suppose you must have shoppers download a plug-in to experience your products. For example, you have an online music store selling CDs. You want to give shoppers the opportunity to hear some sample tracks from a CD before they buy. They will most certainly have to download an audio player plug-in like Real Audio at realaudio.com. If you say your site needs RealAudio to listen to the sample CD tracks, then make sure it links to the download page on the RealAudio Web site.

If you keep it simple you won't give your customer a reason to click his way over to a competitor.

Wrath—Do You Hate Your Customer?

Want to really drive customers from your site? Use frames, have them register, provide no site search engine, and ignore international customers.

Let's take these one at a time (see Figure 14.5).

Figure 14.5

This is a perfect example of the bad use of frames.

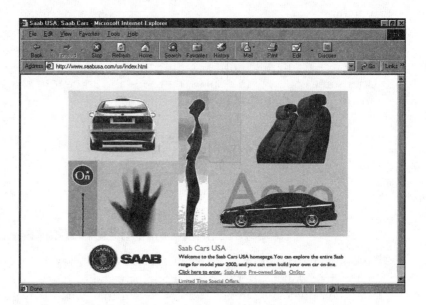

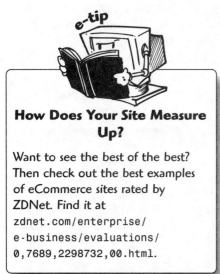

How Does Your Site Measure Up?

Want to see the best of the best? Then check out the best examples of eCommerce sites rated by ZDNet. Find it at
zdnet.com/enterprise/
e-business/evaluations/
0,7689,2298732,00.html.

Framed sites are bad news. Most search engines can't find your site because they hide your real content from the search engine and visitors can't bookmark the page they're actually interested in—only the framed page they're on. Also, customers can get lost easily navigating your site through frames.

If you want to irritate your visitors, count their time onsite in milliseconds by forcing them to register before using your site. Or, forget that the first W in the World Wide Web stands for World. Think globally. Remember that users from other countries can easily access your site. If you want your eBusiness to be truly global, respect other cultures and keep in mind that they might not be familiar with American expressions or respond to American advertising.

Oh, and don't forget to throw in a lot of small pop-up windows giving a pitch after each mouse click to really drive your shoppers nuts.

Be considerate of your shoppers. Tell them which Web browsers to use to best view your site such as "This page is best viewed by Netscape 3.0 and above." And though techno-speak might be familiar to you, many newbies to the Net might not understand it. Don't confuse shoppers new to the Net by using techno-jargon.

If your site commits any of these seven eCommerce sins, immediately say your *mea culpas* and correct them.

The Least You Need to Know

➤ Partner with companies on the Net that supply free and near free resources to set up and run your business.

➤ Don't force customers to sit through a flashy, long splash page before getting to the site's home page.

➤ Tell shoppers upfront—on your home page—that their credit card purchases are secure.

➤ Don't be lazy with security and convenience. Place your Web store on a secure server and provide an easy-to-use shopping cart and site navigation system for your customers.

➤ Framed sites are bad news.

Part 4
Delivering the Goods

"Show me the money!"

You have customers in your store and they're ready to buy. So what forms of payment do you take and how do you take them? You also need to know what information to collect from a customer at the point of sale and the best ways to get it. When you have orders in hand, you have to get them into the hands of your customers. That means pick, pack, and ship the orders.

Choosing the best and most economical way of fulfilling your orders is as important as taking the order itself. And if you think your job is done after shipping the product, think again. Shipping the order is only half the job. Servicing the customer properly after the sale will determine whether that customer buys from you again.

And that, friend, is the key to the long-term success of your eBusiness. Come on in and find out how to deliver it.

Chapter 15

Taking the Order

> ## In This Chapter
>
> ➤ Learn the important elements of an online order form
>
> ➤ Discover the different ways you can take an order at your Web store
>
> ➤ Learn how to protect your sales from fraud
>
> ➤ Learn the different Internet Tax proposals and their effect on your business

Creating a shopper friendly eCommerce Web site and locating it on a server is a lot of work. But that's only the beginning. Your next task is to find and implement the various services needed to quickly and safely make a transaction.

In one way or another you have to be able to take an order and accept payment for it. The customer must be notified that his or her electronic order was accepted and that your company acknowledges the order. Let's face it. Without human acknowledgement, customers want to be secure in the fact that after they purchase from you, their order is not floating around somewhere in cyberspace. Your electronic process of taking an order has to give the same warm fuzzy feeling that they would get placing it with a real person.

Finally, you have to protect yourself from those who would try to steal product from you by placing bogus orders or using stolen credit cards. You might have protected your customer's credit card by using a secure server but that doesn't protect you from fraudulent credit card use.

Break Up Your Order Form

You have to collect a lot of information on your order form. So don't put your entire order form on one Web page. Break it up into logical steps with short pages for billing and shipping address, credit card number, contact information, shipping information, and so on.

The Order Form

The purchasing relationship that you have with a customer starts with the order form. Up until then, your shopper was sold on your Web store and decided to make a purchase from you. Is the order in the bag? Not necessarily. You still can blow it. You still can make the customer abandon his purchase if your order form is not easy, fast, and convenient to use.

Whether the customer fills out a form on your site and pays by credit card or prints the form from your Web page and mails or faxes it to you with their payment, how you design your order form and the order form process itself can make the difference between keeping the sale you made and losing it to a competitor.

So, here are the elements of a good online order form:

➤ Registration Request
➤ Customer Contact Information
➤ Product Information and Order Costs
➤ Customer Billing and Shipping Information
➤ Optional Services Request

Registration Request

Shoppers like convenience and as an online merchant, you want to provide it. One way is to have the customer sign in before starting his or her order. If a customer has ordered before, he or she might already be registered at the site. By registering with your Web store, you can populate or automatically fill many of the order form fields for your customer.

Don't Get Pushy

Asking a customer who is ready to buy to register is one thing. But never ask a shopper to register at your site just to shop. Ask them to register or sign in only when they are starting the purchasing process.

Another use for registration is that you can keep the customer's credit or debit card on file and stored on your secure server. That way, all the customer has to do is supply a password at the time of checkout and they don't have to enter their card number and send it over the Net again.

There are both positives and negatives to customer registration. Some shoppers, no matter how secure you claim your Web store to be, do not like the idea of a merchant storing their personal information. And if you store their card number, they get even more nervous! So, making registration mandatory to purchase at your site might not be a good idea. You could lose a sale that you've worked so hard to get.

Give Your Shopper a Cookie

Another way to track customers who don't want to register and populate the fields of your order form is to use a *cookie*. A cookie is a small piece of information that your Web server sends to a shopper's computer via their browser. Cookies can contain information such as login or registration information, online shopping cart information, user preferences, and so on.

So, give your customers a choice. Let them choose their comfort level. First, make registration an option. Then sell them on registering. Explain how registering their personal information makes shopping at your site faster and more convenient for them. If you have a secure server, tell them that any personal information they give you will be kept secure and private. (You did remember to place a Privacy Policy Statement on your site. Right?) Then let them choose whether to give you their shipping information and/or their card number to store on your site.

When should you ask them to register? Ask them if they'd like to register before they place their order, and if they don't, ask them again after they have ordered.

Customer Contact Information

If your customer has not registered at your Web store, then you'll need to collect his or her contact information.

Your order form should have two separate fields—or spaces—for their name. It should have one field for their first name and one for their last name. After their name, provide a field for their email address. Always collect their email address. This will be the means by which you will do almost all communication with your customer—such as order confirmation, product stock status, and shipping notification.

Finally, ask for their phone numbers. And the word *numbers* is plural for a reason. Always get two phone numbers from your customer—their home phone and their day phone. Why? The first reason is obvious. If you need to contact them by phone you need a number to reach them both during the day and at home in the evening and on weekends.

The second reason is not so obvious and it has to do with fraud prevention.

Getting two numbers from your customer can help prevent the fraudulent use of a credit or debit card. If a customer is using a stolen card number and you suspect that it's stolen, having two numbers available for confirmation helps you decide whether the order is legit or not. If you call and both numbers don't work or the person on the other line did not place the order, then you know you might have a possible fraud on your hands. Contact the customer by email and let him know of the problem. Dollars to donuts, you'll probably never hear from him.

Product Information and Order Costs

Customers need to know at every point of the ordering process what they're buying and how much it will cost. This is why you should supply on your order form information on the product they've ordered. Show them the name of the product, the product code number, its price, and description. And if the product they ordered comes in different colors or sizes, be sure these are listed with the product information.

In a sense, you're verifying that your site knows what the customer ordered even during the ordering process.

And don't make the mistake that some eCommerce sites make. Your order form should automatically generate the product information. Don't make the customer remember the product information and enter it into the order form (see Figure 15.1). Want to lose a sale really fast? Do that.

You should also give the customer the opportunity to choose the shipping method. Allow them to choose whether they want their order shipped by ground or by air—next day or second day—and show them the difference in costs.

Finally, show all the costs before asking the customer to enter his or her credit or debit card. Provide a page before finalizing the order that details what the customer is buying, how much it costs, and the shipping and handling charges. Show the total amount the customer's credit card will be charged or account debited. If they are printing the order form after filling it out, show them the total amount they should write their check for.

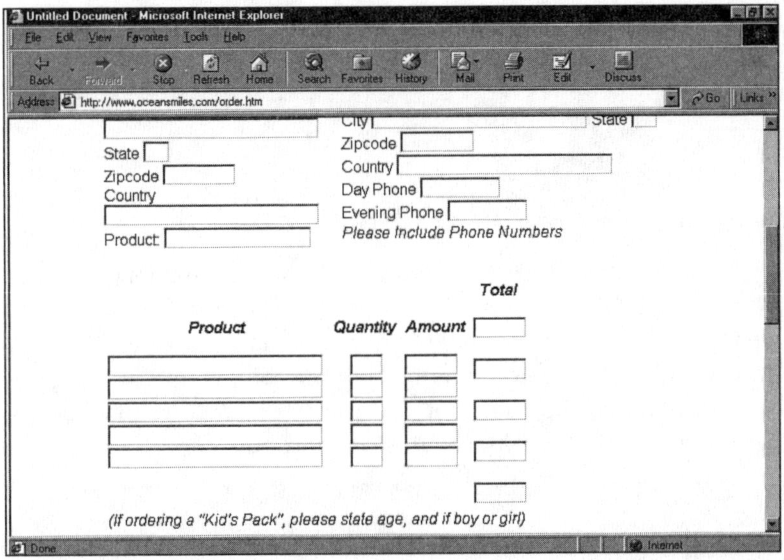

Figure 15.1

Here's a good example of a bad way to design an order form. Never ask the customer to enter the products he is going to buy.

Customer Billing and Shipping Information

After requesting the customer contact information and confirming what he has ordered, you need to collect his billing and shipping address and his credit or debit card number. The customer's billing address is the address to which his credit card bill is sent. Your credit card processing company will compare the billing address against the customer's name and credit or debit card number to verify that the card number matches the billing address. This is the first layer of merchant fraud protection.

You also must ask for the customer shipping address. This might sound redundant but it's not. First of all, the customer might want to have the product shipped to her work and not her home. She might be buying a gift for her husband or family and doesn't want the gift to be opened at home by mistake. Second, the customer might be buying the gift for someone else and would like to have the product shipped to that person.

If the billing and shipping address is the same, you can avoid having the customer type the same address twice by asking them to check a box on the order form that says, "If the billing and shipping address are the same—check this box." Your software can then fill in the shipping address automatically so the customer doesn't have to.

Finally, provide fields for the customer's credit or debit card. They will need fields to enter their card number, the expiration date of the credit or debit card, and what type of card it is—MasterCard, Visa, American Express, Discover, and so on.

Ask for the Customer Credit Card Number Last

On your online order form, ask for the customer's credit card number last. This serves two purposes. First, it makes the customer comfortable that they have all the information they need up to that point to make a final purchase. Second, if the customer abandoned the order form before completing the sale, you've captured his or her contact information upfront that you can use later to send a special offer enticing them to come back to your Web store and buy.

Optional Services Request

Customers like special consideration and perks. So, if your Web store intends to offer special optional services or promotions, they also should be included on your order form. They should be easy to find and use. Here are some examples:

Gift Wrapping   You might want to provide a gift-wrapping service for your customers. Provide this option on your order form. If it's a free service ask them if they would like to have it and confirm it by checking a specific box. If you charge for the service, tell the customer what the charge is and be sure to include it on the total cost page that you present to the customer before accepting the payment.

Coupons and Discounts   If you are running a special promotion in which you distributed regular or electronic discount coupons, have a field where they can enter the coupon code number and have the discount be reflected on the total cost page. The same goes for any frequent buyer discounts that you might apply.

Remember: your order form can make or break a sale. So be sure to include all the elements here to make your customer's buying experience match the shopping experience he or she has had on your site.

How Do I Pay Thee? Let Me Count the Ways

One of the best ways to make it easy for shoppers to buy from your Web store is to provide them with a variety of ways to pay for your product or service. People are different and have different ways of managing their money. Various customers have different comfort levels and different ways they like to pay for merchandise.

Your Web store should cater to this difference and plan to allow your customers a choice between several payment methods to ensure that *everyone* will be able to do business with you.

Like the French say, *Viva la difference!*

The first thing that comes to mind when shopping online is buying online. That's what the Internet is about. And the easiest way to buy online is with a credit or debit card so you must set up your site to accept both. But accepting credit or debit cards are not the only ways the customer can pay for products or services.

Some people will not use a credit card. Not because they're concerned with online security but would rather pay cash for their purchases. So you need to be able to accept checks—both electronically and mailed in—and COD. And you also should be aware of the new payment kid on the block—*eCash* and it's cousin *microCash*. Over the last year or so these new forms of electronic payment have come of age and many Web consumers are starting to use them.

But these are all payment types. You also should consider payment methods. Your eBusiness should be able to take orders online from your Web site, by telephone, fax, and even mail orders. Any and all these payment types and methods should be considered when setting up a payment plan at your Web store.

So, let's take a peek at each one.

Payment Methods

Your site should be set up to take orders through a variety of methods. When a customer arrives at your site, he or she should know that they have the flexibility to place an order with you online or otherwise. Consider offering customers as many of these payment methods as possible.

➤ Secure Online Ordering

➤ Email Ordering

➤ Ordering by Fax or Mail

➤ Ordering by Telephone

Secure Online Ordering

If you are going to take any kind of sensitive financial information from your customers, such as credit or debit card numbers, you must have your Web store on a secure server. All transactions between the customer and your store should be secured by using the *Secure Sockets Layer (SSL)* protocol, which prevents third parties from discovering the credit card information.

Customers can tell if they are entering their card number into a secure Web page by looking in the lower left corner of their browser. They will see right away if the little lock is locked or if the little key is unbroken. Some later browsers also will post a security alert box within their browser stating that they are entering a secure section of the Web site.

Don't risk the chance of giving your eBusiness a bad rep and hurt your chances of making sales in the future by having a customer claim (whether true or not) that he had his credit card number stolen when ordering from your site. There are no ifs, ands, or buts about it. If you accept credit or debit cards for payment, do it on a secure SSL server.

Email Ordering

Email is a very unsecure way to take an order and is not recommended. Still some customers might want this option so here's how to take email orders and still protect the customer's credit or debit card information.

Is There Such a Thing as Secure Email?

Secure email is available using encryption systems such as PGP and S/MIME that are built into most email programs. But this method is not very well known and is bulky to use because of the private and public encryption keys that must be used. If you intend to accept orders via secure email, remember to include your public key on your Web store.

Have the customer email you all the information about his order except his card number and expiration date. Be certain he does include his phone numbers. Then call the customer to get his card number and complete the transaction. Another way, yet still not advisable, is to have your customer send his card number in two pieces in two different email messages.

Ordering by Fax or Mail

To help facilitate fax and mail ordering, you should make your order form printable from your Web site. You can either provide customers with a blank order form, or have the option to print out a completed order form—without their card number—for faxing.

After they have their order form in their hands they can either fax or mail it to you. Be sure that you have a dedicated fax line at your business. This way there will be less chance that a buying customer will get a busy signal—and you won't lose an order.

A new use of faxing is the fax-to-email gateway. This type of Internet service converts a customer's fax into an email message thus relieving you of the need for a dedicated fax number. This eliminates the chance of your customer getting a busy signal when he tries to fax you an order and also allows you to pick up orders from a remote location.

Use a FAX to EMAIL Gateway

If you want to use a fax to email service, check out JFAX (`www.jfax.com`). MessageClick is another service (`messageclick.com`)—and it's free!

Finally, if you're going to give customers the option of ordering through the mail, then be sure your customers can easily find your complete mailing address on your Web site.

Ordering by Telephone

Statistics say that many people shop the Net, choosing a store, locating a product to buy, and then calling the online merchant to place the order. You should make it easy for your customers to do just that.

But accepting phone orders does have a downside. Remember that the Net is global. Not only can you get orders from around your country, but around the world! So if you do give customers the option of phoning in their orders, you would need to man phones 24 hours a day 7 days a week. For a small to medium size business, this is not feasible. You can rely on a simple answering machine or a voice-mail service or outsource your phone orders to a third party answering service. For all these, be sure you offer a toll-free number for customers to use. Also, include a standard telephone ordering number so thatinternational customers can place orders.

A nice solution would be to answer the phones on your time. You can do this by posting your telephone order days and times on your Web store. Another solution is to use the rapidly developing technology of Web and telephony services. A provider of this technology is Instant Call at `www.instantcall.com` (see Figure 15.2). Instead of calling you, you call them.

Here's how it works.

You place a Call Me Now button on your site for when a customer wants to order via telephone. When a customer clicks the button, a message is sent to you with the customer's phone number. You then call him back and take his order.

Figure 15.2

Place the Instant Call's InstantCall button on your site and customers can alert you to call them when they have a question. No additional software or hardware is required.

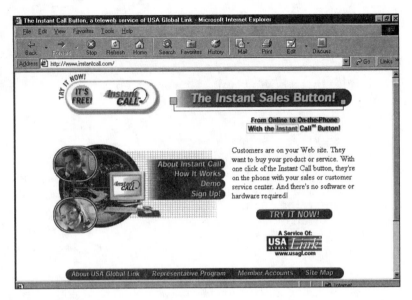

Payment Types

After you've established the different ways customers can place and order with you, you need to consider the types of payment you'll accept. Online merchants can use all the payment types that merchants use in the real world. In addition, there are payment types that are native only to the Net.

By offering customers a variety of ways to pay for their merchandise, you increase the likelihood of making a sale. So, consider offering customers as many of these payment types as possible.

➤ Conventional Payment
➤ Credit and Debit Cards
➤ Digital Cash
➤ Telephone Billing

Conventional Payment

Believe it of not, in this world of instant gratification and freely available credit many people still prefer to pay with cash. You should make this traditional way of paying for products and services available to customers at your Web store. Accepting payment in the traditional way includes paying by check or COD.

When a customer wants to pay by check, he normally uses one of your offline payment methods. A customer sends his order through the mail or faxes it to you. When dealing with checks you run the risk of having the check bounce because of insufficient funds. With payment by check you have one of two choices to make. Either you hold the check until it clears the customer's bank, or you take the risk and ship when you receive the check. You could limit your risk further by using a check verification service.

In the matter of CODs, you can limit your risk by requiring that the customer pay for the product with a cashiers check or money order.

The whole process of sending checks back and forth is not very Net-like and is inefficient. But a new technology has emerged over the last few years that can make the act of paying by check a lot more palatable for Web merchants. This technology is called *Electronic Checks*.

In its simplest form Electronic Check systems merely require the customer to fill out a form at your Web store. This data is then transferred to the merchant where it is converted into a paper check by using blank check forms in a standard office printer. Check out CheckMax (`www.chekfaxx.com`) for one such service. Also, check out ECCHO. ECCHO (`www.eccho.org`) is a not-for-profit national clearinghouse whose primary objective is the development and promotion of electronic check presentment.

e-tip

Accept Checks via Fax, Phone, or the Net

Using software from Virtual Bank Checks, you can print customer checks from any printer and deposit them in your bank. Simply request their account information and print the check in seconds. Find it at `virtualbankchecks.com`.

Credit and Debit Cards

Taking credit cards online is critical to any online merchant because credit cards are still the most popular way for paying for goods and services on the Net. Don't just accept Visa and MasterCard. Accept American Express and Discover, too. The more card types you can accept the more opportunity for a sale you'll have.

Accepting credit cards also gives you the advantage of having funds automatically and electronically deposited in your account within 2–3 days.

Also think about accepting debit cards at your Web store. Debit cards deduct the amount of the customer's purchase directly from her checking account. If you're planning on selling to European customers, accepting debit cards is a must. They are more widely used in Europe than credit cards. And they are catching on fast in the United States. CardData reports the annual growth rate of debit cards is surpassing those of credit cards.

Digital Cash

Digital cash or *eCash* is a Net-native form of payment. The main drawback to digital cash is that both the customer and the merchant need to have an account with a bank that issues it. The bank provides customers with a piece of software called a *purse*. The purse manages the transferring of digital cash. Customers take money from their checking or savings account and convert it into digital cash that is then transferred to their purse software. It's then encoded and stored on the their hard drive until it is spent.

A payment technology that is developing will allow just about anyone to sell anything on the Web. It's called *microCash*. It enables customers to make very small purchases—anywhere from a few pennies to a few dollars—without having to use a credit or debit card or writing a check. This is good for Web merchants because the costs involved in charging a credit or debit card for such a small amount surpasses the price of the sale itself.

What would a Web merchant use microCash for? How about paying for a stock quote; or a news article; or an installment of your new book. Or even for a daily joke. You could open and run a successful Web store selling bits of information for pennies a piece—something you could never do in the real world.

Ain't the Net grand!

Telephone Billing

An alternative to all these payment types is a blend of the old and the new. A company called eCharge (www.echarge.com) has created a payment system called *eCharge Phone* that allows Internet users to shop online and securely charge items to their normal phone bill (see Figure 15.3).

Figure 15.3

With eCharge you can bill a customer's order right to his phone bill.

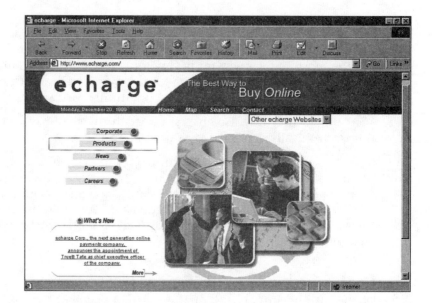

Aside from convenience, one of the benefits of eCharge Phone is that it's so secure. eCharge Phone connects directly from your modem to a switch that automatically captures the billing information. There is no transfer of private data or account numbers over the Internet. The only draw back right now is that you can only charge products up to $300 a piece.

Online Fraud

Building an online business takes a lot of work. Nothing can be worse than seeing all your hard work lost through credit card fraud. Although here has been a lot of discussion in the media about credit card fraud, the fraud committed against online merchants has gone practically unnoticed.

In fact, it's the online merchant who is the true victim of Internet credit card fraud. The Internet itself makes the process of credit card fraud easier in many ways. Visit the newsgroups and you find lists of stolen credit card numbers readily available. There are even programs easily available online that generate new valid credit card numbers!

Why doesn't your bank protect you against fraud? Because your merchant agreement with them says it can't.

Verification Does Not Protect You from Fraud

Don't make the assumption that just verifying a credit card—getting an authorization number—is sufficient fraud protection. All this verification process does is to check that the card has not been reported stolen and that it has sufficient free credit available to fund the purchase.

Transactions by merchants on the Net fall under the heading of MOTO—Mail Order/Telephone Order. Most credit card merchant account agreements leave you, the merchant, 100% liable for fraud committed at your Web site. And that's not all. You're also required to pay the $15–25 charge–backcharge–backcharge-back fee that the bank hits you with when the charge on the customer's stolen card is reversed by his or her bank. If you accrue too many charge–backcharge–backcharge-backs, your merchant account can be terminated. After terminating, it's nearly impossible to get another one.

Not a pretty prospect when you think about it. Just the thought of credit card fraud can take the wind out of your eCommerce sails. So, before you dream of counting all the money you'll make with your online store, you need to protect your online business. It is guaranteed that you will experience an attempt to defraud you either sooner or later.

So, how do you protect yourself? Follow these steps.

How to Avoid Online Fraud

The first level of fraud protection is AVS. AVS stands for *Address Verification Service*. But it has its limitations.

AVS compares the billing address of the customer with the records held by the card issuer. If the card number and billing address match, AVS gives it a thumbs up. The problem is, the card could still be stolen and a thief can ask that the order be shipped to another address.

What About SET?

The credit card industry has been working on a new standard for credit card security that would protect both the consumer and the merchant. The standard is called SET. SET is the *Secure Electronic Transaction* protocol developed by Visa and MasterCard specifically for enabling secure credit card transactions on the Internet. It uses digital certificates to validate the identities of all parties involved in a purchase and encrypts credit card information before sending it across the Internet. However, it is likely to be several years before the use of SET becomes widespread.

AVS has other problems too. AVS only works for addresses in the United States. So, if you have an international order AVS will not help. If you sell software or information that can be downloaded instantly, AVS provides no protection. All a thief has to do is to obtain a valid billing address that corresponds to a stolen credit card number and your instant buy becomes an instant fraud!

Warning Signs of Fraud

So how can you reduce your vulnerability to fraud? By looking for these common warning signs that an order is possibly fraudulent.

Your first red flag is noticing that the bill to and ship to addresses are different. Look out for a billing address that's in one country and a shipping address that is in another. But keep in mind that many legitimate customers will buy a product and have it shipped to an address other than their billing address. Some merchants will not accept these types of orders. The problem here is that you can lose a considerable number of orders using this policy.

A good thing to look out for in these cases is the size and amount of the order. Be wary of big orders, especially for brand-name items. If someone is ordering a high-priced item or a large number of items—like three MP3 Players at once—and the ship to and bill to addresses do not match, then investigate the order further.

Another tip off is the email address. With fraudulent orders the customer's email address is often one of the free email services like Hotmail, MSN, or Yahoo! A thief will do all he can to avoid being traced so an untraceable email address from one of the free services is a great way to hide his identity. A high proportion of fraud orders come from these free email services.

Untrustworthy Email Addresses

You can find a list of free email domains on the AntiFraud Web site that are used most frequently in fraudulent transactions along with an very extensive list of domains that have been used for fraud at `antifraud.com/redflag.htm`.

A red flag should be raised if an order specifies express or next day shipping. Another clue is a suspicious billing address such as 123 Main Street. You can check to see if an address is real by using Yahoo! Maps at `yahoo.com/r/mp`. And finally, if someone places a very valuable order and asks that it be left at the front door, be suspicious. It could be a sign that a thief is using an innocent person's house as a drop-off point. If an order is for a high-priced item, request that it be signed for.

Fraud Prevention Services

For a list of some automatic checking tools for fraud prevention, check out AntiFraud.com at `antifraud.com`. AntiFraud provides a number of antifraud services like Automatic Email Screening and Instant Fraud Alerts, among others. Another fraud prevention service is supplied by CyberSource at `cybersource.com/services/risk/`. Its Internet Fraud Screen automatically calculates your risk associated with an order.

You Suspect Fraud—What Do You Do?

You have a great order but you suspect fraud. If you do, follow these steps:

1. Call the customer. Use the phone numbers you requested and collected from him. When you contact him, don't automatically assume that you're dealing with a thief. The customer could have entered incorrect information and you don't want to offend him and lose the sale. In general though, a thief will not want to have a long conversation with you.

2. If the billing address doesn't match or is incorrect, ask him to give it to you again. If the area code doesn't match the billing address's city, ask him why.

3. Ask the customer for the name and phone number of the establishment that issued the card. Both are usually printed on the back. If the customer cannot supply it, this is a sign that he doesn't physically have the card—just the number.

4. If you still feel uncomfortable with an order even after talking to the customer, ask him for payment in advance.

Remember, it takes a lot of orders to replace just one order lost to fraud. So, it's better to pass on the ones that you're not 100% certain about.

The Least You Need to Know

➤ How you design your order form and the order form process itself can make the difference between keeping the sale you made and losing it to a competitor.

➤ Don't make customer registration mandatory to place an order.

➤ Customers need to know at every point of the ordering process what they're buying and how much it will cost.

➤ One of the best ways to make it easy for shoppers to buy from your Web store is to provide them with a variety of ways to pay for your product or service.

➤ It is guaranteed that you will experience an attempt to defraud you either sooner or later, so use a fraud detection process.

Fulfillment and Shipping

When I was a young lad growing up in New York, my buddy and I would trek down to our local mom-and-pop food store on the corner for groceries. The little old man who ran the small store had no cash register or receipt book—not even a shopping cart. You used a small basket that you would carry through the store filling it with your purchases. When it was time for you to check out, he would write the price of each item on the back of a brown paper bag, tally it up, and place your purchase in the same bag.

Although primitive by today's shopping standards, he provided all the elements that a Web store should provide today: a shopping basket, a checkout process, and a receipt. Even shipping was covered. You delivered the goods to your home yourself.

Over the last 40 years, the old mechanical cash registers gave way to computers with a drawer followed by laser scanners that feed information into a sophisticated database system that tracks pricing and inventory. The Net has evolved too. The few short years that eCommerce has evolved on the Net have seen three generations of the sales-enabling process. The current generation of eCommerce technology is called the shopping cart and often referred to as *storefront* or *store-building* software. We saw these in Chapter 8, "Hosting Your Store for Free." Using just a Web browser, you could add and delete products, change prices, run special sales promotions on certain products, and pick up your orders.

To fully automate the buying process, every shopping cart software solution requires the use of a credit card and the ability of the merchant to accept them. But taking and processing the order is one thing—delivering to a customer is quite another. So let's look at what's involved in taking, fulfilling, and delivering an online order to your customer.

Free Shopping Carts

You don't have to pay for a shopping cart on your Web store. There are dozens of free shopping cart programs that you can easily add to your site. Check them out at www.onlineorders.net/links/Free/.

The Shopping Cart

The first question to ask yourself is, "Do I really need a shopping cart software program to take orders on my site?" If you're selling only a few products in your Web store, you can probably get by with a simple Web page order form. But if you sell more than a few products or offer a service, making the customer switch back and forth from the order form to the product pages will drive him from your site never to be seen again.

So, if you sell a number of products that have a number of different variables connected with them, you need to install a shopping cart on your site. If you're going to do serious eCommerce, a shopping cart is essential. With the proper shopping cart software your customers will be able to

➤ Place an order on the same page that it's pictured and described. A simple Add to Cart button on each product or service catalog page gives your customers the convenience of choosing a product to buy, then letting them continue to shop your store.

➤ Select to buy more than one product at a time and choose different colors and sizes.

➤ Calculate and tally all the items in the cart at one time giving the shopper a running total of what's in his or her cart and what the charges might be.

➤ View the final order including all charges that will be made to their credit card including taxes, shipping, and handling.

When choosing a shopping cart package, be sure you answer these important questions.

Is the package easy to set up? Do you have to place it on your server (which will take some technical knowledge) or do you just "bolt it on" to your site (the credit card order is processed on the shopping cart provider's secure server)? How long does it take to set up the shopping cart? If it's through a service that bolts on to you Web store, then the process should take no more than an hour.

Can products be added and deleted easily and quickly? Does the shopping cart offer the option for different attributes for each product such as size and color? Do you have to manually retrieve your orders or are they faxed or emailed to you? Is the shopping cart connected directly to your credit card service and automatically processed or do you have to process the cards yourself? Will the shopping cart software compute taxes, shipping, and handling? Can it compute international shipping rates and tariffs? When the order is confirmed will it send out a confirmation email to the customer?

If you're using a shopping cart service, what about fees? Are they per sale, per item stored, or a flat monthly rate? Is their server secure?

Pick a Card—Any Card!

Here's an all-in-one site to view a large selection of credit card merchant accounts that you can review for your eBusiness. Check them out at www.onlineorders.net/links/ Credit_Card_Merchant_Accounts/.

Some of the better store-building products are reviewed by Sell-It at sellitontheweb.com. To go directly to the shopping cart reviews, head to sellitontheweb.com/ezine/features.shtml#carts.

Another good shopping cart service is MerchantChecks at merchantchecks.com. They charge a flat rate per month and also will sign you up for a credit card merchant account.

The Cash Register

The shopping cart or the shopping basket is only one of two parts of a shopping cart. The second part is the cash register. The shopping cart keeps track of and tallies the order; the cash register records, processes, and charges the customer's credit card.

Here's how it works.

The customer's credit card information is transmitted through a Secure Socket Layer (SSL) (like we discussed before) to your credit card processing agent. Any fully functioning shopping cart software must reside on a secure SSL server to protect the sensitive credit card information of your customers. If you are hosting through an eCommerce hosting service or are hosting yourself, it's essential that you take the customer's orders on an SSL server.

After your customer has entered his credit card information into your shopping cart's order form and clicks **Confirm My Order**, that information is sent from your SSL server to your credit card processing agent's server—or what's called, the *Payment Gateway*. The Payment Gateway, or credit card processing agent, performs a very important function. The agent is responsible for verifying the customer's credit card information and confirming that there are sufficient funds in the customer's account to cover a purchase.

What's a Payment Gateway?

The Payment Gateway verifies that a credit card is valid and that the cardholder has enough credit in his account to purchase the product he selected. A Payment Gateway is just an agent and does not verify that the card is stolen or being used by someone other than the cardholder.

The Payment Gateway then passes this information on to your bank, which then contacts the customer's credit card issuer that approves or denies credit. This notice is then passed back down the chain to the Payment Gateway and then to you.

For you to accept credit cards and have the customer's card charged to your account thereby collecting your money, you must establish a Merchant Account at a bank. Establishing a credit card Merchant Account can be tricky and fraught with problems if you don't do it right. In addition, there are thousands of what are called field agents that aggressively recruit small merchants into Merchant Account programs that sound great on the surface but have hidden costs that can drive up the costs of accepting credit cards.

Setting Up a Merchant Account—The Rules

You must be very careful when choosing a Merchant Account. If you choose incorrectly, the costs incurred on each and every credit card sale you make could dramatically affect your bottom line.

Rule 1: Know the Fees   Setting up a Merchant Account and the processing of a customer's credit card has certain fees associated with it. It's not done for free. By not knowing what the required fees are, you can make a mistake that will cost you extra money on each and every credit card sale you make.

So, what's it going to cost?

Read the Fine Print

Many credit card field agents use fraudulent tactics to get your business by advertising a ridiculous rate like 1% to clear credit cards, and then you find out that it is 1% on top of 3% from the bank and additional percentages from the Payment Gateway. Make sure you get all the information before signing up for a Merchant Account.

First, there's the Merchant Account setup fee. This can run from a few hundred to a thousand dollars. Most Merchant Account set up fees are in the $400–600 range.

The second fee is what's called the discount rate. Using the word discount makes it sound like you're getting a deal. It's not. This is the percentage of the sale that your Merchant Bank will charge you on each credit card charge. For example, if your customer has purchased $100 in merchandise from you and you're going to charge his card $100, you will have to pay your Merchant Bank a percentage of that sale to process the customer's credit card.

This percentage can range between 2% and 3% for Visa, MasterCard, and Discover and 3% to 5% for American Express. So if your discount rate for a Visa card is 2%, your Merchant Bank will take 2%—or $2—of that $100 customer purchase and deposit the remainder in your bank account. And by the way—that percentage is on top of the total credit card charge—including shipping and handling.

The third fee a Merchant Bank might charge you is a transaction fee. This fee is in addition to the discount fee and is the charge that your Merchant Bank assesses to process the credit card sale. Expect to pay between $0.25 and $0.70 per transaction.

And the fees don't stop there.

Your Merchant Bank might require you to pay a monthly statement fee on top of all the other fees. Statement fees range between $10 to $15 a month. You also might be charged a minimum processing fee of up to $25 a month. This fee is usually waived if your credit card sales meet your Merchant Bank's minimum monthly credit card sales. There also might be a holdback for charge-backs. Your bank might want to hold a sizable deposit against your sales to cover any charge-backs that you incur.

What's a Charge-Back?

A *charge-back* is what your bank does when they reverse a charge on your customer's credit card. Reasons for this include fraudulent or unauthorized use of the customer's credit card or just dissatisfaction with your product and you've refused to take back the product and issue a credit to their account.

Do you have to pay all these fees?

That depends on the Merchant Bank you choose. The credit card business is very competitive and now that eCommerce is the hottest thing in business, many banks are aggressively lowering and even eliminating fees to attract eBusinesses. There are hundreds of credit card programs available to eTailers today and if you do your research, you'll find Merchant Banks that will not charge statement fees, minimum monthly processing fees, or even setup fees. But you have to take the time and make the effort to look around.

Get at least five price quotes. You can find a free impartial listing of Merchant Account Providers and their primary rates and fees at MerchantWorkz at MerchantWorkz.com (see Figure 16.1). Another place to check is the Payment Processing links of About Electronic Commerce Guide Gordon Whyte's site at ecommerce.about.com/shopping/ecommerce/msub10.htm. He has a very comprehensive list of credit card payment processing sites and Payment Gateways.

And don't be afraid to push these providers into a bidding war. With a little research and planning, getting a merchant account can be painless and inexpensive. It also can protect you from less-reputable providers who know they can make a quick buck off a new Web merchant who's new to the game of accepting credit cards.

Finally, you might have to pay additional fees for purchasing hardware or software to send your credit card sale information through the Payment Gateways to your Merchant Bank. That's why it's important to choose a Payment Gateway/Merchant Bank Package.

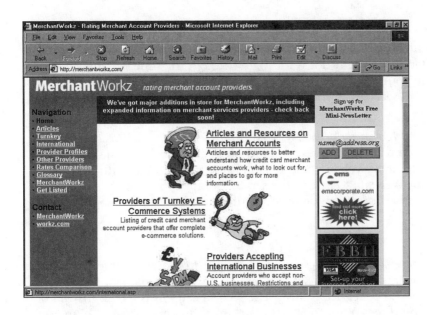

Rule 2: Choose a Payment Gateway/Merchant Bank Package   Don't try to save money by choosing a Payment Gateway that does not have a standing relationship with a Merchant Bank.

Unless you're a financial genius or someone who enjoys the pain of making separate online systems work together, choose a Payment Gateway and Merchant Bank that already work together. In reality, when you choose a Payment Gateway, your Merchant Bank is already chosen for you. You might not get the best price from the Payment Gateway's bank, but you will save yourself a lot of time and expense trying to integrate two systems from scratch. Use Rule 1 as a guide to ensure that you're getting a square deal.

Directory of Payment Gateways

eCommerce Guidebook has a good list of prominent eCommerce companies that provide Payment Gateways for online transactions. Find it at www.online-commerce. com/directory.html.

So look for a Payment Gateway/Merchant Bank Package where the Payment Gateway has prearranged the credit approval system and payment system of a Merchant Bank for you. Pick a package that works with all major credit cards and your account will be credited directly by the Payment Gateways Merchant Bank. Also, remember to find out how funds are deposited in your account. Some Merchant Banks will send a monthly lump sum to your bank, and others will pay on every transaction as it happens.

Do I Need My Own Merchant Account?

If you have a small site, or are on a limited budget or just want to dip your toe into the eCommerce waters, you might not want to go through the time, trouble, and expense of setting up your own merchant account. You can still accept credit card orders for products and services at your Web store just like the bigger sites—and do it securely.

There are a number of Web sites on the Net that offer to process credit cards for you for a flat fee. There are no setup charges, no hardware or software to install, and no monthly minimums to meet. When your customers are ready to buy, you simply direct them from your Web site to one of the service company's secure Web pages. After there, your customer inputs his credit card information and buys your product or service.

So, what's the catch?

First of all, most of these companies accept only credit card orders for information or services. If your online business sells a service, a piece of downloadable information, or software, then this type of service is ideal. The second catch is the fees. Instead of paying merchant account fees of up to 5%, these companies charge fees as high as 10% to 15% of your credit card sale.

One such service company is ibill (ibill.com). They make online sales of intangibles such as access to subscription sites, content, or services easy for merchants who do not qualify for, or want to acquire, a merchant account. Their fees start at 15% and go down to 12% depending upon the volume of your sales.

ccBill (www.ccbill.com) is a similar service to ibill. They also process only credit card sales for services, subscriptions, and downloadable information. ccBill fees vary depending on the volume of sales done during each accounting period. These fees are never more than 14.5% of revenues charged during a one week period. Both of these companies handle all billing inquires and customer service problems relating to them.

ABANX (abanx.com) is a little different from iBill and ccBill. In addition to accepting payment for services and information, ABANX accepts payment for product. ABANX provides your Web store with a centrally located shopping cart system, real-time secure SSL encrypted checkout servers, and handles the majority of billing inquiries including the necessary accounting. Using their Client Administration Interface, you're able to manage your account with ABANX, view any new orders, place refunds, and view your account statement.

ABANX collects 12% of the total amount charged to the customer. There are absolutely no startup costs, no monthly fees, or any other charges to utilize their service.

So, the choice is yours. Either way, you can take and process credit card orders on your site, which is essential to the success of your Web store.

Choosing a Fulfillment Partner

You're making sales and getting tons of orders—but how do you fill them? Your eCommerce site is more than just a catalog and shopping cart that lets your customers choose products and purchase them using a credit card. True, the *e* in eCommerce means electronic, but until the day comes when transporter rooms like in *Star Trek* arrive, you'll still have to move those atoms from a warehouse to your customer's front door.

So the question is, "Who's going to do it?"

Will you have your own warehouse filled with inventory and a staff of shipping and receiving people? Or do you outsource this to a third-party service? My advice is not to go it alone. Though you might have dreams of being the next Amazon, you have to walk before you can run. Outsourcing your receiving, shipping, and handling makes fulfillment and distribution simpler and more efficient—especially for a small to medium size eBusiness. In addition, outsourcing enables you to focus on your core business—selling product. Having to both market and fulfill product will only divide your attention.

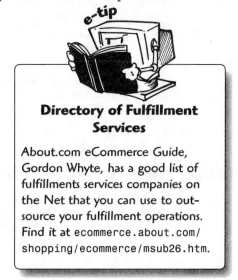

Directory of Fulfillment Services

About.com eCommerce Guide, Gordon Whyte, has a good list of fulfillments services companies on the Net that you can use to outsource your fulfillment operations. Find it at ecommerce.about.com/ shopping/ecommerce/msub26.htm.

Besides, you can always bring fulfillment in-house after your sales and staff get large enough to support a warehousing and shipping operation.

So, how do you choose a third-party fulfillment service? What are the things to consider? They are

➤ **Warehousing**   Find out how large their warehouse is. How many different companies can they service? Do they have an efficient way of separating your company's merchandise from others? It's a very good idea to visit a fulfillment house and check out how their warehouse is laid out and physically see where your merchandise will be stored. Will they charge you for the storage space that your products occupy? How much? Find out how many orders a day they're capable of shipping. Will your business requirements put a strain on their daily shipping capabilities? How much of their shipping capabilities will your business eat up?

➤ **Fees**   How will they charge you for their service? Most fulfillment houses will charge you a setup fee, a monthly management fee, and a pick-pack-and-ship fee. Ask if receiving of your products is included in the monthly management fee or is it an extra charge. If so, is the extra charge based on a per-box basis or a per-hour basis?

➤ **Integration**   An important question to ask is how will they receive orders from your Web store and how will they send their shipping and receiving reports to you. You might ask if the fulfillment house can seamlessly integrate their system into your Web store. The ideal scenario would be this. Your Web store takes the order and sends all the shipping information to the fulfillment house electronically. The fulfillment house fulfills the order and sends a shipping report back to you electronically. Barring that, you might have to collect the order information offline and email or fax the orders to the fulfillment house. In turn, they might have to email or fax you back offline when the products are shipped. Either way, you'll need to know when the product is shipped, what shipping carrier was used (UPS, FedEx, US Post Office), and the tracking number to email to your customer.

Finally, ask about insurance. Are they fully covered for fire, theft, and flood? Make sure that your products are insured while in their care.

Using Your Suppliers for Fulfillment

You don't have to go through the process of finding and negotiating with a fulfillment house to ship your goods. You might be able to eliminate the middleman. If you're buying from distributors or directly from the manufacturers of your product, you might be able to convince them to drop-ship their products to your customers.

Don't Ship It—Drop-ship It!

You should ask whether your product supplier will ship your orders for you instead of warehousing them yourself. This is called drop-shipping. By having your suppliers ship your orders to your customer, you can save a bundle on warehousing and shipping costs for yourself and pass the savings to your customer.

This is a good solution if you don't want to invest your money in inventory and pay storage and fulfillment fees to a third-party fulfillment house. That's how many large eTailers started their business. Take Amazon as an example. They worked directly with the major book distributors who dropped shipped books to Amazon customers.

There's another advantage to having a drop-shipping agreement with your distributors. Because you're not actually buying and warehousing inventory, you can list on your Web store every product that your distributors sell without actually buying them.

This gives shoppers the impression of a much larger store than you have. In addition, you might be able to negotiate a better deal from your distributors. Because you're a customer and it's their goods you're selling, they see you as more of a partner and might charge less for fulfillment than a third-party fulfillment house.

The Tax Man Cometh

It's said that a statesman is a dead politician. And Lord knows we need more statesmen. In the meantime we're stuck with the politicians we have and our wonderful wags in Washington have now taken up the issue of the Internet sales tax.

Currently, Congress has declared a moratorium on taxing Net sales to study the issue. This moratorium will not last forever so you should consider how you'd be collecting taxes on sales made at your Web store. Although the task sounds daunting—collecting taxes for 30,000 existing taxing jurisdictions—there are some solutions if Internet tax legislation is passed.

Two companies are working on a Web-based tax calculation system that they plan to make available to small to medium sized eBusinesses. Both will provide to eBusinesses a tax server that acts like a central data repository for small to medium sized businesses. Taxware at taxware.com will provide a tax server that will charge by the transaction with charges as little as $25 a year. Another tax software vendor, Vertex at vertexinc.com also is considering a Web-based approach.

If Internet tax legislation is passed your Web store will have to charge city, county, and state taxes. So you should prepare for this eventuality. Stay up to date on what's developing on the Net sales tax issue at webcom.com/software/issues/0sii-tax.html (see Figure 16.2).

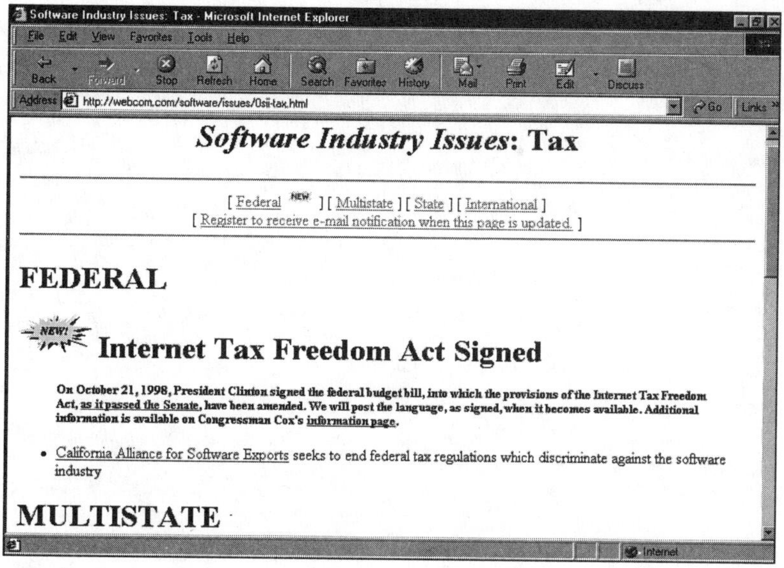

Figure 16.2

As a Web merchant it's important to stay on top of what is happening on the Internet sales tax front. The Software Industry Issues site will keep you up to date.

The Least You Need to Know

➤ When choosing a shopping cart service, check for usability, fees, and security.

➤ The shopping cart keeps track of and tallies the order; the cash register records, processes, and charges the customer's credit card.

➤ You must be very careful when choosing a Merchant Account. If you choose wrong, the costs incurred on each and every credit card sale you make could dramatically affect your bottom line.

➤ There are a number of Web sites on the Net that offer to process credit cards for you for a flat fee.

➤ Outsourcing your receiving, shipping, and handling makes fulfillment and distribution simpler and more efficient.

➤ If you're buying from distributors or direct from the manufacturers of your product, you might be able to convince them to drop-ship their products to your customers.

Chapter 17

Customer Service

In This Chapter

➤ Learn the important elements of customer service

➤ Discover the ways to handle disgruntled customers

➤ Learn how good service, satisfaction guarantees, and the proper handling of returns can increase your business

The quickest way to eCommerce failure is not delivering on what you promise. Your promise to your customers is a good product or service, at a fair price, delivered promptly. But your responsibility to the customer doesn't end there. What you do or do not do after the sale determines whether your customer returns and buys from you again.

Here's another important point. It's five times more expensive to get a new customer than it is to keep an existing one. So, growing your eBusiness includes not only attracting shoppers to your site, but also keeping the customers you have. You keep a customer by providing good customer service. Customers—even potential customers—need to know that you care enough about their business to service them when they have a problem.

In the wide world of eCommerce, customer service can spell the difference between success and failure of your eBusiness.

Service Elements—It's the Customer, Stupid!

We've talked a lot about making your Web store customer-friendly and easy to use. If your site seems difficult to buy from, a shopper will move on to your competitor. But good site design, an easy-to-use shopping cart, quality products or services, the speed of your site, and your selling price are all for naught if the quality of your customer service is below par.

An investment in good customer service is one of the best customer-retention investments you can make. And customer service strategies should be applied at every stage of the purchasing process.

Good customer service is not offered just after the sale. Good service is everything that takes place before, during, and after the sale. Wouldn't you rather influence shoppers to buy when they're considering making a purchase and not just when they're ready to buy? Then, after the sale, wouldn't you want the ability to bring them back again to your site for repeat purchases? A well planned out customer service strategy or online "help desk" can accomplish all of these.

So how do you build good customer service into your Web store? Easy. Walk a mile in your customer's shoes. Ask yourself, "What kinds of service would you expect before, during, and after a sale?"

Customer Service Starts Before the Sale

Picture this. A first-time visitor comes to your Web site. He or she came with a shopping list in hand and the thought of making a purchase. What can you do to make this first-time shopper feel comfortable enough to buy from you?

Here's what.

Create a First Time Visitor icon and place it very visibly on your home page. It's a great way to welcome new visitors and give them a feeling that help is just a mouse click away. The icon brings them to a First Time Visitor Web page that contains a brief description of the customer service that they can expect when they buy from your Web store. OfficeMax has a good example of a First Time Visitor page (see Figure 17.1).

For instance, provide your customer service email address, toll-free customer service phone number, fax number, and your customer service hours. Include your customer satisfaction guarantees and return policies. Tell them how their order will be handled—how fast their order will ship, how you will confirm their order, when it's shipped, and how to track it after it's shipped. Also, provide a link to your FAQs—Frequently Asked Questions—about your products and services and tell the shopper that you have a secure site where they can use their credit card without fear.

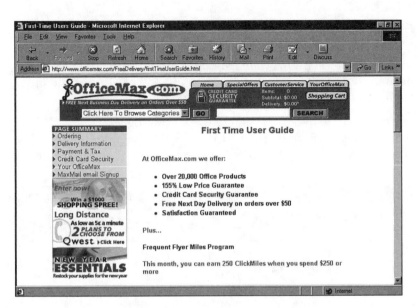

Figure 17.1

OfficeMax invites the First Time Visitor with a User's Guide to their site.

Finally, direct them to the fastest way to place an order on your site such as a list of specials for first time customers or the product or service directory page of your Web store. If you have a product or service search function on your site (if you have lots of offerings—you should), include this on the First Time Visitor page.

If executed properly, your first time visitors will get a nice warm and fuzzy feeling about your Web store and feel secure enough to make that first purchase.

Now, let's look at some other types of customer service elements that you can provide to encourage a shopper to make a purchase. They are

➤ Customer Care FAQs

➤ Dedicated email

➤ Discussion boards

➤ Guarantees and warrantys

Get Your Free Search Engine

Need a search engine for your site? Don't want to pay a lot for it? How about free? Matt Wright's Simple Search Engine gives your site a search engine that can search up to 300 Web pages or so on your site. Find it at www.worldwidemart.com /scripts/search.shtml.

Customer Care FAQs

Customer Care FAQs (Frequently Asked Questions) can be used to list the most common answers to customer service questions that a shopper might have. They not only list in an easy to understand way your customer service policies, but also list the most common customer service problems and how you will solve them.

A company with a plug-and-play help desk is Right Now Technologies at www.rightnowtech.com (see Figure 17.2). Its product is an online help desk that builds a database of questions already asked by customers.

Figure 17.2

Right Now Technologies helps you automatically build a database of questions and answers that are then made live and searchable.

Customer Care FAQs let shoppers answer questions by themselves all in one place. Ask yourself—would you like having to visit one area of your site to learn about a product, then another to buy it, and a third to see how long it will take to ship? Of course not. So place all this information in your Customer Care FAQs.

The easiest way to start building a Customer Care FAQ is to ask yourself what questions would a customer ask most often? Just frame a simple answer for each question and you have your FAQ. Not only will this benefit the shopper but it also will save hours of phone support.

Dedicated Email

When the FAQs are not enough, email comes to the rescue. A dedicated email address for customer service is a must for your Web store and is one of the easiest ways to provide online service and support for your customers. Set up at least one email address for customer questions such as support@*yourbusiness*.com. You might even consider setting up several email aliases to extend your customer care services.

What's an Email Alias?

Email aliases are additional email addresses that point to another email address. All messages sent to an email alias are automatically forwarded to the specified "real" email address. This way you can have more than one email address on an email account.

With email aliases, you can forward customer email to the appropriate person or department in your company. This way you can create different email address for different customer concerns and problems. For example, you can create a separate email address for general customer questions, product questions, order status, and product return requests.

Keep in mind, that receiving the emails is only half the task. You must answer them, too—and answer them in a timely manner. Shoppers and customers expect to have their email answered within 24 hours—at the latest! So check your email regularly throughout the day.

A simpler and easier way for your shoppers and customers to ask questions of you is to provide a Web-based form for each area of concern that when filled out, emails the information to you. The benefit here is both to the customer and to you. With a specific Web-based form for each customer service problem, you can request the type of information that you'll need to more quickly address your customer's questions and concerns.

Discussion Boards

Here's another customer care strategy. Why should you do all the work? Let your customers ask questions to each other. By offering a discussion board on your site, you can give customers and potential customers a way to discuss your product or service with other users.

In addition, you can pick up valuable market research from the comments posted there that can help you design better customer care policies, choose better products, improve

Automate Your Email

For faster customer response compose a series of brief email replies to each of these common questions so you can respond quickly to email inquiries.

your service offering, and build a loyal customer base. This will help build a strong online community (one of the 3 Cs of eCommerce, remember?) on your site. You can even solicit customer feedback and advice, giving your customers the impression that you care about their needs and are willing to make changes to your policies and improve your offering.

Reward Your Customers for Good Advice

Why not reward customers who give you good advice for improving your customer support? Their feedback is the best you can get—and worth it. Hold contests or award rebates on future purchases for the most helpful advice.

Guarantees and Warranties

One of the best ways to build customer confidence in your Web store is to tell the shopper of any product or service warrantees and your satisfaction guarantee.

If you have a satisfaction guarantee (and you should), let the shopper know that right up front. Put it on your First Time Visitor page and in your Customer Care FAQs. To be blunt, you should offer nothing less than a 100% customer-satisfaction guarantee on all the products and services you sell. These guarantees come in three types:

➤ **100% Satisfaction guarantee** Customers must be 100% satisfied with their purchase. If not, they should be able to return the product within 30 days of receipt for either a full refund or a credit on a future purchase.

➤ **100% Product warranty** If your products carry a manufacturer's warranty, say so. If not, consider replacing the product yourself.

➤ **100% Price guarantee** Guarantee that your customer will not find your product or service at a lower price at another Web site. If they do, offer to refund the difference in price.

Consider using one or more of these guarantees to build customer confidence in your Web store and to make more sales.

Serving the Customer During the Sale

Servicing the customer during the buying process is just common sense. You want to remove as many sales objections as you can to allow the shopper to make a buying decision. Right? So, you have to think ahead. Two of the best ways to make a customer comfortable with a purchase at the point of sale is to provide real-time stock status and shipping time information.

If a customer knows the stocking status of a product and when it would ship, you will eliminate many of your customer service problems. Amazon does a very good job of informing the potential customer of what books are in stock and within what time frame they will ship. Keep in mind, that what you promise on, you must deliver. So, if you find that a product offered by a customer is not in stock or if shipping of the item will be delayed, be sure to contact the customer immediately and inform him or her when the product will be shipped.

Sometimes stock status and shipping time estimates are not enough. There are times at the point of purchase when the customer needs additional information to make the sale. This is where live customer care becomes important.

You can offer free live customer support using ICQ at www.icq.com/download/, Yahoo Instant Messaging at messenger.yahoo.com, or AOL's Instant Messenger service at www.aol.com/aim/. Shoppers can download the free desktop application and communicate with you real-time if they have a question.

There are a number of new technologies that enable you to place live customer support right on your Web site that customers click to get in touch with a real live human by phone or by online chat. Services such as LivePerson (see Figure 17.3) at www.liveperson.com offer a pop-up chat box that allows instant customer contact with a real person whereas ActiveTouch by WebEx at corporate.webex.com/about.shtml lets you communicate in real-time with your customers using just your browser and a phone line.

Figure 17.3

With just a click of a button, LivePerson opens a small chat window on your site where customers can chat with a customer service agent and ask questions.

Another service is Instant Call at www.instantcall.com.

When a site visitor clicks the **Instant Call** button on your site, Instant Call phones you and the customer and links the calls for instant communication.

Service After the Sale—The True Test of Customer Care

You might say that service after the sale is where the rubber hits the road. You've spent a lot of time, money, and energy getting the sale—now you have to keep it.

Online customers are a skittish bunch. No matter how comfortable you've made them in buying form your Web store, after that buy button is pressed, they still want to be secure in the fact that their order has been actually received and that their product has been shipped.

To sooth the customer's concerns about an order and to eliminate many email messages to your customer service department, be sure that you send a real-time instant order confirmation to the customer as soon as the order is placed. The order confirmation message should include an order number, what they bought, where it will be shipped, and the total amount of the order including all shipping and handling charges and applicable taxes.

After their order is shipped, another email confirmation should be sent with relevant shipping information and order status. If for some reason, you cannot ship within the time promised on your site, then send an intermediate email keeping the customer informed of the status of his order and when it might ship.

Help Your Customers Track Their Shipment

Here's a good customer service idea. Provide a link on your site to the multitracking shipment Web site at www.fedexground.com. From this site, your customers can track their shipment through more than a dozen different shipping companies including FedEx, UPS, USPS, Airborne, DHL, and a host of smaller carriers.

After the order has been shipped and enough time has elapsed for the customer to receive it, send another email asking if they did receive it and if there were any problems with the order. This proactive approach to customer service will pay off in spades. It shows that you do care about your customers and that you are willing and able to correct any problem that they might have had. In addition, if they respond to your follow up email, some customers might write you a good testimonial that—with their permission—you can print on your Web site.

Finally, despite the best efforts of your customer service strategies some customers are disappointed in the product they bought and want to return it. It's important that you have a no-hassle return policy. Remember, your prime goal is to keep the customers you have so you will have to weigh the return of a product or a refund on a service in light of how valuable your customer is to keep.

Sometimes returns are a blessing in disguise. Okay. Not blessings, but useful for your business. Most times customers will give you their reasons for the return and this information is good feedback on a particular product or the manner in which you sell from your sight. Collecting all the returns data and adding it to your customer service requests will help you identify merchandising problems and opportunities.

Handling Disgruntled Customers

The old adage goes, "A satisfied customer tells no one. A dissatisfied customer tells ten of his friends." And on the Net, a dissatisfied customer can tell thousands of other consumers about a bad shopping experience. But, like product returns, customer complaints—if used correctly—can be a valuable resource that you can turn to your advantage. They can give you valuable insight into problems with your selling process. Accept each complaint for what it is—a chance to learn.

First of all, answer each and every complaint promptly and politely. Before answering with a solution to a customer's complaint be sure that you understand the problem and be as specific as possible in your replies. If the customer is frustrated and complaining, expect the tone of his or her message to be angry and confrontational. That doesn't mean you should be. Respect your frustrated customers and reply to them in an empathetic tone.

But don't stop there.

If you've not received a reply, follow up with the customer to make sure his or her concerns have been addressed by you. This additional email will show the complaining customer that you are willing to come to a mutually agreeable solution to his or her problem. If a customer sees that you are willing to work with him or her, this will go a long way in resolving the issue.

Just remember that every complaint, no matter how illogical, should receive a reply. Your best efforts could turn a complaining customer into one of your best.

Remember that good service is essential and is a promise you make to your customer. So, don't make any promises you can't keep.

Pay Your Customers to Complain

Even negative feedback is useful in running your business. Sometimes it's better than positive feedback. So, run a "Complaint Contest" to elicit feedback on your site and service.

The Least You Need to Know

➤ Good customer service is not offered just after the sale. Good service is everything that takes place before, during, and after the sale.

➤ Customer Care FAQs (Frequently Asked Questions) can be used to list the most common answers to customer service questions that a shopper might have.

➤ A dedicated email address for customer service is a must for your Web store and is one of the easiest ways to provide online service and support for your customers.

➤ Two of the best ways to make a customer comfortable with a purchase at the point of sale is to provide real-time stock status and shipping time information.

Part 5

Promoting Your Online Business

"Build it and they will come." That was the message in the movie Field of Dreams. *But, if you think that all you have to do is build your Web store and customers will flock to your door—you're just dreaming.*

Rising above the din of the World Wide Web with tens of thousands of eTailers vying for a shopper's attention might seem like a daunting task. But have no fear! There are dozens of ways to market your products or services—many of them free—that can drive traffic to your Web store.

So, put on your marketing cap and learn the many ways of promoting your eBusiness to the World Wide Web.

Chapter 18

Marketing Your eBusiness

In This Chapter

➤ Discover how to optimize your site for search engines

➤ Learn the grass-root techniques of Guerrilla Marketing

➤ Discover how to create repeat visitors to your Web site

➤ Learn how to protect your Web store's online reputation

Congratulations! If you've followed me this far, you have one of the best little Web stores on the Net. Unfortunately, odds are that no one has ever heard of it. In fact, too many eTailers work on the assumption in the movie *Field of Dreams*: Build it and they will come.

They won't.

After your Web store is built, you have to give customers a reason to come. That takes marketing—and the right kind. Your Web site is a passive form of marketing that points shoppers toward your products or services. You can't stop there. You must create a marketing plan using a set of active tools that will drive traffic to your Web store.

You've probably heard that registering your site in as many search engines as possible will result in millions of visitors streaming to your new Web store.

It won't.

Start Your Marketing with a Free Sample Marketing Plan

At Bplans.com you can find sample marketing plans that match your business. It takes only five minutes answering a few questions and, voilá—you have a marketing plan that you can build on. Find it at bplans.com/marketingplans/.

Yes, search engines are important, but that's where you start your marketing efforts—not end them. There are literally millions of Web sites on the Web all vying for the Web surfer's attention. You'll have to go beyond them if you are to have a successful marketing plan. To paraphrase Thomas Edison, "Success is 99% perspiration and 1% inspiration". To succeed, persevere and be prepared to sweat!

Now, there are many books written on how to market on the Internet (*The Complete Idiot's Guide to Online Marketing* is one of the best—hint, hint!) and any large bookstore will carry dozens of them at any point in time. But all the marketing advice from all the authors in these books boils down to two marketing objectives.

➤ Make your site visible to consumers on the Web.

➤ Give them a reason to come—and then come back.

Let's take a look at each one.

Hello! Here I Am!—Letting the Web Shopper Know You Exist

Making your site visible to the consumer is your first challenge. So the first question you need to ask yourself is, "How will I get consumers to visit my site?" Let's face it; rising above the din of the Web is a daunting task. But like solving any problem, breaking the tasks down into small pieces greatly increases the odds for success.

Using each of the following marketing strategies one at a time will greatly increase the exposure of your Web store and it's ultimate success.

➤ Search Engine Optimization
  • Placing your store properly in search engines
➤ Grass-Roots Marketing
  • Exchanging links and banners with other sites
  • Registering your Web store with online promotion services
  • Using the Internet newsgroups and discussion lists
  • Using viral marketing

We'll start with the major search engines and optimizing your Web site for them.

Search Engine Optimization

Registering your site at the major search engines is your first and most important step in marketing your Web store. Although there are hundreds and hundreds of search engines, directories, and yellow pages that you can register your site with, you should register your site first with these major search engines.

Be Careful with Free Site Submission Services

Although free site submission services such as SubmitIt! (submit-it.com) provide a way to submit your site to approximately 15 of the most important indexes, be aware that this is a cookie-cutter approach. Because just one submission must be basic enough to fit within the guidelines of all the search engines, you're not able to take full advantage of the differences each have to offer. For example, one engine might allow 75-word descriptions, but you'll have supplied only 25 words to the free submission service.

➤ altavista.com
➤ excite.com
➤ goto.com
➤ hotbot.com

➤ infoseek.com
➤ lycos.com
➤ webcrawler.com
➤ yahoo.com

All these sites search the Web in one of two ways. Either they're a directory such as Yahoo! that searches its own database, or they search actual Web pages looking for keywords residing in the page itself.

There are two recent additions to the search engine world that search the Web a little differently. You also should register with these new search engines. Google! at google.com uses text-matching techniques to find pages that are both important and relevant to a search. Google! keeps track of which pages actually get chosen when presented in a search result. The next time that keyword is searched on, it remembers which pages were selected by the user before and presents those pages high on the search results list. Direct Hit at directhit.com is a similar site that ranks search results according to what other people have selected as the most relevant and popular sites for their search request.

Optimize Your Site for Search Engines

Virtual Stampede will help you build and email to you meta-keyword, description, and title tags that you can cut and paste into your Web pages. It doesn't promise that you'll appear in the top of the search results, but the code it does send you is generic enough for the top search engines. Find it at `virtual-stampede.com/tools.htm`.

There are other places to submit your site that you should consider, such as Associate-It (`www.associate-it.com`). It has a list of the 10 best places to promote your site (see Figure 18.1).

Figure 18.1

Associate-It gives you a list of the 10 best places to promote your site.

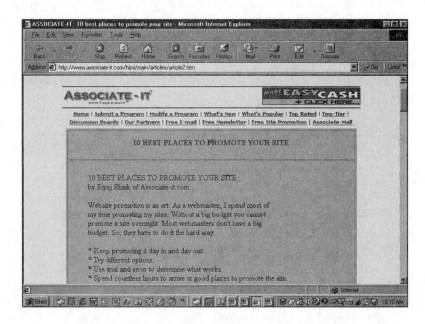

Registering your Web site at the major search engines is relatively simple. The challenge is making your site appear at the top of the search results list when a shopper searches for an eTailer that sells your products or services. To accomplish this feat, you have to optimize your site for the major search engines.

Optimization is more art than science because each search engine uses different search rules. But there are some key things you can do to ensure that your Web store does not come up as site number 1,000 in a search results list. Now, there are many books and online services that claim to guarantee top placement in the major search engines if you use their tricks and services. But the search engines regularly change the ways they search the Web, so many of these tricks do not hold true for long.

If you really want to learn the current tricks of the search engine trade, then visit Search Engine Watch at searchenginewatch.com.

Whatever your choice, you need to know the general basics of how search engines search the Web. As I said before, search engines fall into two basic groups. Some search their own database, such as Yahoo!, and some search actual Web pages looking for keywords residing in the page itself, such as AltaVista. This means you have to know how to register with a search engine directory, such as Yahoo!, and what search engines, such as AltaVista, to look for.

Are You Listed in the Search Engines?

Some search engines make it easy to confirm that your Web page is in their catalogs. With others, it can be more difficult. Here's a way to find out whether your Web pages are listed in the major search engines. Check out the URL checking information along with many other useful tools at Search Engine Watch, searchenginewatch.internet.com/webmasters/.

To optimize for both, you have to keep the following in mind.

Page Titles, Keywords, and Your Web Pages

It's very important that you take care when creating the title, description, keywords, altags, and the first paragraph of your Web pages. The search engines in one way or another will read this text and use it to return a list of search results to the Web surfer making a search.

Don't make the mistake of creating a page title that's good for people but bad for the search engines. Don't use a title for your page such as "mySoftware Store—We Sell Computer Software." With a title like that, you're asking to be overlooked by the search engines. Keep this rule in mind: All your most important keywords must be in the title tag. Make a list of all the keywords that describe your Web store and create a title tag that uses them with the most important words first.

A good title tag for your page would read:

> <TITLE>Productivity software for business and home office use—selling word processing, spreadsheet, database, and presentation software including utilities and accessories—mySoftware Store, your store for business productivity</TITLE>

Notice that your company name is near the end of the title tag. Why? Your page description will probably be truncated by the search engine, so you want your most important information on what you offer upfront.

Another reason for all this verbiage is that the three most important places to have keywords and phrases are your title tag, your metatags, and your first paragraph. You want them to all contain the same important words because this will improve your ranking in a search result. Why? Because all these keywords in all your tags increases your keyword density and improves your rankings.

Now let's look at your metatags.

Don't Forget Your Alt Tags

When placing graphics on your Web page, include a text alt tag for each graphic. An *alt tag* is a small text description of the graphic included in the HTML code with the graphic that the search engines can read when searching your Web page. Search engines can't read a graphic so an alt tag is important. Another advantage of alt tags is that they increase the keyword density on a page.

The metatags are important to getting a good ranking in the search results. Metatags come in two flavors—the description metatag and the keyword metatag. The description metatag is a brief description (about 100–200 characters) of what's on a Web page.

The description metatag looks something like this:

> <META name="description" content="Productivity software for business and home office use—selling word processing, spreadsheet, database, and presentation software including utilities and accessories">

The other metatag is the keywords tag. Create a set of keyword phrases that explain your page or site and list them in the metatag separated by commas.

A good resource for choosing the right keywords is GoTo.com. You can use its service at `inventory.go2.com/inventory/searchInventory.mp` to see how many times a particular keyword has been searched on. This can help you choose keywords for your site that will drive more traffic to your store.

After you have your keywords, turn them into key phrases. Don't repeat a key phrase, and don't repeat any individual keyword more than five times or so. The reason for this is that many of the search engines will penalize you for doing this.

Here's an example of a keywords metatag:

> <META name="keywords" content="productivity software, word processing, accounting software, spreadsheet software, productivity tools for business, home office computer software, virus protection, modems, surge suppressors">

e-tip

Where Do You Rank in the Major Search Engines?

To find out how well your site is positioned with the major search engines, use a service called Position Agent, which will show where you're coming up in the various search engines. Get a free trial at `positionagent.com/free.htm`.

Finally, pay attention to the first paragraph of the Web page you are registering with the search engines. The first paragraph of your Web page should duplicate and expand upon everything in your title and metatags. Make sure the first paragraph has all your key phrases in it. Turn those keywords, key phrases, and title into a welcoming message that will make a good first impression on the consumer visiting your site.

Grass-Roots Marketing

After you've prepared your Web site for the search engines and carefully registered with them, your thoughts now should turn to promotion. Your first question is probably "How can I make a big impact on the Net—fast?" The Web is filled with sites such as ZenithMedia (`zenithmedia.com`) that can point you to useful sites to market your Web store (see Figure 18.2).

Keep in mind that unless you have substantial resources (or happen to be a relative of Bill Gates), promoting your new eBusiness takes a lot of hard work and time to see results. So make the most of your time with these basic grass-roots marketing strategies to launch your eBusiness.

Promotion does not mean advertising. So, before you go out and spend a bundle of money advertising, start your marketing first on a grass-roots level. This gives you a chance to find out what works best for your eBusiness and what doesn't before you put your limited resources toward a full-fledged marketing plan.

Figure 18.2

ZenithMedia will direct you to the most useful sites for marketers on the Net.

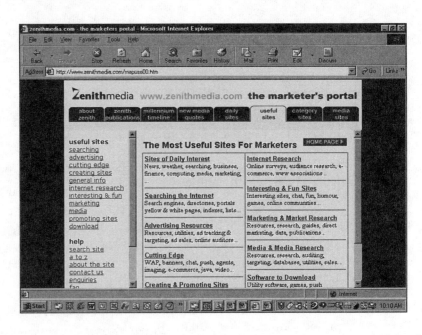

What the Net Is Saying About Your Business

Every day hundreds of thousands of messages are posted on the various news-groups around the Net. Some of those messages might be about your eBusiness. To find out, go to DejaNews at `Deja.com`. Another absolute must for eBusiness is NetWatch at `www.netwatch.ca`. It will search for specific keywords—such as your company name or your competitor's name—in more than 280,000 newsgroups. And NetWatch will email you within hours if one of your keywords appears in any of the newsgroups on the Internet.

Swapping Links and Banners

After registering your site with the search engines, the first grass-roots marketing initiative should be to search for sites that will link to you and vice versa. Swapping links can come in two ways.

> ➤ **Reciprocal linking** Placing links on your page to complementary product sites that, in turn, place links to your site on their page.

(`catalog.com/vivian/interest-group-search.html`) is another site packed with discussion lists to join and TileNet (`tile.net/lists/`) will point you to newsgroups in just about any subject area.

Don't Get Flamed!

It's very important to remember that the newsgroups and discussion boards are *not* advertising vehicles. You cannot post blatant ads on the boards. If you do, you will get flamed—that is, others will respond with negative comments about you and your eBusiness. So don't risk it.

Finally, although you can't blatantly advertise your Web store on the lists and groups, you can still get your Web store some visibility by creating a good sig file.

A *sig* file—or a signature file—is a text tag that you can place at the bottom of the emails that you send out. When you participate in an email discussion group or post to a newsgroup, your sig file can be attached to your message. Created properly, a good sig file can attract shoppers to your Web store. In reality a sig file can act as a small promotional message at the end of each and every posting that you do.

The trick, of course, is to create a compelling sig file. Do this by creating a brief 4–5-line statement that describes a specific benefit your product or service provides, why that benefit is important to your target customers, and why they should respond to you now. It's cheap, fast, and it works.

Viral Marketing—Spread a Cold: Catch a Customer

Let's face it. The best kind of marketing is the kind you don't have to do yourself— especially if you're a small business on the Web with a limited advertising budget. Viral Marketing is like it sounds—call it word-of-mouth, spawning, self-propagation, or organic.

Viral marketing has been around forever. Spreading the word through word-of-mouth was the world's first form of marketing. But the Internet has taken this organic form of marketing to new heights by making communications better and communities of people tighter—thus making word-of-mouth even more effective.

So, how do you spread the word of your Web store virally on the Net? Motivate your customers and visitors to do it. Here's how.

➤**Tell 'em Sam sent you**   Reward your steady visitors for bringing new visitors to your site. Create a special referral program that your steady visitors can sign up for. Have them invite their friends to visit and if they do, have them mention the referrer's email address and the referrer earns something free from your site.

Get Your Visitors to Market You

Here's a good idea to spread the word about your Web store. Ask visitors who like what you offer to email your URL to a friend along with his comments. Place a form on your Web site that can be filled out by visitors and emailed to any address they enter. If you want a free service that does this and is easy to place on your site, check out Recommend It! (recommend-it.com).

➤**Got any good jokes lately?**   I don't know how many times I've forwarded jokes or scam and virus alerts I received in my email to friends and associates. So, create a funny newsletter or an email alert that someone would pass on to friends.

➤**Take my site, please!**   This is similar to "Got any good jokes lately," but in this case you give away your best assets. Don't just send out a notice about new content on your site—send out summaries by email and ask people to forward them on (with copyright and URL attached, of course). A variation on this is to let other sites reprint your content on their site, with appropriate credits and links to yours.

The challenge is to exercise some control over how your message is delivered and how others perceive it. But when you master this technique, your message and your site can spread as quickly as the common cold.

Finally, don't expect a Viral Marketing program to pay off immediately. Like a real virus, viruses don't become epidemics until they reach critical mass. Your virus must propagate through the host population until it reaches a certain threshold of visibility and scale.

Think of it this way. Suppose a real-world virus doubles every year. In the first few years it's scarcely detectable. But within a few years after that it suddenly becomes an epidemic. You should understand that you're playing the same game. Viral Marketing takes time. So be patient, be fruitful—and go out and multiply!

The Downside of Viral Marketing

A downside to Viral Marketing is that you're letting others do your marketing for you. Although this will save you money, your message and your brand are in the hands of someone else. There's a fine line here between spreading the word and diluting your brand. A good example of negative branding as a result of viral marketing is the spam mail that you receive from friends and family. If you've been on the Web any length of time, you could have received emails promising that if you send an email to everyone you know, you will receive a free case of Coke or a trip to DisneyWorld.

Creating Consumer Flypaper—Attracting Shoppers to Your Site

After you have the consumers' attention, you have to bring them to your site. So, your next challenge is to give shoppers a reason to come to your store in the first place—then give them a reason to return. To attract visitors to your site, you have to promote not only your products or services and your unique selling position, but also give the consumer a reason to visit your Web store right now! Auto-HomePage (auto-homepage.com) offers software that creates an auto home page for customers that gives them news feeds, a reminder service, and other services that return them to you Web site (see Figure 18.4).

The marketing strategies to attract consumers to your site fall under two groups. These are the ways to attract Web consumers to your site and keep them coming back.

➤ Promotional Announcements
  • Continually announce special seasonal, event and, limited time promotions.
➤ Loyalty Programs
  • Build loyalty programs to keep shoppers coming back.
  • Conduct surveys to find out what your customers want and need.
  • Attract visitors to your site by giving away something free.
  • Establish a free email newsletter.

Armed with this list of simple but powerful marketing strategies, you can give your Web store the success it deserves.

Figure 18.4

Auto-HomePage offers software that creates an auto home page for customers that gives them news feeds, a reminder service, and much more.

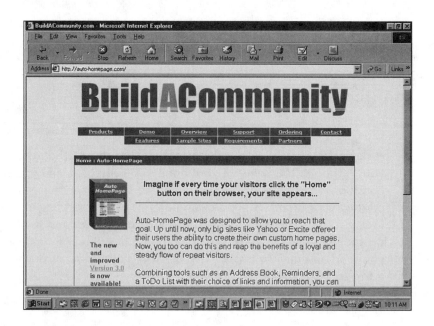

Promotional Announcements

A great way to get shoppers to your Web store is to offer them a timely product or service. Better yet, have them tell you when they would be willing to shop.

First, design your product or service offering around seasonal promotions. Use the major holidays such as Christmas, Hanukah, Easter, Valentine's Day, Father's and Mother's Day to design special sales and promotions to draw shoppers to your site. Then give the shopper who visits your site a chance to tell you when he or she would like to be contacted with offers from your Web store.

Offer shoppers a reminder service. Allow shoppers to enter the details of any event they want to be reminded off, such as a birthday or anniversary. Send this reminder to them via email along with a link to your Web store with products that are made to order for the event they are reminded of. Another idea is to send shoppers at your site an email when a selected product or service they are interested in changes in your store—such as perhaps a price drop or a special limited time sale. We will cover this service in further detail in Chapter 21, "Contests, Give-Aways, and Shopper Services."

In all your promotions, try and give away something a shopper might value. It could be something as simple as a free piece of information that a shopper might find useful. With your promotion, inform him that he can find this free information on your site and send him to that page on your Web store. You might even offer a trial size of a product or a small piece of the service you offer.

If you sell software, offer a shopper a free demo to download from your Web site. If you offer a cooking course, give him the first lesson free.

You could tie these free offers to a customer survey asking the shopper a series of questions that lists his interests and helps you market to him in the future. But surveys can be tricky. It's a well-known fact that the more information you ask people to fill out, the fewer people will complete the form. But there is a way to collect as much information as possible without having the shopper bolt for the mouse button and abandon your survey.

Ask for the information in stages.

First, ask for his email address to receive the free offer. After he enters his email address and hits **submit** and your server has recorded it, direct the shopper to a second page that has a form that asks for more a little more information. After the shopper hits **submit** on that page, direct the shopper to another page and another form to gather further information. Thank him for his help and offer another form on another page.

At each step you'll lose people who won't complete the additional information, but you'll get many who will fill out more information than they would have if you had asked for it all at once. And besides, you will at least have their email address to send them promotional material in the future.

Kibitz with Other eBusiness Owners Like Yourself

The Net can be a lonely place and business owners often talk to other business owners to exchange ideas and get advice. So check out the message boards at BizWeb200. They provide a free forum to discuss issues directly related to Internet marketing. Find it at bizweb2000.com/wwwboard/.

And it goes without saying that you will tell the shopper that his or her information will be kept in the strictest confidence—right? Remember your privacy guarantee?

You can program your own surveys, but that takes some programming skills. An alternative to that is to use one of the survey services on the Net. Zoomerang (zoomerang.com) is a free Internet service that enables businesses to easily conduct surveys using simple to use templates. Another service is ClickToSurvey (clicktomarket.com). ClickToSurvey's service is not free—costs start at $200 per survey and 50 cents a response—and you can set up a survey form right on your site in few minutes.

Loyalty Programs

Getting good responses on your promotional activities is great. But a response is not a relationship. And you get that with loyalty programs. Loyalty programs also are known as incentives, membership clubs, frequent buyer programs, and rewards programs.

How important can a loyalty program be to your eBuinsess?

Jupiter Communications wrote that 56% of online consumers would buy more often if awarded loyalty points. The Harvard Business Review stated that companies could boost profits by nearly 100% by retaining just 5% more of their customers and that cutting defections in half can more than double a company's growth rate.

As you can see, a well-run loyalty program can be of great value to a new eTailer.

A loyalty program can help you identify loyal customers, and a good loyalty program at your Web store can accomplish a number of marketing objectives. First, giving incentives to new shoppers can get them to purchase from your Web store. Second, a loyalty program encourages repeat business. Finally, with a loyalty program, you can track and build customer profiles with every customer transaction associated with your rewards program.

A loyalty program entices shoppers to become customers and then encourages them to purchase more often by offering rewards. Customers are encouraged to buy more by earning points, which they can redeem for special promotions and free products. You can set up a loyalty program yourself—but why bother. There are several good ones already available on the Net that you can join and will perform all the administration tasks necessary to run the program.

Get a Plan, Man!

To stay on top of your marketing, you need to have a marketing maintenance plan. Sell-it-on-the-Web provides you with an Online Marketing Maintenance Plan that's easy to follow and important for you to do. It outlines the marketing tasks you need to do on a daily, weekly, monthly, and quarterly basis. Find it at sellitontheweb.com/ezine/opinion034.shtml.

Beenz

www.beenz.com

Beenz is a new form of Web currency. Your eBusiness can reward shoppers with Beenz for filling out a survey, registering to receive your newsletter, or even each time they buy a product or service from you. Shoppers can "spend" their Beenz on movies, gift certificates, travel discounts, music, and more.

MyPoints

www.mypoints.com

myPoints has more than 200 direct marketing partners, including 1-800-Flowers, Barnes & Noble, Target, Olive Garden, General Cinema, Blockbuster, and CBS Sportsline. It has created a bevy of practical and easy-to-redeem rewards, such as gift certificates. Their Web-based interface enables you to control your own Point awards on your site. Shoppers earn Points from all participating merchants across their network.

NetCentives

clickrewards.com

NetCentives offers its ClickRewards, where shoppers at your site can earn ClickPoints redeemable for frequent flyer miles on 10 major airlines, hotel stays, car rentals—even merchandise.

CyberGold

www.cybergold.com

CyberGold differs from the other loyalty programs by actually rewarding shoppers with cold, hard cash that is conveniently deposited into their checking account.

The Least You Need to Know

➤ All marketing advice boils down to two marketing objectives—make your site visible to consumers on the Web, and give them a reason to come and then come back.

➤ Use metatags to get proper placement in the search engines.

➤ Seek to exchange links and ad banners with other sites.

➤ Use viral marketing to get your customers to market you to their friends and family.

➤ Create and use a loyalty program to get shoppers back to your site and to buy again.

Chapter 19

Speaking the Language of Net Advertising

In This Chapter

➤ Learn the alphabet zoo of Net advertising

➤ Discover the different ways you can advertise your Web store on the Net

➤ Learn how to place banner ads on banner networks

➤ Learn the difference between direct email advertising, newsletter advertising, and eZine advertising

➤ Learn how to measure your ad strategy

A marketing plan provides a strategy to find and attract customers, and advertising is one of the tactics to do it. Unlike some aspects of marketing, advertising is going to cost you. So it's important to know how and where you spend your limited advertising buffet. For that, you have to understand what Net advertising is and how to do it properly on the Net.

Paid advertising is a necessary evil and is used to maintain and increase awareness of your eBusiness, introduce new products, generate new customers, offer special programs, grow market share, and penetrate new markets. The advertising vehicles available to you to promote your site are

➤ **Banner Ad**   An electronic billboard or ad in the form of a graphic image that resides on a Web page.

➤ **Newsletter Advertising**   Placing your promotional ads in electronic newsletters that are emailed to a base of subscribers.

➤ **Direct Email Advertising** Sending your promotional message directly to individuals via email.

➤ **eZine Advertising** An eZine is an electronic magazine that is distributed to you via email. You subscribe to it like any real-world magazine.

So, what will it cost?

Most marketing experts agree that you should devote 3% to 8% of your annual sales to your total advertising and promotional budget. But before you pull out your wallet and get ready to spend ad dollars to advertise, you should first know how to speak the lingo of Net advertising.

The Language of Net Advertising

Like a bunch of eager bunnies, Internet advertising has split, combined, and multiplied into a bewildering array of approaches to advertising on the Web. Using abbreviations such as CPM, CPC, CPA, CPT, and CPS make the novice Net advertiser's eyes glaze over when he sees this alphabet soup of Net advertising jargon. If this is you, don't feel bad. You're not alone.

Everything You Wanted to Know About Banner Advertising

For a good series of articles on banner ads and banner ad networks, check out Wilson Web at wilsonweb.com/webmarket/ad.htm

So, let's go through, step by step, this seemingly incomprehensible zoo of letters. Let's define them and see how using each of them can make the best use of your Internet advertising dollar. There's a New World out there for advertisers on the Net. Accountability is the word and today's Net delivers it in spades—not just audience estimates like in the real world. When you advertise on the Net, you know exactly how well your ad campaign is doing by the number of impressions, click-throughs, and responses (read sales) that you get from your advertising.

Impressions are correlated with awareness or brand advertising. You count impressions by how many times your ad is presented to a viewer. If the intent of your advertising campaign is to raise awareness of your product, service, or brand, then the number of impressions per dollar is of prime importance—that is, you want the most impressions you can get for the lowest ad dollar.

Click-through, in response to an ad by a consumer, simply indicates interest or intent. After he or she clicks your ad or goes to a URL that you've advertised in an email message or newsletter, click-through provides you with an opportunity to offer something for sale or even complete a sale. Other uses include filling out a survey or asking the viewer to take some other kind of action. Look at a click-through like a potential buyer opening a direct mail envelope to read the offer inside. The better the ad, the more potential it has to be acted on. If your intention is to have the viewer click your ad or go to your site, then the number of clicks—or visitors to your site—per ad dollar is of prime importance.

A *response* is indicated by either providing leads for future sales or the sales themselves. A response also could include the downloading of a piece of software. If your objective is to actually make a sale or have the viewer complete an action, then the number of responses per ad dollar is of prime importance.

Now let's see how impressions, click-throughs, and responses play out in the alphabet soup of Net advertising.

CPM or Cost per Thousand Impressions

You want to get the best bang for your ad buck, right? So knowing about CPM—or cost per thousand impressions—is important.

CPM is the number of times your ad is viewed. Another way to say it is the number of eyeballs that see your ad. When you buy based on CPM, you're paying each time a consumer views your ad. Click-throughs to your site and sales are not your prime objective here. Brand or image awareness is. Compare it to the FedEx or UPS commercials on TV. They don't want you to take action right then and there, but to have you remember them when you're ready to ship something.

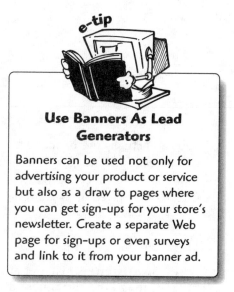

Use Banners As Lead Generators

Banners can be used not only for advertising your product or service but also as a draw to pages where you can get sign-ups for your store's newsletter. Create a separate Web page for sign-ups or even surveys and link to it from your banner ad.

You calculate CPM in this way. CPM is the total ad cost divided by the total possible impressions—or eyeballs that see your ad—in thousands. The lower the CPM, the lower the cost to reach your audience. For example, an ad that costs $5,000 and is seen by 100,000 people will have a CPM of $50.00 (5,000 divided by 100). The ad is costing you $50.00 to reach 1,000 viewers of a Web site or receivers of an email message or newsletter. Today, CPMs can run as low as $3 or as high as $75. Run of site ads have a lower CPM than ads that reside on targeted pages of a Web site. For example, if you sell sporting goods and buy a banner ad on Yahoo! that appears every time someone does a search on sports, that will carry a higher CPM than if your ad appeared randomly across the whole Web site.

CPC or Cost per Click

Impressions are good for branding or making shoppers aware of your eBusiness. But if you want to pay only for consumers who actually open your ad and view it, then you want to buy advertising based on CPC—or cost per click.

CPC is the number of times your ad is clicked or how many people actually go to the URL you are advertising. Your objective is to have them "open your direct mail envelope" and view your offer. Currently, you can expect anywhere from about a half of a percent to a 3% click-through rate on a CPC ad. The rate depends on how strong your offer is to the consumer.

Keep in mind that consumers on the Web are bombarded by literally thousands of ad messages every day in the form of banner ads, email promotions, and ads in newsletters that they subscribe to. Like you and I, consumers have developed a subconscious filtering system to filter out most of these ads. So you have quite a difficult time rising above this din of advertising.

Banner Ads Can Take Orders, Too

You can actually use banner ads to take orders directly in the banner by using rich media. Rich media banners have a built-in order area, expandable order forms, and even secure server technology to protect credit card transactions. Check out Enliven at www.enliven.com.

How can you even up the odds?

➤ **Consistency** First of all, you must run your ads enough times to break through the consumer's awareness level. Most advertising experts claim that you must run the same ad at least three times in the same place before it begins to register with your audience.

➤ **Visibility** There are a number of factors that can influence the impact of your ad and get the consumer to "open it." First is the size of your ad. If you're using a banner ad, then obviously larger ads have more impact. Where the banner ad is placed on a Web page also affects an ad's impact. Having your ad appear "above the fold"—being seen as soon as the page loads without scrolling down to see it—is important for visibility.

CPA, CPT, and CPS

The last group of abbreviations in this advertising alphabet soup is CPA, CPT, and CPS. All three of these fall, more or less, under the same umbrella. Using these schemes you are paying only for an actual response to an offer, not just a view or click-through.

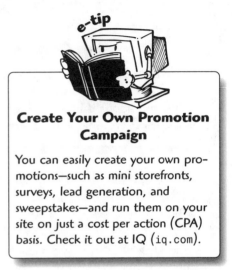

Create Your Own Promotion Campaign

You can easily create your own promotions—such as mini storefronts, surveys, lead generation, and sweepstakes—and run them on your site on just a cost per action (CPA) basis. Check it out at IQ (iq.com).

➤ **CPA (Cost per action)** This is the number of times the desired action takes place on your site, such as a sale, a registration, or a download. Here you want to pay only for those people who actually take action. They've viewed your ad, clicked it, and responded by actually buying something or downloading a piece of software. You can expect normal direct mail response rates from 1% to 3% of those who respond to your ad. If your offer is targeted and on a targeted site, the response could go as high as 5%, 10%, even 25%.

➤ **CPT (Cost per transaction)** This is the cost per lead. This type of banner ad is similar to CPA but you are paying only for those people who click your banner ad and either fill out a registration form or are sent to a page on your site where they can view the full offer.

➤ **CPS (Cost per sale)** Like CPA, you are paying only for leads that generate a sale.

Not every one of these approaches is perfect for everyone. You need to decide what type of action you are willing to pay for, and then negotiate your best deal. Just as there is room on the Web for more than one successful business model, what might suit one content site might not suit another, and what might suit one advertiser might not suit another.

It's good to keep in mind that the number of sites are accelerating on the Web and there is now an overabundance of sites and ad serving companies that are selling ad space. There is literally a glut of ad space on the Web. So be patient. Check out each opportunity against the objectives of your ad campaign. And remember that what might work on one site—impressions or responses—might not work on another.

Advertising Strategies and Placement

The first step in designing your ad campaign is to define your customer. You need to be very specific about the age, gender, marital status, geographic location, religion, political affiliation, occupation, educational level, and so on so that you can buy the proper ad placement.

251

Pay Only for Visitors to Your Web Store

Using the search engine at www.goto.com you pay only for shoppers who go to your site. GoTo gets paid only when a visitor actually clicks the listing. They are very open about this as the cost charged to the advertisers is listed with each entry. Most are only a few pennies a hit.

If you're selling games for children, you don't want to advertise on a site or in a newsletter that sells apparel. So, knowing your customer is of prime importance. The more accurate you can be in defining your most likely customer, the easier it is to refine your message and select the appropriate media to reach them.

Speaking of refining your message, identifying your customer's specific wants and needs is necessary to write the proper copy to get them to act on your message. Sure, you sell computers. But different people use computers in different ways. Do you craft your advertising message to consumers who need a computer for the home, their business, or just to surf the Web? Your customers' different wants and needs will dictate the message you send them.

Finally, be sure that your ad message includes who you are, what you do, and why the consumer should buy from you. Then tell them what they should do next—the call to action—if they are interested in what you are selling.

Now you're ready to buy those ads. Here's how.

Banner Ads and Ad Networks

The first advertising tool to consider in promoting your Web store is the banner ad. A banner ad is like a small billboard that resides on a Web page . The standard full-size banner ad is 250×80 pixels. But even though almost every ad-supported site sells the full-size banner ad, less than 20% of them rely on that alone. At least half of these offer several smaller sizes—usually 120×60 and 88×31. Because of their size and the limited room for your message, it is no surprise that the smaller banner ads are 1/2 to 1/3 lower in cost than the full-size banner ad.

It's a Banner Debate

The debate of the effectiveness of banner ads continues to this day. For the latest on the debate check out AdAge, the authority in advertising at adage.com; AdWeek, the other authority on advertising at adweek.com; and Fast Info, a newly formed association of advertisers, advertising agencies, and others to determine a standard on Internet advertising measurements at fastinfo.org.

How's the availability of banner ad space?

Currently, there is a glut of banner ad space on the Web. In fact, most available banner ad impressions on the Web go unsold. And this situation is unlikely to change for many years, as page views are being created at a much faster rate than new ad spending. So you should be able to buy ad space on most second-tier Web sites for much less than the standard $25 CPM that is asked of today. A small number of large, prominent, and/or special types of sites like Yahoo! and others in the Top 100 Media Metrics traffic report continue to charge high CPMs.

Reduce Your Cost of Advertising

Another way to reduce your cost is to buy ads as ROS (run of site). If you're not looking for specific locations or targeting within a Web site, you can run your banners ROS. With ROS buys, your banners can appear anywhere on the site wherever there is available space.

Computing and Technology and Reference and Education sites charge between $50 and $60 CPM. Business and Finance and Shopping and Auctions charge $40 to $50 CPM. Automotive, Comics and Humor, General News, Home and Garden, Society, Politics, and Sports and Recreation sites charge $30 to $40 CPM. Games, Kids and Family, Movies and Television, Music Portals, Search Engine, Travel, and Regional/Local sites can charge $20 to $30 CPM. Community sites and Yellow/White Pages sites charge $10 to $20 CPM.

If you buy in volume or offer a larger time commitment, you can reduce these charges significantly. Or, instead of trying to lower your overall cost, ask whether the site would be willing to offer you bonus impressions or a free sponsorship of their email newsletter. If you can get some of these add-ons, they might provide you with an opportunity to test that ad vehicle without an additional outlay of ad dollars.

Buying banner ads from individual sites is one way to get your message out. Another is to buy ads on a Banner Network. About.com Guide for Advertising Online at `adsonline.about.com/business/adsonline/msub6.htm` has a good list of interactive ad networks that you can place your banner ad on (see Figure 19.1).

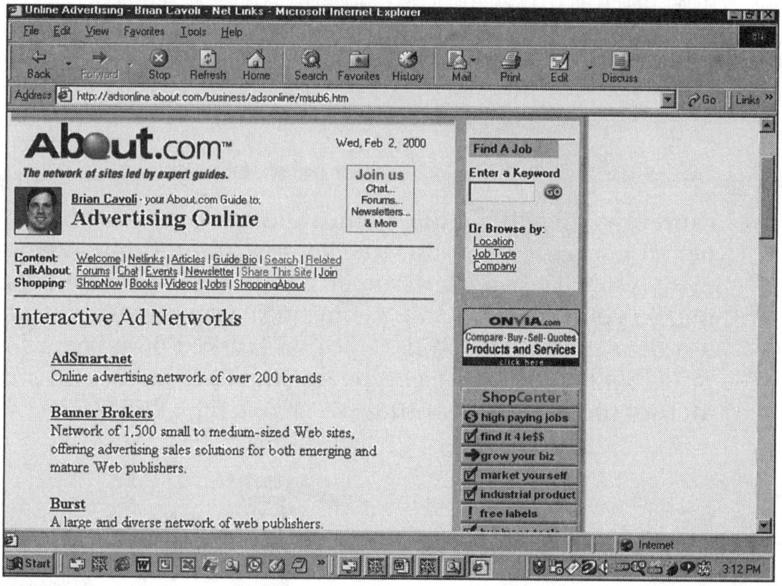

Figure 19.1

If you're looking for a list of advertising networks, check out the NetLinks from Brian Cavoli's About.com Guide for Online Advertising.

Opt-in Email Advertising

Crafting your own message and emailing it to a list of prospects is one of the most cost-efficient ways to advertise. But if you're not careful and don't do your home-work, it could be one of the most costly advertising mistakes you can make. Direct email can be very effective if you know your target market and can find an opt-in emailing list that closely matches your customer profile.

First, be sure that any email list that you rent is an opt-in list. People hate unsolicited email. This is spam, and your offer and your business will leave a bad taste in their mouth. By renting opt-in lists only, you know that the people on those lists have asked to receive email offers in a particular category. This also is helpful to you because you can target your offer and send it directly to those prospects who would be willing to "open" your offer when they receive it.

Direct Email Should Catch the Eye

When sending out a direct email piece, do not use the words FREE or BUY NOW in your message. This is a sure way to get your email message sent to the trash bin. Take the time to explain your offer without the hype. And remember to play up benefits—what's in it for the customer—and not features.

Next, consider the format of your email.

Use ASCII text only. The majority of people who use email have email readers that can read only text. So sending out emails with hyperlinks and graphics embedded in the message could make it unreadable. Keep your message simple and short. Deliver your most important information up-front. People don't have a lot of time, so you have to grab their attention in the first few lines of your message.

People scan the subject lines of their emails first. So, make the subject line your headline. If it's compelling, they'll open your message.

Remember to include a lot of white space in your messages. Be careful with CAPS. Don't overuse them in your message. Make your pitch easy to scan and read and remember to use wide margins—64 characters or less per line. This helps make your message readable with many different email programs.

Finally, before you roll out your email campaign with full list, test your message first by testing one element of your message at a time. Test the subject line or headline. Select a test set of names and see what the response is from your test sample of emails. Then test the body of the message, the layout—even the P.S. at the end.

After you've determined what works, then send your message to the full list.

Both PostMaster Direct at postmasterdirect.com and CopyWriter at copywriter.com/lists provide opt-in email names to use in your direct email advertising campaign (see Figure 19.2).

Figure 19.2

PostMasterDirect offers thousands of opt-in email lists that you can use to send your promotional message to.

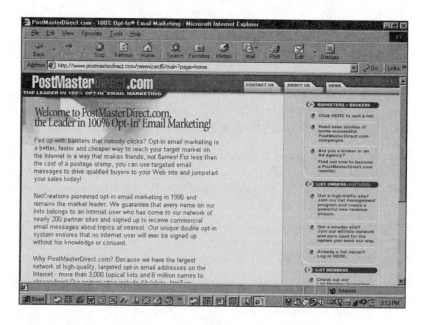

Advertising in Newsletters and eZines

The cyberworld has its equivalent of the printed media of the real world. They are the email newsletters and eZines (electronic magazines). These two media are great places to target your advertising message. There are thousands of newsletters you can advertise in and hundreds of eZines, each focusing on a particular market niche.

Why advertise in an email newsletter or eZine? Why not just stick with advertising on Web sites? Studies show that the average Internet user returns to only 5 to 10 Web sites. To get a better "mind share" of the consumer, you need to send your message to where the customer lives—his or her email box. People who subscribe to newsletters and eZines have specifically asked to receive them. Because of this, your advertising message will be better received.

So how does it work? The most common form of advertising in a newsletter or eZine is the *text flag*. Text flags are featured bits of copy, about five lines or so, which rest amidst the larger content of a newsletter or eZine. They are usually set off from the rest of the text message by lines (=) or stars (*) like this:

```
=====================================================
SATISFIED CUSTOMERS???
Ever wonder what site visitors are saying about your site behind
your back? We can tell you!
From content to commerce to community.
cPulse ^ The (free!) Internet Satisfaction Monitor.
http://www.cpulse.com/default.asp?ref=IC2
=====================================================
```

Two good places to find newsletters to advertise in are PennMedia (`pennmedia.com`) and OakNet Publishing (`oaknetpub.com`). Penn Media offers newsletters in the network that get read such as daily jokes, daily quotes, daily golf tips, and many more. You get up to 50 words for your ad and all advertisements are included in the body of the newsletter. OakNet Publishing offers more than 90 newsletters reaching more than 3.2 million readers in the areas such as Internet and Computing, Family, Kids and Education, Entertainment and Hobbies, and Travel.

Advertising in eZines targeted to your types of customers is another way to reach your specific audience. List City has the Book of eZines (see Figure 19.3) at `list-city.com/ezines.htm`, which is a database of advertising contact information and rates for hundreds of eZines on the Net. And if you publish an eZine, you can join its Advertising Exchange Directory that consists of listings of eZines interested in advertising exchanges.

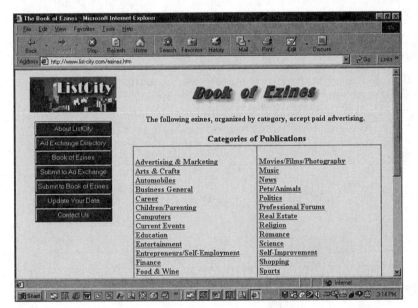

Figure 19.3

The Book of Ezines has contact information and advertising rates on hundreds of eZines.

LifeStyles Publishing at `lifestylespub.com` offers an eZine Broadcast Promotional Package that broadcasts your message thousands of times across targeted eZines for one special pricing. And for a list of all eZines around the world, visit E-Zine-List at `www.meer.net/johnl/e-zine-list`. It currently lists more than 4,000 eZines that you can review.

Measuring Your Ad Strategy

There's a story about a businessman lamenting about his advertising campaign. He said, "50% of my advertising doesn't work. I just don't know which 50%." The bad news is that an advertising campaign does cost money. The good news is that advertising on the Net is easy to track. With the proper tools and strategies, you can see right away if the dollars you're spending are paying off in traffic and sales.

But before you can start measuring the results of your advertising strategy, you need to know what to measure. And what you measure are hits, visitors, and page views.

First, you need to understand the difference between *hits* and *visitors*. When someone claims that they get 100,000 hits on his or her site each day, that does not mean that they get 100,000 visitors. A hit on a page consists of two things—text and graphics. A Web page is most often made up of two elements—the copy on the page and any graphics pictures or images. A hit counts each individual graphic, picture, or image on a page plus all the text on that page.

So when a visitor opens a Web page that has text and three images, it counts as four hits. One for all the text on the page, and one for each image.

The entire page, regardless of how many hits it represents, is counted as one *page view*. A shopper can view any number of pages when he or she visits your store. So one visitor could view several pages in one visit. If you have 100,000 hits a day, and those hits equal 10,000 page views, and if each visitor views an average of 10 pages per visit, you would have approximately 1,000 visitors a day to your Web site. Pretty good numbers if you can get them.

Use Doorways to Track Ad Campaigns

If you're running more than one ad on the Net, a good way to track the results of each one is to create separate Web pages—or doorway pages—on your Web site. Each doorway page has a unique URL that is not accessed through your normal site navigation. You can then create a doorway page for each ad that you are running on the Net—one for each different banner ad, one for each direct email campaign, and one for each newsletter or eZine ad you place.

But approximate numbers of visitors is not good enough. If you really want to measure your advertising efforts, you need to know the exact number of visitors to your Web store that your advertising has generated. In addition, you want to know not just the number of visitors that visited your site but the number of *unique visitors* who came to you site.

A unique visitor is a person who comes to your site only once during a particular span of time. For example, a shopper might visit your Web store, and return two or three times during the day. The shopper made two or three visits to your store, but counts as only one unique visitor. You could set the time between visits to any period you want—per day, per week, or per month. So 50,000 visits to your Web store per month might represent only 10,000 visitors.

Obviously, when evaluating your advertising, you want to know how many unique visitors are driven to your Web store and if they buy. The more unique visitors who are sent to your site through advertising and the more sales that are made from these visitors, the better spent was your advertising dollar.

All well and good. But how do your track these visitors to your site?

That depends on how much you want to pay for tracking software for your site and what you want to track. A quick and easy way to track the number of visits to your site is to place a counter on your home page or the page that your advertising has directed the shopper to. Yahoo! lists a number of sites where you can get a counter for your Web site. Go to Yahoo! at www.yahoo.com and type **access counters** in the search field—you will get a list of access counter sites (see Figure 19.4).

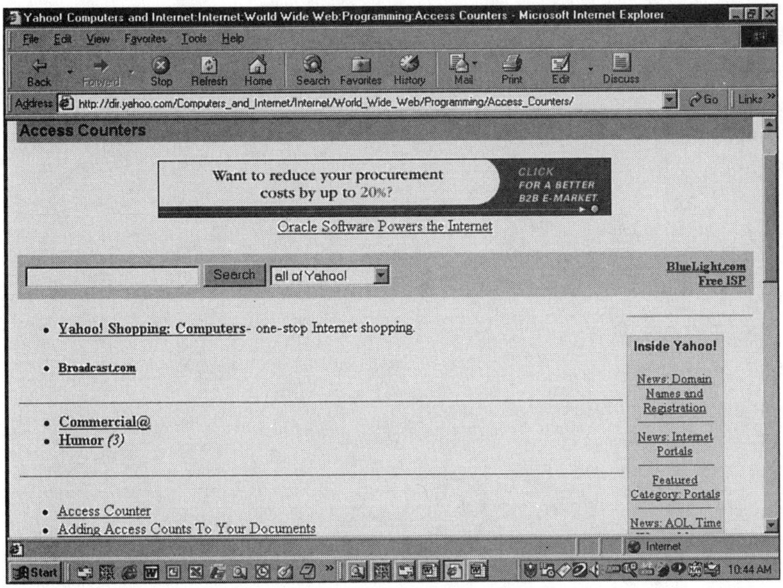

Figure 19.4

At Yahoo! you can find a list of Access Counters that track and analyze your site traffic.

Keep in mind that these counters record only the number of visitors to your page—not the number of unique visitors.

To do some serious analysis of your site traffic and to see how well your advertising dollars are being spent, you need a professional site traffic-tracking program. Many of these can be found again at Yahoo!

The Least You Need to Know

➤ You can measure your ad campaign by tracking the number of impressions, click-throughs, and responses (read sales) that you can get from your advertising.

➤ Any advertising message you create should include who you are, what you do, and why the consumer should buy from you. Don't forget the call to action.

➤ Be sure that any email list you rent is an opt-in list. People hate unsolicited email.

➤ To evaluate your advertising campaign properly, you want to know not just the number of visitors who visited your site but the number of unique visitors who came to your site.

HERE WE ARE!

Chapter 20

Promoting Your Site for FREE!— From Meatspace to Cyberspace

In This Chapter

➤ Learn the free ways to promote your Web store offline

➤ Discover the online ways to list your site on multiple search engines and indexes for free

➤ Discover how free classified ads can promote your Web store online

➤ Learn how participating in communities on the Net can help promote your Web store

➤ Learn how to get others to market your Web store for free

Advertising costs money. There's no way around that. But there are a lot of ways—and I mean a lot of ways—that you can promote your site for free.

Sure, the Big Dogs who inhabit the Web with their bloated advertising and marketing budgets pose a real problem for your company's visibility. But your bark can be heard above those of the Big Dogs, and you can do it without stretching your limited financial resources to the breaking point.

Before spending money on marketing, use the Internet marketing vehicles that are free. Free is good. And unless you're a small business owner who has a spare million or two lying around, or your brother-in-law is Bill Gates, making use of the free marketing opportunities on the Net can help stretch your marketing and advertising dollar.

Spending your time and not your money will help you maximize your Web visibility and traffic and stay within your marketing budget. If you spend your time wisely and follow these strategies, you can go a long way in giving your site the visibility it needs.

So, let's get started.

Meatspace—Start in the Real World

Before you venture into the online world of free promotion, you should start with what can be done offline to assist in the promotion of your business Web site. Most times these promotional vehicles can be done with little or no additional expense.

First of all, spread that URL of yours around. You burned the midnight oil thinking up a cool URL that tells the world who you are and what you do. Good. Now, it's time to tell the world!

Attract More Traffic to Your Site—from Traffic!

Okay, so it's not free. But for $29.95 added to your advertising budget, you can get your URL viewed by hundreds of people a day. Osworth Consulting and Marketing sells a custom URL plate for your car or truck that complements the chrome detailing on any vehicle. The letters are bold and stand out. They are easy to read, even at highway speeds!

Find it at `freetips.com/url_plates/`.

Before you reach for your mouse, make sure you sprinkle your URL on every stitch of printed material that leaves your office. And this includes your company's email address, too. Place both your URL and your company email address on all literature, business cards, letterheads, invoices, and the like. This is a great source of free publicity. So, get into the habit of putting your URL and your main email address on all these materials after your Web site is up.

Next, let the world know that you exist.

This also includes both the Yellow Pages and Business White Pages. If the NBA, CBS, and Disney can do it—so can you. Also, if your business uses a POS (Point of Sale) packaging and/or display (such as at trade shows) you need to incorporate your URL and main email address on them, too.

And remember. There are no additional costs to these free marketing strategies if they occur in the normal process of advertising, reprinting, or maintenance. So use them!

Listing Your Site—Getting the Word Out

In Chapter 18, "Marketing Your eBusiness," we talked about registering your Web site at the major search engines and how to prepare your Web pages for it. We also talked about swapping links and banner ads with other Web sites.

But there are other places to get your site listed that should not be ignored. And most importantly—they are free! The major search engines aren't the only places that should list your Web store. There are many listing services that cater to your particular business niche. There are also promotional opportunities that you should take advantage of that could give your Web site a quick "shot in the marketing arm."

And finally, spreading the word far and wide that your site exists using free multiple listing services won't hurt either. So make sure you list your Web site on:

A Problem to Look Out for with Multiple Submission Services

Some search engines and directories need to be manually submitted to. Be careful using multiple submission services that require you to fill out one form for all search engines and directories.

➤ Multiple Submissions sites
➤ What's New sites
➤ What's Hot and Cool sites
➤ Business listings

Start here with these free services and "spread the word" that your site exists and what you offer the online consumer.

Multiple Submission Sites

Submitting your Web site to the top search engines takes work and should be done separately for each one. There are many "second-tier" indexes that are worth submitting to, using one of the free multiple submission services such as the one at ecki.com (see Figure 20.1), which claims to be the Grandfather of All Links FREE Advertising Directories.

Figure 20.1

Multiple site listing services like Ecki.com can help spread your URL around "second-tier" indexes.

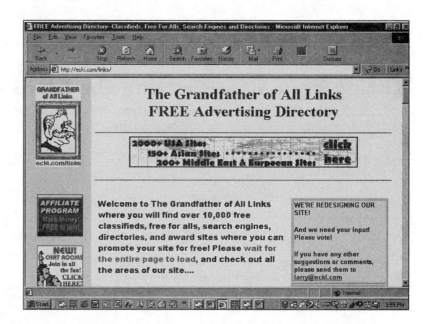

SelfPromotion.com at `selfpromotion.com` leads you through the process of submitting your site to more than 700 different search engines, directories, and indexes. Be aware that using this site will take a fair amount of work. Although site self-promotion is not difficult, it will take some effort, a bit of thought, and a fair amount of patience.

Avoid FFA Sites

Stay away from listing with the Free For All (FFA) sites. Most of them are there for one reason—to collect email addresses so that they can email you advertising messages. Additionally, any click-throughs you do get are of very poor quality.

In addition, some search engines and directories need to be manually submitted to. Certain information that must be entered cannot be automated. SelfPromotion.com alerts you to these engines and indexes so you can manually submit to them and auto-submit to others. When manual submission is required, it's because the site is crucially important and structured so that manual submission is the best way to go, or the site administrator wants you to submit in person.

At JimTools (`www.jimtools.com`) you can use his Search Engine Submitter to submit your Web site URL to the 46 largest engines. Then use his Directory Submitter, which will submit your site to more than 400 of the most important directories.

What's New Sites

Another free service to use in promoting your Web store is the What's New sites. These sites list you for only a few days or weeks but lots of people keep an eye on new Web sites, so it's a good use of your time to register your site with them.

First list your site with What's New Too! at newtoo.manifest.com/submit.html and announce your Web site on their service.

Next, go to What's Nu at www.whatsnu.com and register your site (see Figure 20.2). Its opt-in email subscribers receive a free weekly newsletter notification of hot new Web sites being launched on the Internet—including yours when you register.

Once Is Enough

You can submit your site only once to What's Hot and What's Cool sites. If you try and spam them, they will ban your URL from future listings.

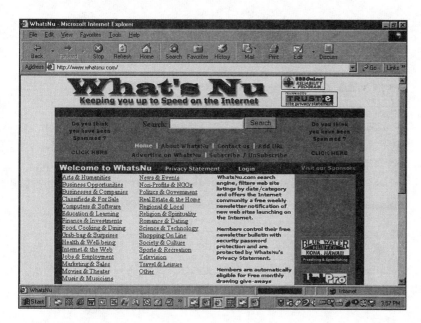

Figure 20.2

Got a new site? Submit it to What's Nu—the biggest What's New site on the Net.

Starting Point at stpt.com/submit/submit.asp is a little different from the others. You can submit your URL to the "New Sites" section of its site in one of 12 categories. Also, Starting Point lets visitors to its site vote to select a daily "Hot Site" from submissions. If yours wins, it sends you an email stating the category and date your site will be featured as a "Hot Site."

What's Hot and Cool Sites

Speaking of hot sites, this is another free device to use when promoting your Web store. Although you're not guaranteed to get chosen as a "Hot" or "Cool" site, it's worth submitting your URL. These sites regularly review submitted sites and promote special sites for a brief time before moving on. Sites are generally selected on good Web design or high-quality content. If you are chosen as a Hot or Cool site, you can expect a lot of hits on your site after it is announced.

Too Cool (www.toocool.com) awards sites are well-designed with great content. You cannot submit a link more than once or submit links of similar nature. The Internet Top 10 at www.chartshow.co.uk lists its Top 10 chart that delivers its weekly Web site Top 10. You can submit your URL to the chart master for review.

Cool Site of the Day (see Figure 20.3) at www.cool.infi.net is the Web's original "Awards" site and is very popular. But because of its popularity, it now charges $14.95 for submitting your site. In exchange for the submission fee, you receive a Cool Site freebie package valued at $45. So, to some extent it is free. Keep in mind that paying the submission fee does not guarantee your selection as a Cool Site of the Day.

Figure 20.3

Cool Site of the Day is the oldest and largest What's Cool site on the Web. Be sure to register your site there.

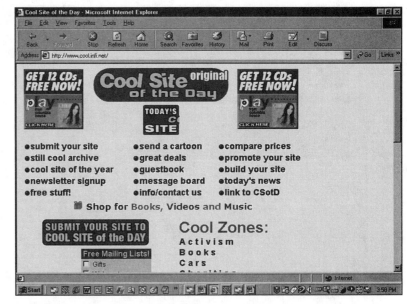

Business Listings and Classified Ads

Sometimes the World Wide Web seems like the "World Wide Wait." But the operative word here is "world," and just because you have a local business doesn't mean you can't attract a global market. Here are some free promotional ideas that can give your business a global presence.

Spend Your Time not Your Money

Taking the time to learn how to promote your site will save you a bundle. Visit sites like VirtualPromote at www.VirtualPromote.com/. It lists free promotional, advertising, and marketing resources that can offer excellent promotional information that can increase traffic to your site. It also has links to other helpful sites.

There are hundreds of business directories—as opposed to general search engines—on the Web where you can list your business by category for free. They range from excellent to so-so, so you will have to determine which ones best fit your business.

Start with eCommerce1 at ecommerce1.com/submit_a_site.htm. Its simple submission form just asks for your business name, URL, and a short description. The WWW Yellow Pages at yellow-pg.com also lets you submit your Web store for free. Its Basic Listing lets you give customer information about your business, including your type of business, address, and phone number. Then register your Web store at ComFind at comfind.com/intro.html.

If you want a more extensive listing of your business, go to BizWeb at bizweb.com/InfoForm. BizWeb allows you to give a more detailed description of your business, including what kinds of payment you accept and a very long list of business types to choose from.

And don't overlook the guides on the Web. There are guide sites such as About.com at about.com, and Suite 101 at suite101.com that might have one or more guide sections that could relate to your business. Send the individual who is responsible for the respective section information about your site with an invitation to visit. If your work impresses the guide, your site stands a good chance of being mentioned on the Guide's site—with a permanent link! Another good reason to approach the guides is that many issue awards to sites that are considered "Best of the Web."

Finally, make use of the free classified ad sites that you can use to promote your particular product offering or service. You can use them to advertise special promotions or sales, alert shoppers to one-of-a-kind deals, give away free or sample products, or do seasonal promotions. Write a compelling enough ad and you'll generate new traffic to your Web store.

Yahoo! Classifieds at classifieds.yahoo.com lets you place free business classified ads in both product and service categories. Netseek Active Ads at netseek.com/classifieds is another free classified ad site where you can place a business classified ad. Its Active

Ads not only allow ad browsing, but readers can click ad titles to go to the advertiser's Web site. Your ad can even display your company and contact information—even send you an instant email.

Banner Ads

Banner ads can be expensive, but you can get them for free by joining a link exchange service. Free banner link services such as LinkExchange (see Figure 20.4) at adnetwork.bcentral.com, BannerSwap at www.BannerSwap.com, and SmartClicks at smartage.com/promote/smartclicks/index2.html can be very useful after you have established traffic to your site.

Figure 20.4

LinkExchange is the oldest and most popular of the banner exchange networks.

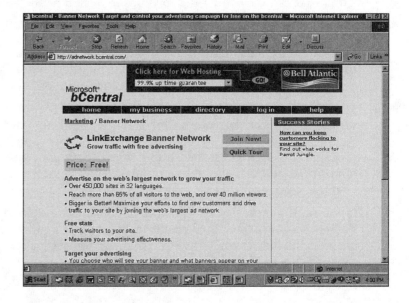

If you decide to use reciprocal linking—banner ad or otherwise—as a promotional strategy, remember to keep the following in mind.

Every link you add to your site is a doorway to another location. After visitors click that link, they might not return to your site. So although you might gain traffic with reciprocal linking, you don't want to show them an exit to your site before you have a chance to show them your offer. So, don't put any kind of reciprocal link on your home page.

Give shoppers a chance to see what you're offering before showing them an exit to other sites.

If you offer links or banners, put them on pages that are at least one level below the home page in your Web site. On your home page, you can get the chance to sell a shopper on your offering (you are selling them as soon as they hit your home page with a product or service offer, right?) before they leave to go to another site.

Web Rings

Another form of reciprocal linking is the Web ring.

Web rings have been around as long as search engines and can give your Web store a traffic boost at the start. A Web Ring provides a fast and easy way for people to navigate the Web within a topic they are interested in. Web sites in a Web ring band together to form their sites into linked circles in a specific subject area. The circle—or ring—leads the visitor to each site through the ring of sites that allows visitors to the ring to reach the sites they are looking for quickly and easily.

The granddaddy of all Web rings is RingWorld at `webring.org/#ringworld`. Member sites in the rings total more than 1,300,000 with the number of different rings totaling more than 80,000. If you are interested in placing your Web store in a ring, join one of the rings in the Business and Economy|Products and Services section at `webring.org/ringworld/bus/products.html`.

A more business-oriented Web ring is LoopLink at `looplink.com`. Unlike RingWorld, LoopLink focuses more on business and online shopping sites. And unlike RingWorld, LoopLink drives additional traffic into all the loops from its home page and through promotional and marketing activities than it does to promote the LoopLink service.

Both RingWorld and LoopLink, of course, are free to join.

Community Participation—Newsgroups and Discussion Boards

No man is an island, and neither is a Web site. Participation in newsgroups, discussion boards, and chat rooms on the Net is a great way to gain visibility for your eBusiness—and it's free!

The trick is to choose the right community participation vehicles and make a contribution to the discussion. Let's take newsgroups and discussion boards for example.

Before the birth of the World Wide Web, online marketers relied heavily on newsgroups. Although they have waned as a marketing vehicle, they still are an important free promotional resource.

With a little time and energy, you can find newsgroups where your product and expertise can lead to visitors and sales. But, remember—you *cannot* post an advertisement stating that you are open for business. That's not how it works, and if you do you will be flamed for spamming the list. To avoid this, first read the postings of the group for a few weeks to get the general nature and feel of the list. This is called *lurking.*

Use a Service to "Seed" Newsgroups

Don't have time to promote your Web store through newsgroups? Yes, it is time-consuming. But you don't have to do it all yourself. Word-of-Net at wordofnet.com will "seed" newsgroups with your promotional messages in the proper way without getting flamed.

Don't Forget To Tell Them Who You Are

Remember to add your signature or *sig* file to each message you post so people can contact you or visit your Web store off the board or list. Keep your sig file to no more than 4–5 lines.

Next, read the FAQs for the list. It will tell you what you can and cannot post to the boards. You might find that some boards do allow you to post a message that reads like an ad. Some newsgroups are formed just for that purpose. They are

➤ alt.business

➤ alt.business.home

➤ alt.business.home.pc

➤ alt.business.import-export

➤ alt.business.misc

Remember, what you're looking for is an opportunity to respond to individual posts for help or enter into an ongoing discussion where your product or service might add to the discussion. If done right, when it's time for those on the newsgroup to buy, they'll remember you first.

For example, if you sell toys on your site and are participating on a toy or children's discussion board. Be prepared to offer advice and news about the toy industry in general and perhaps child safety—not just the toys you sell. If you have an accounting service, offer to answer specific questions on taxes.

Here's a list of the most popular newsgroups among online marketers.

➤ alt.biz.misc

➤ alt.business

➤ alt.business.home

➤ alt.business.misc

➤ alt.internet.commerce

➤ biz.general

➤ biz.newgroup

➤ misc.business

➤ misc.entrepreneurs

In addition to newsgroups, there are two good discussion board sites that have numerous discussion boards on just about any topic that you can monitor and participate in. They are Delphi Forums at `delphi.com` and Forum One at `www.forumone.com` (see Figure 20.5). Delphi Forums is one of the largest discussion boards on the Net and has more than 500,000 individual discussion forums to participate in. Forum One is almost as large with more than 300,000 forums covering thousands of topics.

Read Newsgroups the Easy Way

You don't need a newsgroup reader to read newsgroups on the Net. Visit Deja.com at `deja.com` for easy access to the newsgroups via the Web.

Figure 20.5

Forum One enables you to find targeted news groups or mailing lists through which you might be able to market your product or service—gently!

Community Participation—Discussion Lists, Live Chat, and Newsletters

Besides newsgroups and discussion boards on the Net, there are discussion lists. A discussion list is an email version of the discussion board or newsgroup. But instead of posting your message on a Web site, you send an email to the list. By and large, interactive discussion lists usually offer better quality discussions than newsgroups and discussion boards. These discussions are in the form of emails and show up in your

You've Got a Promotion!

In addition to mailing lists and newsgroups, don't overlook America Online. If your site or product is aimed at the average consumer, AOL's communities can be a great place to promote your Web store.

mailbox every day. When you want to post to a list you have subscribed to, you send an email to the list and the list sends your message out to everyone who has subscribed to the discussion list.

There are business-related lists that offer excellent avenues to expose members of your target audience to your business site, such as TalkBiz.com at `talkbiz.com/bizlist/index.html` (see Figure 20.6). It's hard to gauge how strong a candidate a list is for promoting your eBusiness before subscribing to it and watching it for several days or weeks. So, like in the newsgroups, lurk for a while to learn the rules and see who is participating. Then, join in the discussions after you're comfortable with the format and process.

Figure 20.6

At TalkBiz there is a moderated email discussion list where you can talk with other small business owners about issues concerning your business.

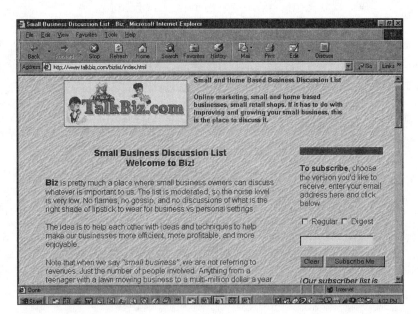

To find a discussion list that addresses your business product or service, go to these Web sites.

First, go to Lsoft at `lsoft.com/lists/listref.html`. It has the CataList, the official catalog of LISTSERV lists on the Net. CataList has more than 33,000 public discussion lists that you can subscribe to. At Lsoft you can search lists by interest, host country, view lists with 10,000 subscribers or more, or lists with 1,000 subscribers or more. Liszt at `www.liszt.com` has more than 90,000 email discussion lists in dozens of topic categories to choose from.

NeoSoft at www.neosoft.com/internet/paml/subjects/ has a smaller database of discussion lists—only about 7,500—but they're worth a look-see because their lists are organized by subject. You are able to find a list easier here that pertains to your eBusiness.

Subscribe and Unsubscribe With Ease

ListTool.com is a free tool that makes the process of subscribing, unsubscribing, and sending commands to 816 mailing and discussion lists easy. You don't have to remember which commands to send to some obscure email address to subscribe or unsubscribe. Find this tool at listtool.com.

Finally, don't forget the live chat rooms on the Net. They can be a great free source of promotion for your new Web store. And besides, you'll be talking directly—and live—to potential customers. Some of the best chat rooms for online businesses can be found at Delphi forums Chat at delphi.com/dir-app/chat/ and at About.com at http://talk.about.com/chatcentral/index.htm.

The Least You Need to Know

➤ Make sure you add your URL and email address on every stitch of printed material that leaves your office.

➤ Although you're not guaranteed to get chosen as a Hot or Cool site, it's worth submitting your URL.

➤ There are hundreds of business directories—as opposed to general search engines—on the Web where you can list your business by category for free.

➤ Don't put any kind of reciprocal link on your home page. Give shoppers a chance to see what you're offering before showing them an exit to other sites.

➤ Participation in newsgroups, discussion boards, chat rooms, and discussion lists are a great way to gain visibility for your eBusiness.

Chapter 21

Contests, Give-Aways, and Shopper Services

In This Chapter

➤ Learn how to run a sweepstakes and contest from your Web site

➤ Discover how to give something free to attract shoppers to your Web store

➤ Learn how to offer coupons and spot discounts on your Web store

➤ Learn the importance of offering gift certificates, reminder services, and gift registries for your eBusiness

Your marketing bag of tricks needs to include more than just an advertising campaign. There are other ways to promote your eBusiness and spend your marketing dollars. The key to your eBusiness success is being able to generate a steady flow of new qualified prospects to promote your product or service to. Contests, give-aways, and shopper services are some of the best ways to do this.

There are basically two things you can accomplish with these types of promotions. You can draw attention to your product or service offer, and you can generate a database of prospects that you can market to later. Either way, these promotional elements should be seriously considered when creating a marketing plan for your eBusiness.

So, let's start with contests.

The Luck of the Draw

Sweepstakes and contests are one of the most popular promotion gimmicks on the Net today. Do a search on Yahoo! for "sweepstakes" and you'll come up with hundreds of sites listing tens of thousands of sweepstakes where consumers can participate. Sweepstakes and contests can increase awareness of your product or service offer and drive traffic to your Web store. In addition, sweepstakes are a great marketing tool.

You can announce your sweepstakes to newsgroups, online sweepstakes groups, and search engines. You could add a feedback form on the sweepstakes page asking for comments on your Web store, product, or service. If you have a new product, consider making that your sweepstakes prize. By using your own products or services as a prize, this will target people who are interested in them. Another marketing trick is to build a list of potential customers by asking them to check a box if they would be interested in receiving emails, newsletters, updates, or possibly receiving catalogs of your products. And don't forget to contact all participants via email when you announce a winner of your ongoing sweepstakes.

Ongoing? Right! You can run a sweepstakes monthly, weekly—even daily. Announcing winners to all participants is great way to keep your Web store and its offerings in front of potential customers.

Create Your Own Sweepstakes

Dynoform lets you create personalized sweepstakes—and here's the good part—their service is entirely Web-based. There's no software installation, and set up takes only a few minutes from their site. Find it at dynoform.com/dynoInfo.asp.

Great promotion tool, right? So what's the downside? How about hefty fines and even jail time. Keep in mind that although sweepstakes and contests can be an effective marketing tool, you must structure them properly to ensure compliance with federal and state laws. But we'll discuss this a little later.

For now, how do you begin? As with any good marketing promotion, you need to plan the event carefully. To have a successful sweepstakes promotion, you need to

➤ Consider your promotion goals

➤ Know your target audience

➤ Design the structure

➤ Promote your sweepstakes

First step—determine your goals. That's easy. You want to drive traffic to your site. But after potential customers are there you can use your sweepstakes for any number of things, such as gathering feedback on your Web site and product offering or building a mailing list of prospects (always ask if they want to be included in future mailings).

Next, you want to target your sweepstakes to make the most of your promotion. Match your promotion to the goals you are trying to achieve and the audience you are trying to attract. Are you after a general audience? Then offer a general prize such as cash, a CD player, VCR, or TV. Something almost everyone can use. If you want to target your offer to those consumers that use your particular product or service, then make the prize either your product or service, or a similar one. The prize in this case qualifies the player for you. Although you'll attract fewer entrants, the ones who do enter will be more likely to purchase your product or service in the future.

Finally, give some thought to your prize. You don't have to offer a large expensive prize, such as a trip around the world or a new Porsche, to get a good response. But don't skimp on your prize, either. If you offer prizes such as coffee mugs, mouse pads, or T-shirts, your sweepstakes will get lost in the thousands of contests on the Net today.

Have a Pro Manage Your Sweepstakes

Sweepstakes Online is one of the largest sweepstakes sites in the world. They will build, maintain, and promote your sweepstakes for you. Find it at sweepstakesbuilder.com/packages.htm.

Run Your Own Incentive Program without the Programming

IQ Commerce Corp at www.iq.com bundles services and technology required to run incentive marketing promotions online from your site or others. It aims to bring the costs within range of smaller eCommerce operators. Fees start as low as $1,000 per month.

Structuring Your Sweepstakes

After you've determined your target market, prize, and goals, it's time to actually structure the sweepstakes.

First up are the rules. Listing the rules on your site is very important in conducting a sweepstakes. At the bare minimum you should

➤ Include the number of entries allowed (one per entrant or as many times as they like).

➤ Mention whether the sweepstakes is run daily, weekly, monthly, or just one time.

➤ Mention any restrictions or limits, such as age limits, if open to U.S. residents only or international.

➤ Tell entrants when the sweepstakes ends and when the prize will be awarded.

➤ Detail any and all information required for entry such as name, address, zip, phone, email address, and so on.

Next, give some thought to the entry method. Will they email their entry to you in response to your advertisement or posting? Or are they required to go to your Web site and fill out a form. The latter is preferred if you want to ask some questions or get some feedback from the entrants or find whether they want to receive more information, a free email newsletter, or a free catalog.

Announce Your Sweepstakes to the Web

A good place to announce your sweepstakes is to post a message on the Usenet newsgroup called `alt.consumers.sweepstakes`.

In addition, make sure the following information is on your sweepstakes page:

➤ Provide information about your company or at least a link to your "About Us" page on your site.

➤ Give entrants a full description of the prize you're offering. Let them know exactly what they might win. For example, if they win a cruise or a weeklong stay in Disney World, is the airfare included?

➤ Make sure you provide a way to contact you in case an entrant has questions about your sweepstakes.

➤ Display a set of the official rules that address in detail the elements that make up the structure of your sweepstakes. Every legitimate sweepstakes must have a set of official rules. The official rules should state exactly how the sweepstakes is structured and any restrictions or limitations about your promotion.

The last thing to consider is how to promote your sweepstakes across the Net. There are a number of Web sites where you can post your sweepstakes and announce it to the world. You add your sweepstakes to sites such as Sweepstakes Online at `www.sweepstakesonline.com` (see Figure 21.1), the Contest Catalog at `contest.catalogue.com/contests/`, Click & Win at `members.aol.com/FTellez/win.htm`, and Games & Giveaways at `www.freestuff2000.com/giveaways`.

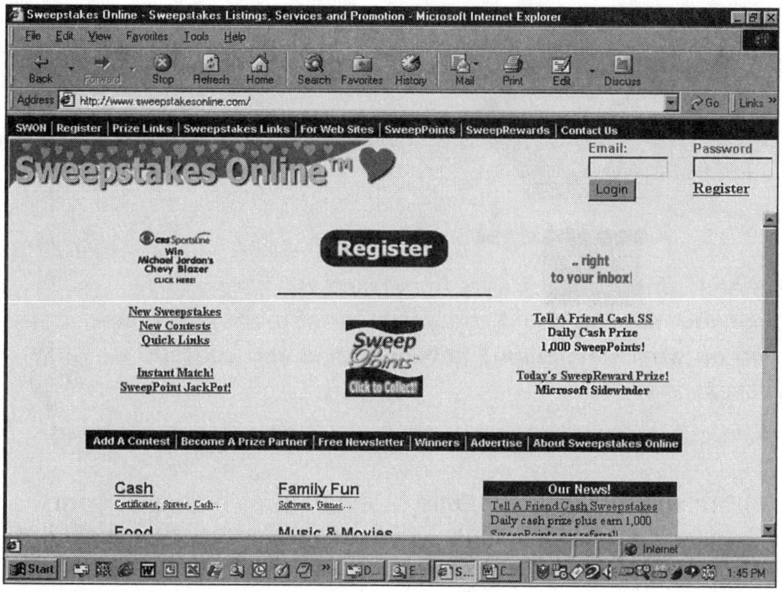

Figure 21.1

At Sweepstakes Online you can list your company's sweepstakes promotion on its site.

Keeping It Legal

Adhering to the law is extremely important here, and structuring your online sweepstakes to be legal is your first concern. And it goes without saying that before you run an online sweepstakes to promote your eBusiness, you should seek good legal council first. The key point to remember is that a sweepstakes is *not* a lottery. If your online sweepstakes is considered by law officials to be a lottery—you're breaking the law!

So what's the difference between a sweepstakes and a lottery? A sweepstakes invites eligible participants to register for a chance to win a prize. A drawing at the conclusion of the sweepstakes usually awards prizes. A lottery consists of a prize, chance, and consideration. It's the "consideration" part that makes lotteries illegal in most states. Although the definition of a consideration differs from state to state (you need that lawyer again), generally, *consideration* means that a willing participant is required to purchase something or pay for access to be eligible to enter the contest. Another example of consideration might be the requirement of the participant providing detailed consumer information to be eligible.

Keep It Legal

Keeping your sweepstakes and contest legal is very important. A mistake in the execution of your contest could cost you a lot of money in fines—even jail time! So, keep up on what's happening in sweepstakes and contest law at Arent Fox at `www.arentfox.com`.

Finally, you must offer an *Alternative Method of Entry* (AMOE). Allowing participants to enter offline via mail or fax is a form of AMOE. Why should you do this? Including an AMOE for your online sweepstakes might decrease the risk that a regulator will view a sweepstakes promotion as an illegal lottery.

Besides the risk of legal action, if you run your sweepstakes improperly, or if the participants feel that it was run unfairly, you risk a public relations nightmare that will be hard to overcome. Just because you are a small business, don't think that you're safe by flying below the "radar screen" of state and federal regulators. Don't be lulled into a false sense of "safety in numbers." Seek legal advice and run your sweepstakes properly.

List Your Freebie at FreeShop

A great place to list your incentive offer, free products, services, coupons, and other incentives, is at FreeShop.com. Find it at `freeshop.com/Advertising/advertise.htm`.

Give-Aways

Stuart Brand, creator of the Whole Earth Catalog, once said, "Information wants to be free." Online merchants have been using a variation of this idea for years—give something free, then sell something. This also is known on the Net as the Yoda Principle—"Give then Take." Although this idea is not new to commerce (businesses have been using loss leaders for decades—selling products below cost to get shoppers into a store) it's the right formula for the Internet.

A good example of this strategy is the free virtual bouquet that many flower sites offer visitors. Come to their site, send a free virtual bouquet via email and perhaps become a paying customer of real flowers in the future. In a similar vein, you can send a virtual greeting card to anyone on the Net by using many of the greeting card sites. Their hope is to have you buy their real greeting cards at some later date. Another example is the search engine optimization services. They will give you a free report on where your site appears in different search engine search results in hopes of selling you their search engine optimization service after you see how badly your site ranks against your competitors.

Give-aways also provide an opportunity to cross-promote with other noncompeting Web stores. You can offer one of your products or a compatible service free to other Web stores. For example, if a site sells auto accessories, and you sell insurance products, you might offer a free comparison insurance quote. Or if a site sells running shoes, you might offer a free pair of athletic socks with each purchase. The trick here is to get the customer from the other site to visit your site to get the free product or service. The partner Web store gets the sale and you get additional visitors.

Besides giving away a product, information, or service, offering discount coupons is another strategy to attract shoppers to your Web store. At first you think of coupons as used only in the real world. And, yes, you can offer coupons on your site that can be printed off and used in your real-world store. But if you're a pure Net-based eCommerce company, how can you make effective use of online coupons?

Why not offer them directly on your site. And here's how.

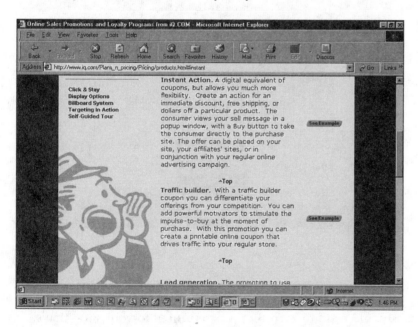

Figure 21.2

Using Iq.com's Instant Action service, you can create the digital equivalent to an offline coupon.

Iq.com (refer to Figure 21.2) has a product called Instant Action that is the digital equivalent of offline coupons. Using Instant Action, you can create any size "teaser" graphic that when clicked, pops up an electronic coupon describing your offer. It might be an immediate discount on one of your products or an offer of free shipping for a limited time. The consumer views your message in a small pop-up window, and when ready to take action, clicks a Buy button. The customer is sent directly to your site to take advantage of the offer. You can place your electronic coupon on your own site or on the banner ads you place on other sites. Research by Forrester at www.forrester.com has shown that the average click-through rates for online banner ads with coupons are 20%, compared to .065% for standard banner ads.

Finally, if you want to add a free service to your site that will attract traffic, consider adding free electronic postcards to you Web store. Postcards Now! at nowtools.com/ postcards (see Figure 21.3) has a free service that gives you the ability to add virtual greeting card capabilities to your Web site. Postcards Now! has more than a thousand postcard images to choose from. You can send free personality-cards from its Web page, or you can link to any category from your Web site. If you would rather run the postcard software yourself from your own Web site with your own images, you can purchase software from Postcards Now! for $99.00, which includes installation.

Figure 21.3

Postcards Now! gives you the ability to add virtual greeting card capabilities to your Web site.

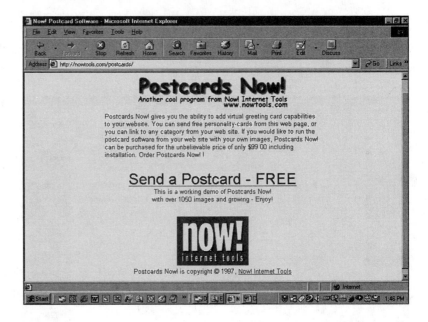

Shopper Services

"Stickiness" is all the rage these days with eCommerce, and for good reason. Constant advertising can get expensive, and as a small to medium-sized eBusiness, you need to continuously find ways to keep shoppers returning to your site—that's called *stickiness*. Three of the best are

➤ Reminder services

➤ Gift registries

➤ Gift certificates

Web consumers are a busy lot. They have a lot to think about and more to remember. That's why Web-based reminder services are so popular. Your Web store can share in this popularity if you place a reminder service on your site.

The most popular kinds of reminder services are those that send out email messages alerting a consumer about an upcoming event such as family birthdays, anniversaries, seasonal gift-giving reminders, and special one-time events such as baby showers and weddings. The best way to offer a reminder service is via email. Set up a page on your site where consumers can fill out a form listing the different days, times, and events that they would like to be reminded of. Capture this information in a database and send out email reminders a week ahead of time. In the email, inform them of the event they wanted to be reminded of and—if you can—suggest a product or service you offer on your Web store that fills their need.

But a reminder service need not be limited to these events. If you sell automobile accessories, you can attract consumers to your site offering an oil change reminder service. If you sell jazz CDs, alert subscribers to your service when new Jazz CDs are released. If you sell movies, offer a service to alert shoppers when new releases are due. And if you sell outdoor supplies to hunters, remind them of when certain hunting seasons begin. If you think a little, you can find a reason for a reminder service for any product or service that you offer.

Gift registries are another fast-growing segment on the Net. You can invest in creating your own gift registry for special occasions, or you can join one of the universal gift-registry sites on the Net to offer your products. Both WishClick at `wishclick.com` and eWish (see Figure 21.4) at `www.ewish.com` not only let consumers create gift registries, but also supply their universal gift registries to online merchants such as yourself.

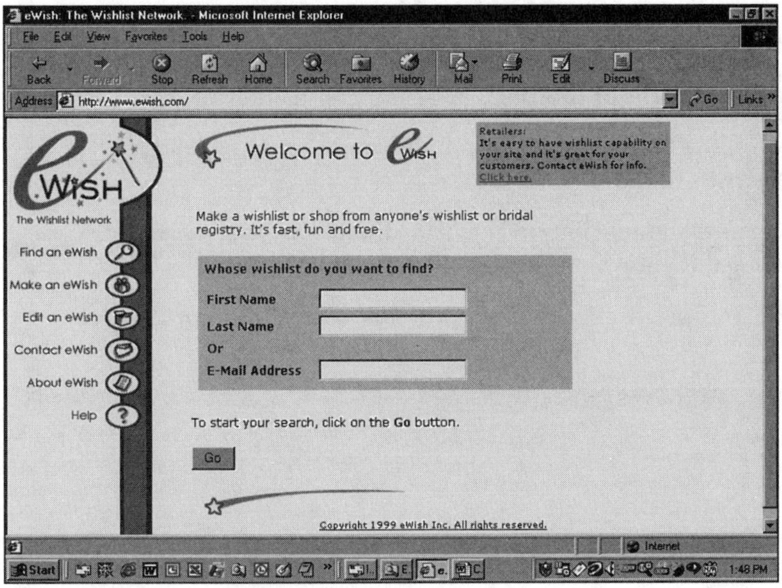

Figure 21.4

You can offer wish list capability on your site using eWish's universal gift registry.

In addition to increasing sales, a gift registry can help you make future inventory predictions based on how many people add your products to their wish list.

Finally, why not print your own private-labeled currency? That's what gift certificates are because they can be spent only at your store. Gift certificates can be offered directly from your site or can be sent by your visitors to anyone they want via email. And here's an idea. Many times shoppers cannot spend the full amount of the gift certificate. In that case, offer to donate the remainder after the sale to charity. Makes them feel good and your store look good.

Have Other Sites Sell for You

Start your own affiliate program. The idea behind an affiliate, or associate program, is to recruit other Web sites to help you sell your products or services by paying them for each visitor or sale they bring you. Find out how at www.theaffiliateprogram.com.

The Least You Need to Know

➤ Sweepstakes and give-aways can draw attention to your product or service offer and generate a database of prospects that you can market to later.

➤ You don't have to offer a large, expensive prize—such as a trip around the world or a new Porsche—to get a good response.

➤ Adhering to the law is extremely important, and structuring your online sweepstakes to be legal is your first concern.

➤ Give-aways provide an opportunity to cross-promote with other noncompeting Web stores.

Chapter 22

PR—Getting the Word Out

In This Chapter

➤ Learn what Public Relations is and how to create a Buzz

➤ Learn how to write an effective press release

➤ Discover where to send your press releases online

➤ Learn the do's and don'ts of news releases

Online publicity is an important element of your marketing plan if you're to rise above the noise level on the Net. But getting that publicity is not easy—it takes a lot of work, and can be froth with dangers. It takes a lot of planning and preparation and is definitely *not* a one-shot effort. A well-thought-out publicity plan gives your eBusiness the kind of portrayal you want in the media and your community. Over the long haul, good portrayal generates good credibility for your eBusiness.

The goal is to generate important coverage of your eBusiness at exactly the right time and in exactly the right place.

Although Public Relations (PR) is a part of marketing, it's really not marketing. Marketing manages demand whereas PR manages your company's image and its awareness on the Net. Online PR is not the process of submitting your Web store to search engines. Good PR appeals to people, not machines. Good PR builds awareness and visibility with minimal cash.

The history of the Web—short that it is—is filled with stories of how an eCommerce Web site was mentioned in *USA Today* or on *Good Morning America* and received instant awareness—and tons of shoppers! You can do that, too.

Creating the Buzz

The Buzz is one of the most important and most elusive forces in all of marketing. If you've got something to sell and are either short on cash or rolling in dough to promote it, creating a Buzz about it will get you millions of dollars in free publicity. Buzz is extremely influential and after it spreads, can boost your Web store's awareness considerably.

Get a Free PR Consultation

Spread the News offers an online 10-question survey to help determine the best way to generate publicity for your venture. After the survey is completed, Spread the News will provide a free mini-PR consultation based on your answers.

Find it at `capital-connection.com/prsurvey.html`.

When you create a Buzz, it means that people are talking about you. You're mentioned in news articles, compared in features, talked about in chat rooms, and mentioned in newsgroups. It's the Holy Grail of marketing and is the marketing goal of every business today.

So how do you create the Buzz? By putting out timely press releases, interviews, and stories that showcase your eBusiness. And that means getting the attention of journalists.

Now, journalists are a fussy bunch. They're harassed daily by companies and individuals asking them to write about their latest "can't-live-without" product or service. But much too often, the news releases they do get are dry, boring, and have no connection to what interests them. Journalists respond to clever writing and news releases that describe how a new product or service is a solution to a business or consumer trend or problem. They respond to releases that piggyback on late-breaking stories that show how a company's product or service relates to current news.

What do you need to know to create a Buzz? First, learn how to write a compelling and timely press release. Second, know where to send it and how. Before you start, check out PR Resource at `www.prweb.com` (see Figure 22.1). It can provide you with information on what you need to know for effective PR.

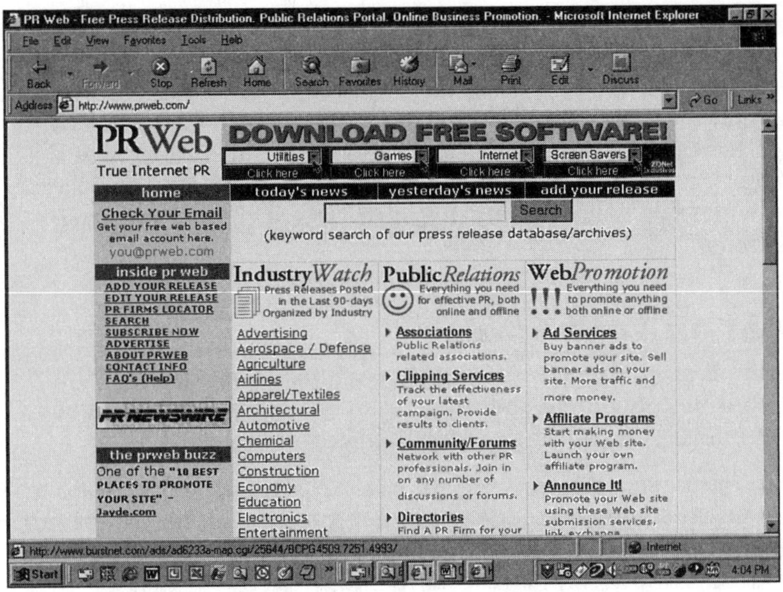

Figure 22.1

PR Resources is loaded with information on what you need to know for effective PR.

The key elements of a good publicly plan include a number of elements.

➤ **State Your Key Message Advantages**   In any release you send out, you need to make sure that the main advantages of your product or service are clearly defined and stated. It's your Unique Selling Position again! If you did a good job defining it way back in Chapter 4, "Creating a Unique Selling Position," you should have no problem pulling your key messages out of it for your news releases. Your goal is to have these key messages reported or implied in any news story about your eBusiness.

➤ **Target Your Publicity**   Make a list of all magazines, newspapers, radio stations, and TV stations that would most likely carry your company story. You want to target these news outlets and make sure that what you do and the news you release match their audience interests. And remember to not just target a new source—target a particular department or individual within it.

➤ **Media Calendar**   Good PR is not a one-shot deal. A good public relations plan is designed to map out a strategy for several months to a year. For PR to be effective, you need a steady stream of it. You need to craft your news releases not only for publication, but to get interviewed for a timely story as well. So look at your product or service, and then look at a calendar. Prepare to send out news releases that show how your product or service relates to holidays—such as Christmas, Easter, Valentine's Day, or Halloween—and seasonal times—such as swim and vacation season in the Summer, back to school in the Fall, winter activities in the Winter, and fashions in the Spring. Design both your marketing campaign and your public relations campaign to coincide with these events. Alert the media at each one of these points with news releases. The object here is to get the press coverage—or better yet—get an interview.

Knowing what is considered news and what's not is key in getting your news releases read. Simply stating that your Web site is open for business, or if you have redesigned your site, or have added new staff is not in itself newsworthy. What is newsworthy is focusing on something that's already prominent in the news or is about to become so. Issue a report related to your site's main theme, or conduct a survey and issue a report on the findings, buck a trend in the marketplace, announce an award you've won, or announce that when you reach a company milestone, such as celebrating your one millionth customer.

Place a Press Room on Your Site

A must for your Web store is an online Press Room. If a media outlet picks up your news release, it might want to know more about you than what's contained in your release. This is where an online Press Room on your site becomes invaluable.

Reporters have quotas to meet every day, or week, or month. They have little time to search throughout your entire site looking for the contact information they need for a story. When reporters find no contact information for background materials for the press, they can only assume that the company has little to say to the media.

So, what to do? Create a set of materials for the press at your Web site that describes who you are, what your company does, how does it sell, and the key personnel in your eBusiness. Make sure to include all contact information—your Web site URL, email addresses of key personnel, physical address, phone numbers, and fax numbers. This information needs to be in your Press Room on your Web site. If reporters can't reach you, they might write about your competitors rather than about you.

Let a Bot Send Out Your Responses

A good way to respond to press inquiries from your Press Room is to use an automated *bot*. Autobots at autobots.net will send instant replies to your prospects and will follow-up, up to 10 times, on your predetermined intervals all automatically! All for free!

Online Press Rooms not only provide useful information to journalists, but they could save you time answering routine questions about your company such as the CEO's professional background or the date of your most recent merger agreement with Amazon or Yahoo! Put that information in your Press Room and make it easy for journalists to find it. But don't stop there. Why not publish articles on you site giving the world your vision of where your particular eCommerce niche is going and how you plan to meet the needs of its consumers? If your eBusiness has been mentioned in an article or if the press has interviewed you, include links to those articles from your Press Room as well.

Finally, have a place in your online Press Room where journalists can request to be informed about future developments of your company. Gather their names, the media outlets they work for, email addresses, physical addresses, phone numbers, and fax numbers. Also, ask them how they would like to receive news releases in the future—via email, fax, or snail-mail. In this way, you can develop over time your own targeted media list.

Writing the Press Release

Writing a press release is more art than science. And to be read, it must be done right. Here's how to do it right.

The biggest challenge is to know what journalists consider genuine news and what they consider fluff. Being so close to your eBusiness, you can easily lose perspective and what you see as earthshaking news to you will get the automatic delete from journalists. Issuing too much company fluff as news will eventually result in your future news releases being ignored. Sort of like the boy who cried wolf too often. So, remember to make your release newsworthy by solving a problem or filling a need. Pinpoint what that need or problem is and write the release from that perspective.

Stay on Top of What's Happening in Public Relations

iPR is a free monthly electronic newsletters about interactive public relations and media relations on the Internet. Included with your subscription to iPR are queries that it receives from reporters who need sources for stories on which they are working. The subscription form for iPR is at xpresspress.com/ipr.html or you can subscribe by sending your name and email address to joinipr@xpresspress.com.

Along with making your press release newsworthy, you need to keep the following in mind when writing your release:

➤ **Create an unmistakable opening** The first line of your press release should read

FOR IMMEDIATE RELEASE

in all caps. This lets the reporters know the news is authorized for publication on the date they receive it.

➤ **Write a headline that gets straight to the point** Write a headline using a combination of lowercase and capital letters, keeping your headline to 10 words or less. Remember, what you say here determines whether the reader will read the rest of the release.

➤ **Create a strong leading paragraph** The first part of your lead paragraph should include the City it was released from or where the event took place, the newswire it was released over, and the date of the release. It would look like this: DENVER—(BUSINESS WIRE)—Jan. 31, 2000. All releases must include a date because reporters do not always use releases immediately. Your lead paragraph should then answer the who, what, where, when, why, and how of the event. The lead paragraph is really an abstract or summary of the whole release.

Check Everything Thoroughly

Don't trust your word processing program to catch errors in grammar and spelling. Have a few people read the release before sending it to a reporter or news agency.

➤ **Give the journalist reading the release the reason why it's important to his/her readers** Here's where you give a detailed explanation from the reader's perspective. Add all background information, quotes from objective or third-party sources, comparisons with competitors, and so on. If you're sending your release inside the text of an email message, format it in the style of the most common email reader. Stay away from HTML tags, tabs, or columns. These are not read well by text-based email programs.

➤ **Include a brief company summary** Mention your company expertise in your niche, your location, years in business, and so on. Keep it short. Don't include your annual report.

➤ **Include complete contact information** Give a contact name, email address, and your URL. The contact name you supply should be someone who's available and capable of answering questions from the press.

➤ **Close the release** Close with the characters -30- or ###, which are style conventions that let the reporter know they have reached the end of the release.

Finally, keep it short. No longer than one page in length—about 500 words maximum.

An example of a well-formatted press release can be found at www.oneminuteshopper.com/oms2/about/PX10_13_99.html.

Where to Release?

Okay. You've done a good job of writing your release and it's ready to go. So, how do you get it out?

You can send it out yourself if you use one of the wire services. In addition, there are several PR companies on the Web that will send out your release to particular targeted media outlets. Obviously, the biggest advantage to sending out your own release is that it's free. Also, you might be able to target your releases a bit more than you can by using a commercial service. On the other hand, there are some advantages to using a service to distribute your releases. Journalists might be more receptive when a press release comes from a known source. A release from an unknown company might be immediately discarded.

One place where you can post your press release for free is at PR Web at prweb.com/submit.htm (see Figure 22.2).

Figure 22.2

Post your press release for free at PR Web.

Media Outlets for Your Release

At Gebbie you can find links to all types of media outlets including radio, TV, daily newspapers, weekly newspapers, and magazines on the Internet. Find it at www.gebbieinc.com/index1.htm.

If you want your release to be sent out over a well-known and credible newswire you have to spend the dollars and send your release through the PR Newswire at prnewswire.com and the Business Wire at Businesswire.com.

PR Newswire is one of the longtime leaders in paid news release distribution. PR Newswire requires an annual fee and reaches 300 Web sites, online services, and leading databases where content might be published or archived. Along with leading journalist's email boxes, Business Wire, the other industry giant, offers a wide range of services parallel to those of PR Newswire. It too requires an annual fee.

If you don't want to pay PR Newswire or Business Wire's annual retainer fee, there are publicity companies on the Net that send out press releases on demand without any retainer fees. Unless you plan on sending out news releases on a very frequent basis, these types of companies are your best bet.

URLwire

www.urlwire.com

URLwire pulls from a collection of more than 3,000 contacts across 100+ subject interest areas (and in 30+ countries). It will personalize between 200–300 separate email news releases, each with content specific for the recipient. It also will build a Web-based version of your news, so that the many online news pointer services, such as Newslinx, Internet-Watch, NewsHub, and others can point to it in their daily headlines if they so choose (see Figure 22.3). Costs range from $795–$2,000. The average campaign is about $900.

Internet Wire

internetwire.com/release/index.htx

Internet Wire sends releases worldwide to 9,000+ technology media via email, top daily and national newspapers, premier technology and business periodicals, major television, radio outlets, and industry user groups. There are no word-count restrictions or membership fees. You also have automatic posting and linking for 90 days on the Internet Wire site. Cost is $225 per release.

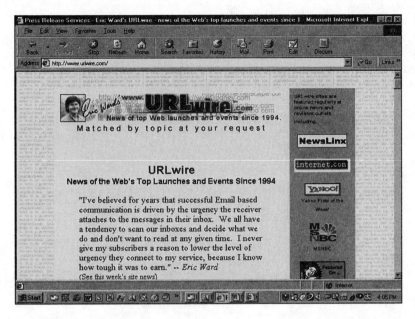

Figure 22.3
URLwire will send your release to more than 3,000 contacts across 100+ subject areas.

Internet News Bureau

www.newsbureau.com/services

Internet News Bureau distributes to the INB Aggregate List (A-List) that includes 2,600+ journalists who subscribe to receive Web-related material (see Figure 22.4). To better serve the journalists who subscribe to INB's service, INB consolidates its material into the daily INB Press Release Digest. In addition to the A-List, INB offers Target Modules that enable a company to reach journalists who cover other topics and industries, and Custom Media Relations services for expanding media exposure beyond INB subscribers. Cost is $250 per release. Price goes down for prepaid multiple releases. Targeted releases start at $80.

Xpress Press

www.xpresspress.com

Xpress Press is an email information service personalizing news delivery to journalists based on their exact areas of coverage. All news releases are sent in separate messages to reporters who can quickly evaluate the content of the news, follow-up immediately by phone, or incorporate the content into working print articles, broadcasts, or Web pages.

More than 9,000 reporters covering more than 400 news beats in 36+ countries currently subscribe to its feed. These subscribers include Xpress Press National and regional U.S. and Canadian-based daily and weekly newspapers; UPI and AP wire;

International Wires and Daily Newspapers; business, trade, and consumer magazines; and online industry-specific Web sites and publications. Also included are electronic business and industry-specific newsletters, radio and television stations including the top 25 U.S. markets according to Arbitron rankings and freelance and nationally syndicated writers, editors, and columnists. Cost is $225 per release.

Figure 22.4

The Internet News Bureau will distribute your release to 2,600+ journalists who subscribe to receive Web-related material.

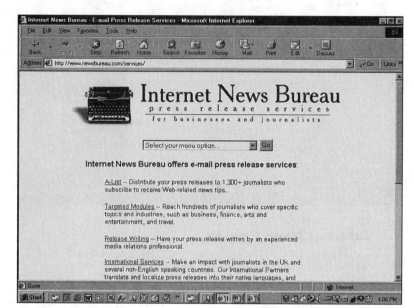

WebPromote

www.webpromote.com/products/prelease.asp

WebPromote distributes press releases to 7,000 individual writers, tech reporters, editors, broadcasters, freelancers, and press professionals. This includes local, regional, national, and international coverage. Media includes top daily and national newspapers, premier technology and business periodicals, major television, radio, and industry user groups. Cost is $395 per release.

PR Do's and Don'ts

Mounting and administrating a good publicity camping takes a lot of work. So mind these Do's and Don'ts of news releases and your publicity efforts will pay off where it counts—bringing qualified shoppers to your Web store for minimal expense.

Here they are.

➤ DO make your press releases short and to the point.

➤ DO include all necessary contact information.

➤ DO spell check your release. And do it twice just to make sure!

➤ DO keep typefaces large and legible and readable both for email and for faxes.

➤ DO write a clear and meaningful subject line. The subject line should reflect the contents of your release.

➤ DON'T write unclear press releases. If it doesn't make sense to the reader, it will not be used.

➤ DON'T send a release to a publication without knowing the audience or what the publication is all about.

➤ DON'T send attached files. Don't send a word processing document or a zipped file that the contact needs to download, unzip, read into his word processor, determine the compatibility, print, review, and so on.

Keep these Do's and Don'ts in mind, and your publicity efforts can pay off big time for your Web store.

The Least You Need to Know

➤ The goal of public relations is to generate important coverage of your eBusiness at exactly the right time and in exactly the right place.

➤ Journalists respond to clever writing and news releases that describe how a new product or service affects their readers.

➤ The key elements of a good publicly plan include stating your key message advantage, targeting your publicity, and a year-long thought-out campaign.

➤ Your releases must be newsworthy to be read and printed by journalists.

➤ A must for your Web store is an online Press Room.

Chapter 23

10 Ways to Drive Customers *Away* from Your Site

> ### In This Chapter
>
> ➤ Learn how to treat your shoppers with respect
>
> ➤ Find out what shoppers expect when they arrive at your Web store
>
> ➤ Discover what information to keep private and what you should reveal to your shoppers

Your Web site is here to serve your customers—not impress them. You job is to design a site and offer a shopping experience that gives consumers a quick, safe, and easy way to purchase something from your Web store.

So before you sit down with your Web consultant, and before your Web designer puts pointer to screen, be sure the 10 ways to drive customers *away* from your site are avoided.

Confuse Your Customers

Rodney Dangerfield gets no respect. He told his psychiatrist that he had suicidal tendencies. His psychiatrist said that from now on Dangerfield had to pay in advance.

That might be funny to you, but treating your customer with no respect will drive him away from your site for sure. And one sure-fire way to drive him away is to confuse him.

Keep your navigation simple. You're there to sell. Customers are there to buy. Make it easy for them to find your products and buy them. If they can't find what they want and order it in three mouse clicks, you run the risk of losing them. So, organize your site material logically from the customer's point of view. Be sure to include clear directions for navigating the site from your home page. Remember that the home page of your Web store serves a variety of functions. It's a map of your store, a welcome mat, and a marketing message all in one.

People get lost easily, so include a "Return Home" link on every page of your site. Include a FAQ page and have links to the FAQ on every page where you think a customer might have a question about your store or service. Anticipate the needs of your users. If your site has a lot of product to sell, provide a search engine to easily find it.

Go light on the technical jargon and don't adopt a hipper-than-thou attitude in your writing. Shoppers want information—not a sales pitch. Don't persuade. Inform.

Finally, look at your URL. See that WWW in front of it? It stands for the *World* Wide Web. So think globally. Users from other countries can easily access your site. If you want to make an international sale, respect cultures other than your own. Remember—they might not be familiar with American slang or expressions. So, keep the wording simple.

Stay Anonymous

Here's another cute trick that will drive customers from your site—stay anonymous. It never ceases to amaze me when the only means of contact on a shopping site is an email address. Come on! We all have an address. Use it. Put your company mailing address, phone number, fax number, and customer service number on your site. And, while you're at it, don't forget to give your customers several ways to order from you—online, by phone, fax, and mail.

Why? People want some indication that your company is real. Supplying just an email address or a P.O. box could seriously impact your sales. But if you're running a business out of your home, you may have little choice.

Also, consider putting a picture of you and your team on your Web store. Make your Web site seem more personal and you more approachable. Be sure that you have an "About Us" section on your Web store that tells the shopper who you are and what your store is about. Use this area of your site to drive home your Unique Selling Position and why the shopper should buy from you.

Offer at Retail

Shoppers believe that because an online merchant doesn't have a brick-and-mortar store, his overhead is low and he can pass these savings on to them in the form of lower prices. I know. I know. That server farm you have taking up the space of a small condo costs as much, if not more, to set up and maintain as a storefront in a strip mall. But shoppers don't believe it. So don't sell at retail. Sell at some kind of discount—at least a 10% off suggested retail price or more.

If you can't offer a discount on the first sale, then offer some value-added service; perhaps a coupon good for a free item or a discount on a future purchase. You might consider partnering with another Web merchant selling products that are compatible with yours. If so, offer shoppers a "bundled" price of your product or service with your merchant partner's product or service.

Frame Your Page

If you really want to drive customers away, then frame your pages.

Frames are a way to display several sections of several pages all at once. This is done by dividing the screen into several segments, or *frames*.

Frames are bad for two reasons. First they confuse the shopper and second, it makes it nearly impossible for a shopper to bookmark a framed page if he wants to return to it again later. When he does bookmark it and return, he only sees the framed page in his browser, losing any and all frames that surrounded the framed page originally.

Frames on your merchant site should be used for only one reason—to keep your navigation bar in front of your customers so they can find their way back to your site when you send them to another. For example, if you have set up reciprocal links or banner exchanges with other sites, a one-frame navigation bar directs customers back to your site from the site you sent them to.

Surprise Them with Shipping Costs

Shoppers don't like surprises. Before you put your customers through your order taking process, let them know what the actual shipped price of their order will be.

You can do this in one of two ways. First, present the customer with the full amount of his order *before* you ask for his credit card. If you can't have offer that calculation, then have complete shipping and handling charges listed on your Web store—and make that list easy to find. This is even more critical for your international customers.

If you want to sell to international customers, then you have to let them know it. Give them the international shipping costs *before* they reach your order form.

Manual Order Forms

Speaking of order forms, here's a way to stop a customer's order dead in its tracks. The customer searched for, found, and is about to order your product. He reaches the order entry screen and it asks him to fill in the product name, code, description, and price of the product! Now the customer has to navigate back to the product page—or forbid, multiple product pages—to retrieve and record the information. Their response? "Fuhgetaboutit! I'm outta here!"

So, invest in a shopping cart software program that keeps track of what the customer is going to purchase and fills in the product information for him. These programs can be bought easily on the Web, and some are even free. If you're not technically adept at installing it on your Web store, hire a programmer for a few hours to do it. But do it!

Make Them Wait

The WWW stands for the World Wide Web—not the World Wide *Wait*. Shopping sites are a challenge to design. You want to keep page-download times low while at the same time customers want to see what they are getting. Don't use bells and whistles just because you can. People don't want to have to download anything to view your site. But if you must use plug-ins, tell them where to get them. Be sure to include links to the software necessary for a full appreciation of your site. If you say your site uses RealAudio, then be sure it links to a download page for RealAudio.

As bandwidth increases, this issue will become less relevant; but until then, heavy use of graphics, video, and audio programs is time-consuming for the user.

Next, keep in mind that people want simplicity over cool graphics. Faster loading is better than eye candy. So keep your graphics small. Small is better where images are concerned. Try and keep them less than 10 kilobytes each and your download time will speed up. If heavy graphics are necessary to display your offerings, at least be sensitive to customers with older systems. Offer a text-only option for viewing your site.

Finally, remember the three-click rule. It should take no more than three clicks to access the information they need. That means three clicks to a buy button.

Neglect to Address Privacy

You want to keep your personal information private, right? So do your customers. Privacy concerns are a big thing these days and shoppers are worried about how their personal information will be used when they give it to a merchant. So create and state your privacy policy and have a link to it from your home page where shoppers can easily find it.

Keep Security a Secret

Don't skimp on security. These days, there's no way to hide that your site doesn't sit on a secure server. Both Internet Explorer and Netscape Navigator tell the consumer when they are on a secure page of a site—and when they're not.

The words "secure server" can have a very calming effect on shoppers. Use a secure server for all your transactions—and tell your customers this when they use their credit card at your site. Put this information in your FAQs and even a separate page on your Web site. Explain to them that their credit card transaction is secure.

SPAM Your Customers

Finally, after you have a customer, you don't want to lose him. Keeping in touch with previous customers and prospects through emails and newsletters will keep your Web store in front of their mind. But you can overdo it.

Never spam your own customers. Offer your customers the option of receiving notifications of sales or new products, but be sure you have permission before sending anything. Unsolicited email is more likely to generate more annoyance than sales.

As for frequency, try not to contact customer more than once a month, unless they have opted-in to a more frequent promotional program with you first.

There you are. Avoid these 10 all-to-common pitfalls, and you have a good chance of making that sale and retaining your customers. After all, isn't that what you went online for?

The Least You Need to Know

➤ Keep your navigation simple. Make it easy for shoppers to find your products and buy them.

➤ Invest in a shopping cart software program that keeps track of what the customer is going to purchase and fills in the product information for him.

➤ If heavy graphics are necessary to display your offerings, at least be sensitive to customers with older systems. Offer a text–only option for viewing your site.

➤ It should take no more than three clicks to access the information they need. That means three clicks to a buy button.

➤ Never spam your own customers. Keeping in touch with previous customers and prospects through emails and newsletters will keep your Web store in front of their mind. But don't overdo it.

Important Resources on the Web

This appendix provides a list of Net-based resources that will broaden your understanding of eCommerce and provide valuable information that will help you succeed in your online business. These eBusiness resources will help your growing enterprise compete by using sound business practices, establishing business and marketing relationships, building product and service quality programs, and entering international markets.

The resources listed here take a variety of formats. Many are standard Web addresses whereas others are mailing lists. To subscribe to the mailing lists, simply send an email to the address listed, unless instructed otherwise.

Email Discussion Lists

AdverTalk

dms_AdverTalk@fiestanet.com

AdverTalk is an email discussion group for small businesses to discuss issues and offer solutions related to small business marketing, including advertising, public relations, database marketing, and sales channels.

BizSupport

join-bizsupport@marketserv.com

BizSupport is the Business Opportunities Support Forum on MarketServ.Com. BizSupport is an unmoderated list on the topic of business opportunities and support of sales organizations.

E-Marketing

www.webbers.com/emark/

This list discusses electronic marketing techniques.

E-Tailer

etd@gapent.com

E-Tailer's Digest is a resource for retail on the Net and is published in a moderated digest form every Monday, Wednesday, and Friday. The E-Tailer's Digest topics include any, and all, subjects that pertain to retailing. To subscribe, send email with a subject of SUBSCRIBE_ETD.

FrankelBiz

www.robfrankel.com/frankelbiz/form.html

FrankelBiz is the Web's only listserv devoted exclusively to doing business on the Web instead of talking about it. List members exchange reciprocal discounts, offer business leads, and do business with one another. Sponsors offer products and services at discounts to members.

GB Internet Marketing

subscribe@digitalnation.co.uk

The GB Internet Marketing Discussion List deals with all aspects of Internet Marketing relevant to the United Kingdom.

GINLIST

listserv@msu.edu

GINLIST has its own Web page. GINLIST (Global Interact Network mailing LIST) focuses on discussion of international business and marketing issues.

GLOBAL_PROMOTE

join-global_promote@gs4.revnet.com

This list is a forum for the discussion of issues relating to sales and marketing in the worldwide Internet marketplace.

GLOBMKT

`listserv@lsv.uky.edu`

Subscribers discuss global marketing issues in this forum.

HBBM-L

`HBBM-L-Request@InternetWantads.com`

The Home Based Business Marketing List, HBBM-L, is an open, unmoderated list geared toward marketing discussions and issues for home-based business owners. To subscribe, send the command SUBSCRIBE HBBM-L in the body of the mail.

HTMarCom

`majordomo@listserv.rmi.net`

HTMarCom has its own Web page. The list is dedicated to discussing the marketing of technology products.

I-Advertising

`listserv@guava.ease.lsoft.com`

This list offers a moderated discussion on all aspects relating to Internet advertising, including online media planning, media buying, campaign tracking, industry trends and forecasts, creative development, and cost estimates.

IESSlist

`majordomo@ix.entrepreneurs.net`

IESS (Internet Entrepreneurs Support Service) is a discussion group for entrepreneurs and businesses doing business on the Internet.

I-NET-PRODUCTIVITY

`listserver@netpartners-marketing.com`

The discussion group called I-NET-PRODUCTIVITY is a self-moderated list to discuss topics relating to using the Internet to improve any company's ability to market and sell on the Internet. To subscribe, type `subscribe I-NET-PRODUCTIVITY` in the body of the message.

Interad

`interad@iponline.com`

This name refers to Internet Advertising. The purpose of this list is to promote discussion and exchange ideas on the use of the Internet for advertising. To subscribe, email the words `subscribe Interad` in the subject line or message body.

International-Business

`majordomo@globalbiz.com`

Discusses topics that concern business owners and marketing professionals as they relate to the Internet and the World Wide Web.

Internet Sales

`join-i-sales@gs2.revnet.com`

Internet Sales has its own home page. The goal of the Internet Sales Moderated Discussion List is to provide meaningful and helpful information to those engaged in the online sale of products and/or services.

I-Sales Help Desk

`www.audettemedia.com/i-help/`

This discussion list was spun off from the successful I-Sales list at the end of 1997. It too is targeted at those involved in online sales, but focuses more on helping people solve specific problems.

Marketplace

`www.onelist.com/subscribe.cgi/marketplace/`

Marketplace is a mail list for trading marketing ideas, and for home-based entrepreneurs. You will be able to plug your business on a weekly basis.

MKTRSRCH

`Listserv@listserv.dartmouth.edu`

MKTRSRCH is an open, unmoderated discussion list covering the topic of primary and secondary market research.

MKTSEG

maiser@mail.telmar.com

The purpose of this list is to allow and encourage an exchange of ideas and information relating to advertising and marketing to target segments.

NetMarket-L

listserv@citadel.net

The NetMarket-L list is unmoderated. It is for entrepreneurs, Webmasters, and pioneers—those of us who are testing out new ideas and marketing concepts on how to best promote our business, products, and services on the Internet.

NEWPROD

majordomo@world.std.com

NEWPROD is a mailing list devoted to the discussion of New Product Development in both product and service industries.

Online-Advertising

www.tenagra.com/online-ads/

The Online Advertising Discussion List focuses on professional discussion of online advertising strategies, results, studies, tools, and media coverage.

PRFORUM

listserv@indycms.iupui.edu

Corporate and PR communications is the theme of this list.

Product_Dev

product_dev-request@msoe.edu

The Product_Dev list is for discussing new product development.

Proposal-L

majordomo@ari.net

Proposal-L facilitates discussions regarding the development of business proposals, responding to Government RFPs, best practices, production, marketing, contracts, training, tools, and resources for planning, writing, producing, and delivering proposals.

Retailer-News

`majordomo@mailing-list.net`

The Retailer News Digest mailing list is a moderated discussion list for retail business owners, managers, and salespeople.

SMBIZ

`smbiz-list-request@dandyweb.com`

The Small Business Discussion List is for all small business owners, workers, marketers, and developers. To subscribe send the message `subscribe`.

SYSOP-Group

`listserv@property.com`

The list is geared totally towards the business aspects of online services and marketing. Marketing, obtaining advertisers/sponsors, and new users is its only purpose.

Sales-Chat

`sales-chat-request@listserv.direct.net`

The Sales-Chat List was formed to provide a discussion forum for people involved in selling or interested in selling. Send email with the one line message `subscribe sales-chat`.

SERVNET

`listserv@asuvm.inre.asu.edu`

This list is multidisciplinary and has been set up for discussions of service.

Webcontentstrategy

`webcontentstrategy@lists.fourleaf.com`

This webcontentstrategy list is for Web-based content business owners, executives, and advisers to discuss strategy and funding issues. Subjects discussed are strategic or financial, rather than trading or operating in nature.

WTB

`www.listhost.net:81/guest/RemoteListSummary/WTB`

The Women-Talk-Business list is set up as a discussion list for business topics.

eBusiness Publications

American Demographics Magazine

`www.marketingtools.com/`

Online reproduction of the print version of *American Demographics Magazine*. The best demographic information online. A necessity for any good marketing plan.

Boardwatch Magazine

`boardwatch.internet.com/`

Guide to Internet access and the World Wide Web.

Business@Home

`www.gohome.com/`

Online version of print magazine devoted to those working at home. This is an online gathering spot and information resource for the working-from-home community.

CLICKZ

`www.clickz.com`

This column is published each business day and includes an eclectic mixture of online marketing news, opinions, and interviews.

CNET

`www.cnet.com`

As well as carrying all the latest technical news online, CNET publishes a weekly summary that provides links to all the major Internet stories from the previous week.

eCommerce Alert

`www.zdjournals.com/eca/`

A biweekly newsletter, an interactive Web site, and an email alert service.

Entrepreneur Magazine

www.EntrepreneurMag.com

A wide range of articles and suggestions for starting, managing, and maintaining a small business.

Fast Company

www.fastcompany.com

Contains plenty of articles about emerging businesses. The Web site is well organized, expansive, and covers up-to-date issues for today's entrepreneur.

INC. ONLINE

www.inc.com

The award-winning Web magazine for growing companies.

Interactive Week

www.interactive-week.com

Covers a variety of aspects of the Internet and interactive technology.

Internet World

www.iw.com

Weekly publication covering Internet news, marketing, infrastructure, and eCommerce development.

Net Magazine

www.netmag.co.uk/

Popular European Internet magazine.

Netguide

www.netguide.com/

Covers new sites, best sites, live events, and Internet tips and tricks.

Sales Doctors Magazine

www.salesdoctors.com

Online sales magazine featuring articles on sales, service, marketing, and management.

Small Business Journal

www.tsbj.com/

The Small Business Journal Magazine has tons of small business articles and information.

Upside Magazine

www.upside.com/

Dedicated to providing its customers with high-quality, insightful media products that uniquely position the company as a leader in the information technology field.

Web Commerce Today

www.wilsonweb.com/wct

Monthly email newsletter on selling products directly over the Internet.

Web Developer

www.webdeveloper.com/

Covers HTML, Java, JavaScript, and Web site management.

Wired Magazine

www.wired.com/

Internet culture and business magazine.

Yahoo! Internet Life

www.zdnet.com/yil/

Covers entertainment, news, and useful Internet sites.

Promotions, Submissions, and Search Engines

Add Me

www.addme.com

A free promotion, submission, announcement site that will submit your site to 34 various Web directories and search engines on the Internet.

Link Exchange

www.linkexchange.com/

A free cooperative service helping over 250,000 Web site owners get targeted exposure.

Netcreations

www.netcreations.com

Provides Internet promotional services, software development, and Web publishing.

Position Agent

www.positionagent.com/

Monitors Web site search engine rankings on top search engines.

Search Engine Watch

www.searchenginewatch.com

This site contains everything you ever wanted to know about search engines, including how they work and how to improve your site's ranking.

Submit It!

www.submit-it.com/

Announces your site to the top search engines and directories on the Web.

What's New Too

newtoo.manifest.com/WhatsNewToo/submit.html

This site promises to post your listing within 36 hours.

General Resources

Builder.com

www.builder.com

If you're building a Web site yourself, CNET's Builder.com has an abundance of articles and advice to assist you.

Domain Name Availability

www.networksolutions.com/cgi-bin/whois/whois

Checks the availability of a domain name.

Emarketer

www.emarketer.com

This site aims to be the definitive online marketing resource. It includes news, statistics, and step-by-step guides to succeeding online. A weekly newsletter also is available.

Incorporation and Trademarks

www.corpcreations.com

Incorporation and Trademark services online (for all 50 states plus offshore).

NUA Internet Surveys

www.nua.ie/surveys/moreinfo.html

NUA publishes a weekly email newsletter that summarizes all the latest Internet surveys and statistics. This newsletter is an invaluable resource if you want to know who's online and what they're buying.

Web Site Garage

www.websitegarage.com/

Has a large package of services including an HTML checker, site promotion tools, and a graphics optimizer.

Wilson Web

www.wilsonweb.com

This site contains a wealth of links to articles relating to every aspect of Web commerce. Much of the information is free, although some areas are accessible by paying subscribers only.

Glossary

ADSL (Asymmetrical Digital Subscriber Line)   This strange-sounding name is the phone company's answer to cable modems. Unlike a cable modem where many subscribers are on the same line, an ADSL circuit connects two specific locations and is much faster than a regular phone connection and could be faster than a cable modem.

AltaVista   One of the top 10 search engines. It indexes actual Web pages, not just Web sites (see *Yahoo*). When you do a keyword search, it returns Web pages instead of Web sites.

Anonymous FTP   Anonymous FTP enables users to access an FTP site for downloading without a password. With regular FTP, you must enter a user ID and a password to access the site.

auto-responder   An email feature that sends an email message to anyone who sends it a blank message or a message with certain key words.

backbone networks   This is the backbone of the Internet that consists of central networks with high-speed computers to which all the other networks of the Internet are connected. Once maintained by the National Science Foundation, they now have been privatized and maintained by companies such as Sprint and MCI.

bandwidth   The transmission capacity, usually measured in bits per second (BPS) of a network connection. Video streaming and other multimedia applications require a high bandwidth.

banner   An electronic billboard or ad in the form of a graphic image that resides on a Web page, many of which are animated GIFs. The newer banners are interactive with the capability to take an order through the banner ad.

baud   The Baud rate refers to the speed of a modem. Common speed for modems today are 14.4, 28.8, 36.6, and 56K. Cable modems and ASDL approach the speeds of a T1 telephone line.

bot   Small pieces of software that search the Net looking for sites—or product pages if they are shopping bots.

BPS (bits per second)   A measurement of how fast data is moved from one place to another, usually in thousands of bits per second (Kbps) or million of bits per second (Mbps). A 28.8 modem can transport 28,800 bits per second.

browser   Software program like Netscape or Internet Explorer that enables you to browse the World Wide Web and access the millions of pages that it contains.

C++   Superset of the C programming language that adds object-oriented concepts. Java, another programming language, is based on C++ but optimized for the Internet.

cable modem   A modem connected to your local cable TV line. The bandwidth of a cable modem far exceeds the bandwidth of the 28.8 Kbps and can be as fast at a T1 connection.

cache   An area of your computer memory or directory on your hard drive. This is the place where your browser stores viewed Web pages. When you return to a page, the browser gets this page from the cache, saving you download time.

CGI (Common Gateway Interface)   An interface that allows scripts (programs) to run on a Web server. CGI-scripts are used for a variety of purposes, including Web page forms and shopping carts. The most popular languages for CGI scripts are Perl and C.

CGI-bin   The name of the directory on a Web server where CGI-scripts are stored.

chat   You can "talk" in real time with other people in a "chat room," but the words are typed instead of spoken.

click   Used in online advertising. A "click" is when someone clicks on a banner ad or link. The click rate is the number of clicks on an ad as a percentage of the number of times that the ad was downloaded with a Web page. A click rate of 1% means that 1% of the people who downloaded the page clicked on the ad.

client/server   The Internet is a client/server network. The client is the computer that requests a service or a piece of information from another computer system, or server, on the network. The PC you use to access the Internet is the client. The Web server you view pages on is the server.

co-location   If you want to have your server on a high-speed connection, or want someone else to maintain it, you co-locate your server with other servers at a hosting service.

cookie   A cookie is a small piece of information that a Web server sends to your computer hard disk via your browser. Cookies contain information such as login or registration information, online shopping cart information, and user preferences. This information can be retrieved by other Web pages on the site so that your site experience can be customized.

cracker   A person who breaks the security of computer systems in order to steal or destroy information. A nonmalicious cracker is called a *hacker*.

cross-posting   Posting one message to several newsgroups at a time. This can be used by commercial enterprises to promote their business with unsolicited messages. Can also be considered spamming the newsgroups.

cyberspace   First coined by author William Gibson in his novel *Neuromancer*, cyberspace is used to describe the Internet.

data encryption key   String of characters used to encode a message. Someone can only read this encoded message with another related key.

dedicated line   A direct telephone line between two computers. Dedicated lines have permanent IP numbers whereas dial-up connections are assigned a new IP number every time you log on.

dial-up   Temporary connection over a telephone line to the computer server of your ISP in order to establish a connection to the Internet. You get a new IP number every time you log on.

DNS (Domain Name Server or **Domain Name System)**   A Domain Name Server maps IP numbers to your URL on the Web. When someone types `www.mybusiness.com` into their browser, the DNS searches for your Web site's IP address, such as 208.12.111.89, and displays your Web page.

domain name   A unique name that identifies an Internet site like `mybusiness.com`. A domain name always points to one specific server on the Internet where your Web site resides.

download   The transfer of data from a server on the Internet to your PC. You can use your browser or an FTP program to download files to your computer. When retrieving your email, you're downloading your email to your computer.

e-cash (electronic cash)   A currency that can be exchanged over the Internet. It requires the buyer to purchase the electronic currency from a special bank via check, credit card, or debit card. He then can use it to purchase goods from Internet vendors who accept e-cash.

email (electronic mail)   A message containing text or HTML sent over the Internet from one person to another or to a large number of email addresses using a mailing list.

317

email address   An electronic mailing address. Email addresses are in the form of *user@domain*, such as `frank@aol.com`.

email alias   These are additional email addresses that point to another email address. All messages sent to an email alias are automatically forwarded to the specified "real" email address. This way you can have more than one email address on an email account.

encryption   Procedure that scrambles the contents of a file before sending it over the Internet. PGP (Pretty Good Privacy) is a commonly used encryption program. The recipient must have software to decrypt the file on their end.

FAQ (Frequently Asked Questions)   A Web page that contains the most common questions and answers on a particular subject.

firewall   Internet security to protect a local area network (LAN) computer system against hackers. A combination of hardware and software acts as a firewall to separate the LAN into two parts. The data you want to have public is available outside the firewall, whereas sensitive data, such as credit card numbers, is kept inside the firewall.

flame   The email equivalent of hate mail. Such hate messages are usually sent to the victim's email box tens and even hundreds of times. Sophisticated Internet users use this technique against businesses that send them SPAM (unsolicited email).

frame   Enables Web designers to break the browser window into several smaller windows, each of which can load different HTML pages. Using frames, Web designers can create navigation bars and advertisements that stay onscreen as you click through a site. If used incorrectly, frames can be a great annoyance to your visitors.

freeware   This is any kind of software that is distributed or downloaded free of charge for unlimited use.

FTP (File Transfer Protocol)   FTP is used to download files from another computer as well as to upload files from your computer to a remote computer. Through (regular) FTP, you can login to another Internet site, but you must have a user ID and a password. Anonymous FTP servers don't require usernames or passwords, but you can't upload files to anonymous FTP servers.

GIF (Graphics Interchange Format)   Common graphics file format on the Internet. This format can display only 256 colors at the maximum of 8 bits—therefore a GIF is mostly used to show clip-art images.

gigabyte - Gb   A gigabyte = 1 billion bytes.

GUI (Graphical User Interface)   Windows and Macintosh operating systems use a GUI where the operating system is displayed to you with icons on your computer screen. GUI is not like DOS and UNIX, which use command-line text commands.

hacker   An expert programmer who uses his skills to break into computer systems or networks just for the fun of it or to expose security risks. Unlike a cracker, a real hacker doesn't want to harm anybody or anything.

hit   A single request from a browser to a server. All text on a Web page is a hit, and each individual graphic on a page is also counted as a hit. If a Web page consists of text and three graphics images, then one Web page would serve up four hits.

home page   The main page of a Web site. A Web site containing only one page is also called a home page.

host   A host is any computer that allows another computer to retrieve information or access its files. An example of a host is the server on which a Web site is stored.

HTML (Hypertext Markup Language)   The coding language used to create hypertext documents on the Web. HTML is a way to format text by placing marks or tags around the text. The tags <i></i> around a piece of text will make it appear italic.

HTTP (Hypertext Transfer Protocol)   The Web protocol for moving hypertext (HTML) files across the Internet. The http:// in front of your URL tells a browser to transfer your Web site files (pages) to a computer for display. When it reads https://, that signals that you are on a secure Web page—for example, an order-entry page requesting a credit card number.

hyperlink   A highlighted word (hypertext) or graphic on a Web page. When you click a hyperlink, it could take you to another place within the same page, to another page on the site, or to a different Web site entirely.

hypermedia   Pictures, videos, and audio on a Web page that act as hyperlinks.

ICQ ("I Seek You")   A communications network on the Internet. If you want to know whether your friends are surfing the Web right now, ICQ does the searching for you, alerting you in real time when your friends sign on. AOL Instant Messenger and Yahoo! Messenger are two other instant messaging services.

impression   Each request from a user for a Web page on a particular server. Counting the impressions is a good way to measure the popularity of a Web site. If a user views three Web pages on your site, that counts as three impressions.

information superhighway   U.S. Vice President Al Gore's term for the Internet.

Internet   A network of computer networks. The Internet evolved from the ArpaNET (a U.S. military network) to an academic research network, to the current global commercial network. Other names for the Internet are the Net, cyberspace, and the information superhighway.

Internet Explorer   The Web browser from Microsoft. Also known as IE.

InterNIC (Internet Network Information Center)   The InterNIC is the entity that keeps track of domain names. When you want to register a new domain name, you do it through InterNIC.

intranet   A private company network of computers using the same protocols as the Internet, but only for internal use.

IP (Internet Protocol)   These are the common rules that provide the basic Internet functions. Internet Protocol enables computers to find each other.

IP address   A unique 32-bit Internet address consisting of four numbers separated by dots, such as 208.56.111.89. Every server connected to the Internet has a unique IP number.

IRC (Internet Relay Chat)   A chat network where the words are not spoken but written. All words typed by any user are seen by everyone who is in that chat room or channel at that moment. (see *chat*)

IRL   Stands for "In Real Life" or "meatspace."

ISDN (Integrated Services Digital Network)   Digital telephone system that can provide high-speed (up to 128 Kbps) transmission of voice and data.

ISP (Internet service provider)   An ISP provides Internet access to its members. Every time you log on, your ISP connects you to the Internet.

Java   A platform-independent programming language, invented by Sun Microsystems, that Web developers use to create applets. Java-enabled Web pages can include animations, calculators, scrolling text, sound effects, and even games.

JavaScript   JavaScript has nothing to do with Java. JavaScript is a scripting language designed by Netscape. JavaScripts are embedded into HTML documents.

JPEG (Joint Photographic Experts Group)   An image compression standard optimized for full-color (millions of colors) digital images. Almost every full-color photograph you see on the Web is a JPG file, whereas GIFs are used to display clip-art images.

Kbps (kilobits per second)   Measure of data throughput. A 28.8Kbps modem transfers data at about 3.6KB (kilobytes) per second.

KB (Kilobyte)   Approximately a thousand bytes (1,024 bytes).

LAN (Local Area Network)   Computer network limited to one single location—usually an office.

link   A link can bring you to another Web page or another Web site. (see *Hyperlink*)

Linux   A free UNIX-based operating system for personal computers. It competes with Windows.

listserv   This is a mailing list. Similar to newsgroups but unlike newsgroups, list-servs operate via email. When you send an email message to this group, your email is copied and sent to all subscribers.

location   Internet address as displayed on your browser. When you type in the URL of a Web site into the location bar of your browser, your browser will take you to this page.

log file   File that contains detailed recorded events of a computer system, such as server access numbers, number of visitors, and error log files.

mail server   Server that handles incoming and outgoing email. This server is normally different from a Web server.

Mbps (megabits per second)   Measure of data throughput in millions of bits per second.

meatspace   Cyberspeak for the real world—anything outside of cyberspace.

megabit   About one million bits. Exactly 1,048,576 bits.

MB (megabyte)   About one million bytes. Exactly 1,048,576 bytes or 1,024 KB.

metatags   Text tags added to a Web page that includes data such as title, author, content, or key words. These tags can be read by search engines.

mirror or **mirror site**   More or less an exact copy of another WWW or FTP site. Mirror sites are created when the traffic on the original site is too heavy. They are usually on servers that are located in different geographic areas.

online mall   A collection of virtual stores on one Web site. Sometimes the online mall may host a Web store and at other times it only provides a link to their Web store.

Navigator   A Web browser from Netscape and the browser that made the Web what it is today.

Net   Short for the Internet.

netiquette (network etiquette)   Informal code of good manners on the Internet, such as typing in mixed case (typing in all uppercase is deemed as shouting). Spamming is not good netiquette.

netizen   A responsible citizen of the Internet.

network   Group of computers that are connected together so that they can share resources and exchange data.

newsgroup   Discussion group on Usenet among people who share a mutual interest. There are thousands and thousands of newsgroups covering almost every possible subject.

news server   Computer of your ISP that gathers Usenet newsgroups. From this server you can download the newsgroups you're interested in.

OC-1 to OC-48   OC stands for Optical Carrier, a standard for fiber optic transmission. They range from transmission speeds of 51.85 Mbps (OC-1) to 2,488 Mbps (OC-48).

Perl (Practical Extraction and Report Language)   Perl is a computer language used for writing CGI scripts.

plug-in   Small piece of software, usually from a third-party developer, that adds new features to a Web browser.

POP (Post Office Protocol)   Internet protocol used by your ISP to handle email for its subscribers. A POP account is another word for an email account.

portal   A Web site that attracts visitors by offering free information or free services on a daily basis. When you are on a portal site, you can use this site as a basis to explore the Web. The most famous portals are AltaVista, Excite, HotBot, Lycos, InfoSeek, and Yahoo.

posting   A single message posted to a newsgroup, bulletin board, or mailing list.

redundancy   This is a form of protection against system failures. For example, if you want to be sure that you'll always have a power supply, you can set up two power supplies so that one takes over if the other one fails—or, you may have a mirror site for your Web site on another server.

router   Computer that acts as an interface between two networks. A router sends data packets back and forth between networks.

search engine   An online database that enables Internet users to locate sites that have the information they need. Every search engine has its own strategy for collecting data, so one particular search usually produces different results on different search engines. Yahoo and AltaVista are two different types of search engines. (see *AltaVista* and *Yahoo*)

server   A computer that has a permanent connection to the Internet. Web sites are stored on a Web server, and email is stored and sent through an email server.

service provider   A subscriber is connected to a service provider through a modem, and the service provider connects to the Internet through other networks.

shareware   This is software that is purchased on approval. The customer downloads it for a predetermined trial period and will have to pay the creator if he wants to use it beyond that period.

Shopping Cart   A Shopping Cart is a program that lets visitors make selections from more than one product page before checking out of your Web store.

shouting   Typing in all capital letters in a chat room or on a discussion board or newsgroup. This is deemed as bad netiquette.

Sig (signature file)   A small ASCII text file of four or five lines that is automatically attached to the end of an email message that includes additional information about the sender like your name, address, phone numbers, and Web address (URL).

SMTP (Simple Mail Transfer Protocol)   Main protocol to send and receive email between servers on the Internet.

snail mail   Slang word for sending mail using the Post Office.

spamming   Posting an unsolicited commercial message to a newsgroup or sending unsolicited email.

spider   Small piece of software, also know as a *bot*, used by some search engines to index Web sites. Spiders search the Web to find URLs that match to the given search string.

SSL (Secure Sockets Layer)   Protocol that enables you to send encrypted messages across the Internet. SSL uses public key encryption to pass data between your browser and a given server, such as when submitting credit card information. A URL that begins with https indicates that an SSL connection will be used.

streaming media (streaming audio/video)   Technology that enables you to play audio or video while it is still downloading.

surfing   Browsing the World Wide Web.

T1   A telephone line that can transmit information at 1.544 Mbps.

T3   A high-speed, high-bandwidth telephone line connection to the Internet. A T3 line can deliver information at 44.736 Mbps—the equivalent of 28 T1 lines.

TCP/IP (Transmission Control Protocol/Internet Protocol)   A suite of communications protocols that defines the basic workings of the Internet. In fact, TCP/IP is *the* protocol of the Internet because it's the language by which all Internet computers talk to each other.

Telnet   Internet protocol that enable you to connect your machine as a remote terminal to a host computer somewhere on the Internet. To Telnet into a remote machine, you have to enter a user ID and a password.

323

timed out   When you request a Web page and the server that hosts the Web page doesn't respond in a certain amount of time, you may get the message "connection timed out."

UNIX   Multiuser computer operating system. The Internet and the World Wide Web grew up on UNIX. UNIX is still the most common operating system for servers on the Internet.

upload   Sending files from your computer to another computer through the Internet. When making changes to your Web store, you must upload your new pages via FTP to your Web server from your computer.

URL (Uniform Resource Locator)   Address of any resource on the World Wide Web, such as your Web store's home page: http://www.*mybusiness*.com.

Usenet   Worldwide decentralized distribution system of newsgroups. There are at least 15,000 newsgroups available through the Internet.

User ID   Unique identifier that you must enter every time you want to access a particular service on the Internet. The user ID is always accompanied by a password.

VRML (Virtual Reality Modeling Language)   A method for creating 3D environments on the Web. On a VRML page, it is possible to move around through a virtual room, see all sides of a product, and try on clothing. To see VRML pages, your need a VRML plug-in for your browser.

Web page   One single document on the Web. A Web page can consist of text, graphics, and pictures.

Web site   A collection of Web pages that form a complete site.

Webmaster   A person in charge of maintaining a Web site.

wetware   Slang for the human brain.

World Wide Web   An Internet client-server system to distribute information based upon the hypertext transfer protocol (HTTP). Also known as WWW, W3, or the Web. Created at CERN in Geneva, Switzerland, in 1991 by Dr. Tim Berners-Lee.

WYSIWYG   Stands for "What you see is what you get."

Yahoo   One of the Top Ten search engines. Yahoo is one type of search engine. Yahoo is a directory of Web sites and searches by site category, not by Web pages (see *AltaVista*). It can be found at yahoo.com.

Zine or **eZine**   This is short for online magazine. They're a good place to target-advertise your site.

Index

J-K

L

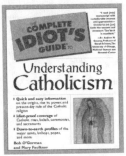

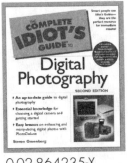